D1590741

North American Bird Folknames and Names

by

James Kedzie Sayre

Bottlebrush Press

Foster City,

California

United States of America

Copyright © 1996

All Rights Reserved

Bottlebrush
Press

Bottlebrush Press
Post Office Box 4554
Foster City, CA 94404
United States of America

Copyright © 1996

ISBN   0-96450-39-05

Library of Congress Card Catalog Number
95-94257

Printed in the United States of America
All Rights Reserved

Printed and bound by Godar & Hossenlopp Printing Company, South San Francisco, CA.

Bottlebrush Press

Painting of Sparrow Hawks on front cover from *Color Key to North American Birds* by Frank M. Chapman, New York: Doubleday, Page & Company, 1903, Drawing by Chester A. Reed.

Table of Contents

Dedication

This book is dedicated to my mother, Audrey St. John Bowers and to my father, Robert Kedzie Sayre, both of whom imbued me with a love of ornithology and of the English language.

This book is also dedicated to Holly Menkel Warnke, who has greatly encouraged me in this endeavor, and who has provided many constructive editorial comments during the creation of this book. She was the motivating force that moved this essay from the state of a private list to its present published form.

This book is also dedicated to my brother, Richard Stone Sayre, with whom I shared a childhood in Ridgewood, New Jersey and Mount Lebanon, Pennsylvania in the innocence of 1940's and 1950's suburbia. This book is also dedicated to the memory of my sister, Marilyn St. John Sayre Kremen.

Thanks is given to the staffs of public libraries and university libraries who were helpful in finding reference materials. The reference librarians at the Burlingame Public Library, Burlingame, California and Foster City Public Library, Foster City, California were especially helpful in obtaining materials through the inter-library loan program.

All errors, mistakes and omissions in this text are solely the fault of the author. The author, however, has depended on earlier sources being truthful in their listings of folknames and names of North American birds.

Preface

This book was written by an amateur birdwatcher to fill a void in modern American bird literature: a book devoted exclusively to the listing of North American bird names and folknames that have been used over the past three hundred and seventy-five years. Many of the older folknames are dropping out of usage in our modern times with the homogenization of modern mass culture. The professional ornithologists have also played a role in the phasing out of the older more colorful and localized folknames, in their unending pursuit of the rationalization of both common names and scientific names of birds.

My original inspiration was finding an old book, entitled, *Bird Neighbors*, written by Neltje Blanchan, and copyrighted in 1897, 1904 and 1922. In the book's text, placed beneath the common name and the scientific name, was a short list labeled, "Called also:." I found that many of these names are interesting and amusing. I decided to research the subject of old folk-names for birds in my local library. Nothing. I checked in other city public libraries. Again nothing. Finally, I checked several University libraries in the San Francisco Bay Area. Again I found no published books that were devoted exclusively to North American bird names. I did find books listing bird names for England and for Australia. I decided to take it upon myself to research, write and publish this book and to fill a hole in the field of American bird literature.

The most dedicated collector of American bird names was W. L. McAtee, a federal government biologist, who over a period of forty years, accumulated many thousands of bird names. He had created a manuscript for a book to be entitled, "American Bird Names: Their Histories and Meanings."
Some of these names were published in naturalist and ornithological journals in the mid-1950's. He listed many roots or origins of the names that he listed in those pages. [McAtee].

This book was originally written on the Macintosh Classic computer using Microsoft Word as the word processing language. Each bird name was individually highlighted and set as an index entry to create the long index at back of this book. It was formatted in FrameMaker on a Quadra 605 Macintosh computer. Draft copies were printed on a Hewlett Packard DeskWriter at 300 dpi.

Introduction

Birds have fascinated people for thousands of years. Their flight, their colorful plumage, their beautiful songs have all been of great interest. Since the coming of the Europeans to the New World several hundred years ago, birds have played an important part in man's perception of the natural world. Birds are the most colorful, noisy and visible part of the animal kingdom. Early settlers named some of the new birds they saw after familiar species which they had seen in their old world homelands. A good example is the American Robin, which was named after the English Robin, although it was a completely different species. The English Robin, Erithacus rubecula, is about five inches in length, while the American Robin, Turdus migratorius, is about ten inches in length.

With the coming of modern mass communications in the 20th Century, birds have assumed a less dominant role in the everyday consciousness of the average person. The coming of daily newspapers, radio, movie theaters, television, and video has led to the natural world becoming a smaller and less dominating part of everyday life. The advent of refrigeration, air-conditioning, private automobile travel and excellent local weather forecasting has also contributed to this trend. The great migration from the countryside into the industrialized cities lowered the contact that the average person had with the natural world. Farmers had to focus on the natural world, and especially the weather for their survival and prosperity. In the cities, the natural world is often just a minor impediment in the lives of its residents.

Part of this passing Americana, is the decline in the use of local and regional folknames for our native birdlife. This book will attempt to list and document some of these names.

American birds have many interesting, funny and fanciful names from our dim and distant past. Birds have been named after their appearance, their song, their behavior, their nesting style and other characteristics.

At the end of the text, a bibliography lists all of the original sources of the names gathered in this list. The interested researcher is referred to the original texts for some detailed analysis of the origin of bird names in North America. The first settlers (the North American Indians) had their own names for birds. The English and other European settlers brought over their knowledge and memories of English and European birds; some names were transferred to similarly appearing American birds. Some French Canadian and Gaelic Canadian bird names have been included in the listings. Some Mexican Spanish and Caribbean Spanish bird names are included as they were listed in the source literature. Local folknames for North American birds which winter in the Caribbean are also included. This book covers the birds that breed or regularly visit north of the US/Mexico border, including United States, Canada, and Alaska. The birds that reside in the Hawai'ian Islands have also been included, due to the islands long association with United States.

Etymology of Bird Names

Etymology is the study of the origins of words. Since this book is written in English about bird names that are almost all in English, this discussion will deal with the origins of Modern English words. The word etymology itself is derived as follows: [Middle English *etymologicus*, Old French *etymologicus*, Latin *etymologia* and Greek *etymologia*. Its roots are Greek *etumon*, literal sense of a word + *-o -logy*, a science or branch of knowledge]. The etymology of the word English itself, is described as follows: [Middle English *English, Englische*, Old English *Englise, Ænglise, Englisc*, from *Engle, Ængle*, plural, the Angles].

Similarly, the etymology of the word England is similarly derived: [England, Old English *Engla* + *land*, the land of the Angles].

Modern English, (A. D. 1780 - date), traces its roots directly back to Early Modern English, (A.D. 1500 - 1780), Middle English, (A. D. 1100 - 1500), and Old English, (A. D. 450 - 1100). Old English used to be called Anglo-Saxon. Some experts put the division between Old English and Middle English at 1066, the date of the successful Norman invasion. Old English is one of the West Germanic languages. Old High German gave rise to High German. Low German gave rise to Old Frisian, which gave rise to Frisian, Old English which gave rise to Middle English, Old Saxon which gave rise to Plattdeutsch, and Low Frankish, which gave rise to Dutch and Flemish.

Latin, the predecessor to the modern Romance languages, which include French, Spanish, Portuguese and Italian is the other great source of words in modern English. Latin itself has been characterized as having several stages including Early Latin, Latin, Vulgar Latin, Late (or Medieval) Latin and Modern Latin. Much of the early infusion of Latin into English came after the Norman invasion and conquest of England in 1066.

British Bird Name Origins

Bird names that were brought over to North America by the colonial immigrants from England had linguistic roots that stretched back into Middle English, Old English, Old French, Old German, Old Norse, Spanish, Portuguese, Latin, Greek, Egyptian, Sanskrit, and Hindi. The following is a listing of many common British bird names, with etymology enclosed within brackets. When possible, individual species referred to by the generic name are listed. If many birds have the same root name, then an example is selected. The scientific names, root words, word of the same meaning in other languages and cognates are all shown in italics. All spelling variations for the italicized root words are listed. With the exception of Scandinavian words with umlauts, diacritical marks for pronunciation have been omitted for ease of reading. Alternative etymologies are listed within parentheses. [Ayto][Barnhart][Champlin][Dwelly] [Fowler][Klein][McDonald][McKechnie][Neilson][Newfeldt] [Onions][Onions][Partridge][Peterson][Skeat][Soukhavnov] [Swann][Sweet][Thatcher][Weekley].

albatross - refers to Black-browed Albatross, *Diomedea melanophris.* [Latin *albus*, white, + Early Modern English *alcatras*, alcatraz, frigate-bird, pelican, Portuguese *algratross*, *alcatra*, Portuguese *akatraz*, cormorant, albatross, (from Portuguese *alcatraz*, bucket, water jar, *alcatruz*, bucket of a water wheel), Spanish *alcatraz*, *alcatra*, pelican, Arabic *al-qadus*, machine for drawing water, jar, pitcher, Arabic *al*, the + *ghattas*, a sea eagle, Greek *kados*, jar, water vessel, Hebrew *kad*, *kadh*, water jar, bucket, named for the size and shape of the bird's pouch, based on the old tale that the pelican carried water to its young in its pouch].

auk - refers to Little Auk, *Alle alle.* [from Scandinavian source, Norwegian *alk*, Old Norse *alka*, auk, razor bill, compare: Danish *alk*, *alke*, Swedish *alka*, auk;].

barn owl - refers to Barn Owl, *Tyto alba*. [barn Middle English *bern, berne*, barn, Old English *bern, beren*, barn, from *bere-ern, bere*, barley + *ærn*, a place, a building, a house + owl, Middle English *ule, owle, oule*, Old English *ule*, compare: Dutch *uil*, Old High German *uwila*, Middle High German *iuwel, iule*, Old Saxon *uwila*, German *eule*, Danish *ugle*, Old Norse *ugla*, Latin *ulula*, screech owl, Latin *ululare*, to howl; reflective of bird's call, the owl's call was considered similar to a wolf's howl, from bird's predilection for barns and other old buildings].

bittern - refers to Bittern, *Botaurus stellaris*, and Little Bittern, *Ixobrychus minutus*. [Middle English *bitor, bitore, bitour, bittour, bitoure, botor*, Old English *bitoure, bittour, bittourn, butoure, botor, botour, buttour, bytoure, buttoure*, Old French *butor*, Anglo-Latin *bitorius, butorius*, Vulgar Latin *butitaurus*, Latin *butio*, bittern + *taurus*, bull, Pliny said that in Gaul the bittern was called *taurus*, i.e., "ox" because its voice resembled the bellowing of oxen, named for its cry].

blackbird - refers to European Thrush, *Turdus merula*. [black Middle English *blak, blakke*, Old English *blac, blæc, blacc*, dark, black, ink, compare: Old Saxon *blac*, ink, Old Norse *blakkr*, black, dark, swarthy, Old High German *blah*, black, Swedish *black*, ink, Dutch *blaken*, to burn with a black smoke, Latin *flagro*, to blaze, burn, glow, flame, Greek *phlegein*; + bird Middle English *bird, brid, bred*, Old English *bridd, brid*, bird, young bird, from Old English *bredan*, to breed, so called because of its black color].

bullfinch - refers to Bullfinch, *Pyrrhula pyrrhula*. [bull Middle English *bul, bule, bole*, Old English *bula*, bull, Old Norse *boli, bole*, bull, compare: Dutch *bol, bul*, German *bulle*, Middle Dutch *bulle, bolle*, Middle Low German *bulle*; + finch Middle English *finch, fynch, fincq*, Old English *finc*, finch, compare: Dutch *vink*, Old High German *fincho, finco*, Middle High German *vinke*, German *fink*; refers to bird's large head and stout beak].

bunting - refers to Reed Bunting, *Emberiza schoenichus*, or Corn Bunting, *Miliaria calandra*. [Scottish *buntlin, corn buntlin*, Middle English *bunting, buntyle, bountyng*, plump, name may reflect bird's plumpness].

buzzard - refers to Buzzard, *Buteo buteo*. [Middle English *busard, bsard*, Old French *busat, buisart, busart, busard, buse, buis-on, bus-on*, Late Latin *busio*, Latin *buteo*, a kind of hawk or falcon].

chaffinch - refers to Chaffinch, *Fringilla coelebs*. [chaffinch Middle English *chaffinche*, Old English *ceaffinc*, from *ceaf*, chaff, husk + Middle English *finch, fynch, fincq*, Old English *finc*, finch, compare: Dutch *vink*, Old High German *fincho, finco*, Middle High German *vinke*, German *fink*;].

chukar - refers to Chukar, *Alectoris chukar*. [Hindi *cakor*, Sanskrit *cakora, cakorah*].

coot - refers to Coot, *Fulia atra*. [Middle English *coot, cout, cote, coote*, Welsh *cwta-air*, literally, short-tailed hen, compare: Dutch *koet*, Middle Dutch *cuut, coet*; unknown origin, possibly echoic of bird's cry].

cormorant - refers to Cormorant, *Phalacrocorax carbo*. [Middle English *cormoraunt, cormeraunt*, Old French *cormoran, cormaran, cormarent, cormareng*, raven of the sea, Latin *corvus*, raven, crow + *marenc*, marine, of the sea].

crake - refers to Corncrake, *Crex crex*. [Middle English *crak*, Old Norse *kraka*, crow, *krakr*, raven, reflective of bird's cry].

crane - refers to Crane, *Grus grus*. [Middle English, Old English *cran*, crane, Old German *kraen*, compare: Dutch *krann*, Old German *kraen*, Low German *kraan*, Welsh *garan*, Old Norse *trana*, Latin *grus*, Greek *geranos*; name may be reflective of bird's cry].

creeper - refers to Tree Creeper, *Certhia familiaris*. [creeper, creep Middle English *crepen, creopen*, Old English *creopan*, to creep, to go bent down, to crawl, compare: Dutch *kruipen*, Old Norse *krjupa*, to creep, Greek *grypos*, curved; + *-er*, Old English *-ere*, suffix].

crossbill - refers to Crossbill, *Loxia curvirostra*. [cross Middle English *cros, crois*, Old English *cros,* Old Irish *cross,* Old Norse *kross*, Latin *crux*, a cross + bill Middle English *bille, bile*, Old English *bile*, beak, bird's bill, *bil*, to strike, in old legend, the bird twisted its bill trying to draw out the nails that held Christ to the Cross].

crow - refers to Crow, *Corvus corone*. [Middle English *croue, crowe*, Old English *craw, crawe, crawa*, a crow, Old English *crawan*, to crow, compare: Middle Dutch *crayen*, Dutch *kraai*, German *kruähe*, Old Icelandic *kraka*, crow; reflective of bird's hoarse cry].

cuckoo - refers to Cuckoo, *Cuculus canorus*. [Early Modern English *cuckow*, Middle English *cuccu, coccou, cukkow*, Old English *coccou, cuccu, cukkow, cocow, cuckow,* Old French *coucou, cucu*, Latin *cuculus*, Greek *kokkux, kokkyx*, Sanskrit *kokilas, kokila*, from the bird's cry].

curlew - refers to Curlew, *Numenius arquata*. [Middle English *curleu*, Middle French *corlieu, courlieu*, Old French *corlieu, corlue, courlis*, from the bird's cry, which sounds like "curlew"].

dipper - refers to Dipper, *Cinclus cinclus*. [dipper, dip Middle English *dippen, duppen*, to baptize, *dipen*, to immerse, Old English *dyppan*, dip, baptize, to plunge in, *dippan, duppan* to immerse, compare: Old Norse *depa*, Swedish *doppa*, Old Saxon *dopian*, Dutch *doopen*; Gothic *daupain*; + *-er*, Old English *-ere*, suffix].

diver - example: Great Northern Diver, *Gavia immer*. In North America, divers are usually called loons, although diver is a folkname for them. [dive Middle English *diven, duven*, Old English *dyfan, dufan*, to immerse, to dip, to sink, to submerge, compare: Old Norse *dufa, dyfa*, to dive or dip; + *-er*, Old English *-ere*, suffix, named for its habit of diving].

dotterel - refers to Dotterel, *Eudromias morinellus*. [dotterel Middle English *doterel, dotterel*, dote Middle English *dotien, doten*, to be foolish, Middle Dutch *doten*, to be silly or crazy, to dote, Old Dutch *doten*, to be silly, compare: Dutch *dutten*, doze, dote, Icelandic *dotta*, to nod from sleep; + diminitive suffix - *erel*, bird named for its supposed stupidity in being easily captured].

dove - examples: Rock Dove, or Pigeon, *Columba livia*, and Turtle Dove, *Streptopelia turtur*. [Middle English *dove, duve, dofe, douve*, Old English *dufe, dufa, dufan*, dark-colored, obscured, compare: Old Saxon *duba*, Dutch *durf*, Danish *due*, Gothic *dubo*, Old Swedish *duva*, Old Norse *dufa*, Old Irish *dub*, black].

duck - example: Tufted Duck, *Aythya fuligula*. [Middle English *doke, douke, duke, duk*, Old English *duce*, a duck, a diver, literally, a ducker, compare: Dutch *duiken*; named for its habit of diving under water while feeding].

dunlin - refers to Dunlin, *Calidris alpina*. [from *dunling*, dun Middle English *dunn*, dark or obscure, gray-brown, Old English *dunn*, dun, dark brown, Old Saxon *dun*, brown, compare: Gaelic *donn, duinne*, brown, Welsh *dwn*, dusky; + *-ling*, Common Germanic, diminutive *-ling*, small].

eagle - example: White-tailed Eagle, *Haliacetus albicilla*. [Middle English *egle*, Anglo-Norman *egle*, Old French *egle, aigle*, Old Provencal *aigla*, Latin *aquila*, black eagle, Latin *aquilus*, dark-colored, blackish].

egret - refers to Great White Egret, *Egretta alba*, or Little Egret, *Egretta garzetta*. [Middle English *egrete*, Anglo-Norman *egrette*, Old French *egrette*, *aigrette*, egret, tuft of feathers, Old Provencal *aigreta*, heron, *aigron*, Old High German *aigron*, *heigir*, heron, from Teutonic source].

eider - refers to Eider, *Somateria mollissima*. [eider Old Norse *ædur*, *æthar*, *aethr*, eider, compare: Danish *edder*, *eder*, Norwegian *ejdar*, Swedish *eider*, Dutch *eider*, German *eider*, Sanskrit *atris*, water bird;].

falcon - example: Red-footed Falcon, *Falco vespertinus*. [Middle English *faucon*, *facon*, Old French *faucon*, *falcun*, *faulcon*, Late Latin *falco*, *falcon*, *falconem*, (named for its curved, sickle-shaped talons), Latin *falx*, *falcis*, sickle, hook-shaped, compare: Old High German *falcho*, Old Norse *falki*;].

finch - refers to Chaffinch, *Fringilla coelebs*. [Middle English *finch*, *fynch*, *fincq*, Old English *finc*, finch, compare: Dutch *vink*, Old High German *fincho*, *finco*, Middle High German *vinke*, German *fink*;].

flamingo - refers to Greater Flamingo, *Phoenicopterus ruber*. [Portuguese *flamengo*, flamingo, Portuguese *flamma*, flame, Spanish *flamenco*, a Fleming, flamingo, Spanish *Fleming*, Old Provencal *flamenc*, flamingo, Old Provencal *flama*, flame, Latin *flamma,* flame, + Germanic suffix *-ing*, named for its bright colors].

flycatcher - refers to Spotted Flycatcher, *Musciapa striata*. [fly Middle English *flye*, *flie*, *fleen*, *flien*, *fleyen*, Old English *flyge*, *flege*, *fleoge*, Old English *fleogan*, to fly, move quickly, flee, Old Saxon *flioga*, fly, compare: Old High German *fliogan*, Old Norse *fljuga*, Dutch *vliegen*; + catch Middle English *cachen*, *cacchen*, Anglo-English *cachier*, Old French *chacier*, Late Latin *captiare*, *capteare*, *capere*, to take, Vulgar Latin *captiare*, Latin *captara*, to catch (an animal) + *-er*, Old English *-ere*, suffix].

fulmar - refers to Fulmar, *Fulmarus glacialis*. [Hebrides dialect, Old Norse *full*, *ful*, foul, unpleasant, + *mar*, sea mew, gull, named for unpleasant odor, from its own oil glands and from its food].

gadwall - refers to Gadwall, *Anas strepera*. [Origin unknown].

gannet - refers to Gannet, *Sula bassana*. [Middle English *gant*, *ganat*, *gante*, *ganot*, gannet, seabird, Old English *ganot*, *ganote*, *ganet*, gannet, solon goose, sea fowl, fen duck, sea bird, compare: Dutch *gent*, Old High German *gannazza*, *ganzo*, gander;].

godwit - refers to Bar-tailed Godwit, *Limosa lapponica* or Black-tailed Godwit, *Limosa limosa*. [Old English *god*, good + Old English *wihta*, *wiht*, an animal, literally, good eating].

goldeneye - refers to Goldeneye, *Bucephala clangula*. [golden Middle English *gilden*, Old English *gylden*, gold(en); gold Middle English *gold*, Old English *gold*, gold, to gleam or shine, compare: Old Norse *gull*, German *gold*, Dutch *goud*, Old Saxon *gold*, Gothic *gulth*, Sanskrit *hiranya*, gold, *hari*, yellow; + *-en*, suffix + eye Middle English *eye*, *eie*, *ege*, *eige*, Old English *ege*, *eage*, *eag*, eye, eye of needle, compare: Old Saxon *oga*, Old Frisian *age*, Frisian *each*, eye, Old High German *ouga*, German *auge*, Dutch *oog*, Old Norse *auga*, Latin *oculus*, eye, Greek *okkos*, eye, Sanskrit *aksi*; named for its gold-colored eye].

goldfinch - refers to Goldfinch, *Carduelis carduelis*. [gold Middle English *gold*, Old English *gold*, gold, to gleam or shine, compare: Old Norse *gull*, German *gold*, Dutch *goud*, Old Saxon *gold*, Gothic *gulth*, Sanskrit *hiranya*, gold, *hari*, yellow; + finch Middle English *finch*, *fynch*, *fincq*, Old English *finc*, finch, compare: Dutch *vink*, Old High German *fincho*, *finco*, Middle High German *vinke*, German *fink*;].

goose - refers to Greylag Goose, *Anser anser.* This goose is the ancestor of the modern domesticated goose. [Middle English *gos, gose, goos,* Old English *gos,* goose, compare: Dutch *gans,* goose, Old Frisian *gos,* Frisian *goes,* goose, Middle High German *gans,* goose, Old High German *gans,* goose, Irish-Gaelic *geis,* swan, Old Norse *gas,* Latin *anser,* Greek *chen,* Sanskrit *hamsa;*].

goshawk - refers to Goshawk, *Accipiter gentilis.* [Middle English *goshauk,* Old English *goshafuc, goshafoc, gos-hafoc,* from *gos,* goose + *hafoc,* hawk].

grebe - refers to Little Grebe, *Tachybaptus ruficollis,* or Great Crested Grebe, *Podiceps cristatus.* [French *grebe,* unknown origin].

grosbeak - refers to Pine Grosbeak, *Pinicola enucleator,* or Scarlet Grosbeak, *Carpodacus erythrinus,* also called Common Rosefinch. [French *grosbec,* from *gros,* large, thick + *bec,* beak].

grouse - refers to Black Grouse, *Tetrao tetrix,* or Willow Grouse, *Lagopus lagopus,* also called Red Grouse. [Early Modern English *grewes, grows, grous,* possibly from *gorse,* heath (or from Latin *grus,* a crane), or from another origin].

guillemot - refers to Guillemot, *Uria aalge.* [French *guillemot,* diminutive of *Guillaume. Guilaume,* William, a proper name].

gull - example: Common Gull, *Larus canus.* [Middle English *gull,* of Celtic origin, Old Cornish *gullan, guilan, gwilan,* gull, (Old English *gul,* yellow, literally, a yellow bird, from prominent yellowness of gull chicks, compare: Icelandic *gulr,* yellow, Danish *gul, gaul,* yellow;) compare: Welsh *gwylan,* seagull, *gilbin,* to weep, wail, Breton *gwelan, goelann, goelan* gull, Old Norse *gulr,* Cornish *gullan,* gull; named for its cry].

gyr falcon - refers to Gyr Falcon, *Falco rusticolus*. [Middle English *gerfaucoun*, *gerfaucon*, *girfaucoun*, Old French *gerfaucon*, *girfaucon*, *gerfauc*, Old Norse *geirfalki*, falcon, spear, Late Latin *gyrofalco*, from *gyros*, a circle, so called from its flight, compare: Old High German *gir*, vulture; + falcon Middle English *faucon*, *facon*, Old French *faucon*, *falcun*, *faulcon*, falcon, Late Latin *falconem*, Latin *falco*].

harrier - example: Hen Harrier, *Circus cyaneus*. [harry Middle English *hergien*, *haryen*, *herien*, *harien*, Old English *hergian*, to make war, to ravage, to lay waste, to plunder, make raid, Old English *here*, an army, predatory troop, band of thieves, compare: Old High German *herion*, Middle High German *hern*, to ravage, to plunder, Old Norse *herja*, to plunder, to make a raid; + *-ier*, French *-ier*, suffix].

hawk - refers to Sparrow Hawk, *Accipter nisus*.[Middle English *hauk*, *hauek*, *havek*, *havec*, Old English *hafoc*, *heafoc*, *heafuc*, *habuc*, *hebuc*, Old Norse *haukr*, compare: Swedish *hök*, Danish *høg*, Middle Low German *havec*, Middle Dutch *havik*, Dutch *havik*, Old High German *habuh*, German *Habicht*, hawk;].

heron - refers to Grey Heron, *Ardea cinerea*. [Middle English *heron*, *heroun*, *heiron*, *hern*, *heyrun*, *heyroun*, *hayroun*, *heiroun*, Old French *heron*, *hairon*, *haigron*, *hegron*, heron, compare: Old High German *heigir*, *heiger*, *heigara*, *heigir*, heron, Old Norse *hegri*, *heri*, heron, of Teutonic origin; from bird's cry].

ibis - refers to Glossy Ibis, *Plegadis falcinellus*. [Middle English *ibin*, *ybyn*, Latin *ibis*, Greek *ibis*, ibis, (Egyptian *hb*, *hbj*, *heb*, *hib*, *hab*, a sacred bird of Egypt + Greek suffix, *-is*)].

jay - refers to Jay, *garrulus glandarius*. [Middle English *jay*, Old French *jay*, *gai*, *geai*, *iay*, *gay*, jay, (possibly from Old French *gai*, gay, so called from its gay plumage), Late Latin *gaius*, a jay, Vulgar Latin *gaius*, Latin *Gaius*, a proper name, Latin root name imitative of bird's call].

kestrel - refers to Kestrel, *Falco tinnunculus* or Lesser Kestrel, *Falco naumanni*. [Early Modern English *castrel, kistrell, kestril*, Middle English *castrel, castrell*, Old French *cresserelle, cresserele, quercerelle*, kestrel, clacker, Vulgar Latin *crepicella*, a rattle, Latin *crepitaculum*, a rattle, Latin *crista*, crest, name reflects bird's cry].

kingfisher - refers to Kingfisher, *Alcedo atthis*. [Middle English *kyngys fyschare*, king's fisher, Old English *cyng*, king + *fiscere*, fisher].

kinglet - old common name for Gold-crested Wren, *Regulus cristatus*, now named Goldcrest, *Regulus regulus*. [kinglet, king Middle English *king*, monarch, chief ruler, Old English *cing, cyng, cyning, cynn*, king, a tribe, compare: Old Saxon *kuning*, Dutch *koning*, Old High German *kuning*, German *könig*, Old Norse *konungr*, Danish *konge*; + *-let* Middle English, Middle French *-el*, (Old French *-elet*, Latin *-ellus*) + *et* Old French *-et*, suffix].

kite - refers to Red Kite, *Milvus milvus*, or Black Kite, *Milvus migrans*. [Middle English *kite, kyte*, Old English *cyta, kyte*, kite, bittern, compare: Welsh *cud*, Breton *kidel*, a hawk; name reflects bird's cry].

kittewake - refers to Kittewake, *Rissa tridactyla*. [kittewake, cattiwake, name from bird's cry].

knot - refers to Knot, *Calidris canutus*. [Middle English *knot, knotte*, Old English *cnotta*, compare: German *knoten*, Danish *knude*, Latin *nodus*, a knot, unknown origin].

lapwing - refers to Lapwing, *Vanellus vanellus*. [Middle English *lappewinke, lapwinge, lap wynke, leepwynke*, lapwink, Old English *læpwince, hlæpewince, hleapewince, hleapan, hledpewince*, lapwing, one who turns about in flight or running, literally, 'a wavering leap,' Old English *hleapan*, to leap, jump, + Old English *wincian*, to wink, compare: *wancol*, wavering; present form uses: + wing Middle English *winge, wenge, weng*, Old Norse *vænht, vængr, vǣngr*, bird's wing, compare: Swedish *vinge*; refers to bird's slow irregular flapping flight].

lark - example: Skylark, *Alauda arvensis*. [Middle English *lark, laverke, laverock, larke*, Old English *laferce, læwerce, lauricæ, lawerce, lauerce*, lark, compare: Danish *lerke*, Dutch *leeuwerik*, Old Swedish *lærikia*, Low German *lewerke*, Old High German *lerahha*, Old Norse *laevirki, lævirki*, German, *Lerche*, lark; unknown origin, possibly echoic].

linnet - refers to Linnet, *Carduelis cannabina*. [Middle English *linet*, Old English *linete, linece*, from *linetwige*, linnet, Old French *linette, linot, linotte*, from *lin*, flax, + -ottus, Roman diminutive suffix, Latin *linum*, flax, so called from its habit of feeding on the seeds of flax and hemp].

magpie - refers to Magpie, *Pica pica*. [magpie, Middle English *magpye, magot, magot pie* (from bird's habit of picking maggots from the backs of sheep), *mag*, nickname of *Margaret*, French *Margot*, a magpie, diminutive of French *Marguerite*, Latin *margarita*, a pearl + pie Middle English *pie*, Old French *pie*, Latin *pica*, magpie].

mallard - refers to Mallard, *Anas platyrnchos*. [Middle English *malarde*, Old French *mallart, malart*, a wild drake, Old French *male*, male, Flemish *maskelaar*].

martin - refers to Sand Martin, *Riparia riparia*, or House Martin, *Delichon urbica*. [Middle English *martoune*, from the proper name *Martin*, Middle French *martin, Martin*, Latin *Martinus*, Latin *Mars*, god of war].

merganser - refers to Red-breasted Merganser, *Mergus serrator*. [Modern Latin *merganser*, Latin *mergus*, diver, gull, a kind of diving duck + Latin *anser*, goose, duck].

merlin - refers to Merlin, *Falco columbarius*. [Middle English *merlion*, *meriloun*, Old English *marlin*, *marlion*, Anglo-French *merilun*, Old French *esmerillon*, diminutive of *esmeril*, merlin].

nightingale - refers to Nightingale, *Luscinia megarhynchos*. [Middle English *nigtingale*, *nihtegale*, *nihtingale*, Old English *nihtegala*, *nihtegale*, night Middle English *night*, *niht*, Old English *niht*, *næht*, *neaht*, night + Old English *galan*, to sing, compare: Dutch *nachtegaal*, Old Saxon *nahtigala*, Old High German *nahtigala*, German *nachtigall*;].

nightjar - refers to Nightjar, *Caprimulgus europaeus*. [night Middle English *night*, *niht*, Old English *niht*, *næht*, *neaht*, night, compare: Old Saxon naht, Old High German naht, Old Norse nott, natt, Gothic nahts, Old Slavic nosti, German *nacht*, Latin *nox*, night, Greek *nyx*, *nyktos*, Sanskrit *nakta*, *nakti*; + jar, *jar*, *chirr*, *gerre*, *ier*, *charre*, harsh sounds, Middle English *charken*, to creak, Old English *cearcian*, to gnash, named for sounds made by bird].

nutcracker - refers to Nutcracker, *Nucifraga caryocatactes*. [nut Middle English *nutte*, *nute*, *note*, Old English *hnutu*, compare: Old Norse *hnot*, Old High German *nuz*, Old Irish *enu*, Welsh *eneuen*, Dutch *noot*, German *nuss*, Latin *nux*, *nucis*; + crack Middle English *craken*, *craken*, to crack, to crash, to break, Old English *cracian*, to crack, Old English *cracina*, to resound, compare: Gaelic *crac*, *cnac*, crack, break, crash, German *kracken*, Dutch *kraken*; + -er, Old English -ere, suffix].

nuthatch - refers to Nuthatch, *Sitta europaea*. [Middle English *notehach, notehak, notehagge, nuthake, notehache, nuthak,* literally, nut-hacker, nut Middle English *nutte, nute,* Old English *hnutu,* compare: Old Norse *hnot,* Dutch *noot,* German *nuss*; + hatch Late Middle English *hache,* Medieval French *hach(er),* to cut up, from *hache,* ax, or from hack Old English *hacke(n),* Old English (to) *haccian,* to hack to pieces, an allusion to bird's ability to crack nuts].

oriole - refers to Golden Oriole, *Oriolus oriolus*. [oriole New Latin *oriolus,* French *oriol,* Old French *oriol,* Middle Latin *auerolus,* golden, diminutive of Latin *aureus,* golden, Latin *aurum,* gold].

osprey - refers to Osprey, *Pandion haliaetus*. [Late Middle English *ospray,* Old French *ospres, ospreit,* Latin *ossifraga,* the osprey or bone-breaker].

ouzel - refers to Ring Ouzel, *Turdus torquatus*. [ouzel, ousel Middle English *ouzel, osul, osel, ouizle, uzzle, ousel,* Old English *osle,* blackbird, compare: Old High German *amsala,* German *amsel;*].

owl - example: Barn Owl, *Tyto alba*. [Middle English *ule, owle, oule,* Old English *ule,* compare: Dutch *uil,* Old High German *uwila,* Middle High German *iuwel, iule,* Old Saxon *uwila,* German *eule,* Danish *ugle,* Old Norse *ugla,* Latin *ulula,* screech owl, Latin *ululare,* to howl, the owl's call was consider similar to a wolf's howl; reflective of bird's call,].

oystercatcher - refers to Oystercatcher, *Haematopus ostralegus*. [oyster Middle English *oistre,* Old French *oistre, uistre,* Latin *ostrea, ostreum,* oyster, Greek *ostreon,* oyster, Greek *osteron,* bone, *ostrakon,* hard shell + catch Middle English *cacchen,* Anglo-English *cachier,* Old French *chacier,* Latin *captare,* to seize + *-er,* Old English *-ere,* suffix].

partridge - refers to Partridge, *Perdix perdix*. [Early Modern English *pertridge*, Middle English *pertrich*, *partrich*, *partriche*, *pertriche*, Scottish *partrick*, Old English *pertriche*, Old French *perdriz*, *perdix*, *pertris*, *perdrix*, Latin *perdix*, partridge, Greek *perdix*, from flight sounds].

pelican - refers to White Pelican, *Pelecanus onocrotalus*, or Dalmatian Pelican, *Pelecanus crispus*. [pelican, pelecan Middle English *pelican*, *pellican*, Old English *pellican*, *pellicane*, Old French *pelican*, Late Latin *pelicanus*, Latin *pelicanus*, *pelecanus*, pelican, Greek *pelekan*, Greek *pelekus*, *pelekys*, axe, Sanskrit *parasus*, axe, Assyro-Babylonian *piliqqu*, axe, Sumerian *balaq*, name reflecting bird's bill shape].

peregrine - refers to Peregrine, *Falco peregrinus*. [Middle English *pelegrim*, Old French *pelegrin*, Late Latin *pelegrinus*, travelling abroad, Latin *peregrinis*, foreign, Latin *peregrinus*, foreigner, *per*, through + *ager*, territory, country, field, so called because of its long migrations].

petrel - refers to Storm Petrel, *Hydrobates pelagicus*, or Leach's Storm Petrel, *Sula bassana*. [petrel French *petrel*, Late Latin *Petrus*, Peter, Latin *Petrus*, Peter, Greek *Petros*, Peter, reference to St. Peter's walking upon the Lake of Gennesareth, from the bird's seeming ability to walk on water (feeding on surface swimming organisms)].

phalarope - example: Red-necked Phalarope, *Phalaropus lobatus*. [French, Modern Latin *phalaropus*, Greek *phalaris*, a coot + *pous*, a foot].

pheasant - refers to Pheasant, *Phasianus colchicus*. [Middle English *fesan*, *fesant*, *fesaunt*, *faisant*, Anglo-Norman *fesaunt*, Old French *faisan*, *fesan*, *fesant*, *faisant*, Provencal *faisan*, Latin *phasianus*, Latin *Phasianus*, the Phasian Bird, Greek *phasaianos*, the Phasian bird, after *Phasis*, river of Colchis, where birds collected at the river's mouth, on the Black Sea, in what is now Georgia].

pigeon - refers to Wood Pigeon, *Columba palumbus*, or Rock Dove, *Columba livia*, commonly known as Domestic Pigeon. [Middle English *pigeon, pejon, peion, pyion, pegeon, pygeon, pichon, pijon*, pigeon, dove, Middle French *pigeon, pijon*, Old French *pijon, pyjoun, pipion*, young bird, young dove, Late Latin *pipo, pipio, pipire*, chirping bird, Latin *pipio*, squab, young bird, Latin *pipire*, to peep, of imitative origin].

pintail - refers to Pintail, *Anas acuta*. [Middle English *pinne, pyn*, Old English *pinn*, a pin, a peg, Latin *pinna*, wing, feather, compare: German *pinne*, Dutch *pin*, Middle Low German *pinne*, Old Norse *pinni*; + tail Middle English *tail, tayl*, Old English *tægel, tægl*, tail, compare: Old Norse *tayl*, Old High German *zagal*, Swedish *tagel*, Gothic *tagl*, hair; named for its long central tail feathers].

pipit - example: Meadow Pipit, *Anthus pratensis*, or Tree Pipit, *Anthus trivialis*. [Early Modern English *pipit, pippit*, name is probably a reflection of the bird's call].

plover - example: Ringed Plover, *Charadrius hiaticula*, or Little Ringed Plover, *Charadrius dubius*. [Middle English *plover, pluver*, Anglo-Norman *plover*, Old French *plovier, pluvier, plevier*, rain bird, Vulgar Latin *pluviarius*, Latin *pluvia*, rain, named because flocks usually arrived in rainy season].

pochard - refers to Pochard, *Aythya ferina*, or Red-crested Pochard, *Netta rufina*. [unknown origin].

ptarmigan - refers to Ptarmigan, *Lagopus mutus*. [Greek *pteron*, wing + Scottish-Gaelic *tarmigan, tarmachan, termigan, termagant, tormichan, termigant*, ptarmigan, unknown origin].

puffin - refers to Puffin, *Fratercula arctica*. [Middle English *poffin, pophyn, puffon, puffoun, pofin*, Cornish, possibly from Middle English *puf*, puff, reflecting bird's plump appearance or large beak].

quail - refers to Quail, *Coturnix coturnix*. [Middle English *quaille, quayle, quaile*, Old French *quaille, caille*, Medieval Latin *quaccula, coacula*, Middle Latin *quaccola, cuacula*, compare: Dutch *kwakkel*, Old High German *quahtela*, name is a reflection of the bird's cry].

rail - refers to Water Rail, *Rallus aquaticus*. [Middle English *raile, rayle, rale, rayl*, Anglo-Norman *radle*, Middle French *rale, raale, raaler*, to rattle or screech, Old French *raille, raale, raalle*, Vulgar Latin *rasclare, rascula*, to grate, reflective of bird's call].

raven - refers to Raven, *Corvus corax*. [Middle English *raven, reven, reaven*, Old English *hrefn, hræfn*, Old Norse *hrafn*, compare: Middle Dutch *raven*, Dutch *raaf*, Danish *ravn*, Middle Low German *rave*, Old High German *hraban, rabo*, Middle High German *raben, rabe*, German *rabe*, Latin *cornix*, a crow, Greek *korax*; name reflective of bird's harsh call].

razorbill - refers to Razorbill, Razorbilled Auk, *Alca torda*. [razor Middle English *rasoure, rasor, rasour*, Old French *rasor, raser, rasour*, to scape, Vulgar Latin *rasdre*, Late Latin *rasorium*, a scraper, Latin *radere*, scrape, to shave + bill Middle English *bil, bile, bille*, Old English *bile*, beak of a bird, named for its rather short, sharp bill,].

redpoll - refers to Redpoll, *Acanthis flammea*. [red Middle English *red, reed, read*, Old English *read*, red, compare: Old Saxon *rod*, Old Norse *rathr, rjothr, rauor, rjoor*, Danish *rød*, Old Frisian *rad*, Frisian *rea(d)*, red, Middle Dutch *root, rood*, Old High German *rot*, Middle High German *rot*, Gothic *rauths*, Gaelic *ruadh*, reddish, ruddy, red-haired, Latin *ruber, rufus*, red, Greek *erythos*, Sanskrit *rudhira, rohita*; + poll Middle English *pol*, head, especially back portion].

redstart - refers to Redstart, *Phoenicurus phoenicurus*. [red Middle English *reed,* Old English *read,* red, compare: Old Saxon *rod,* Old Norse *rathr, rjothr, rauor, rjoor,* Danish *rød,* Old Frisian *rad,* Frisian *rea(d),* red, Middle Dutch *root, rood,* Old High German *rot,* Middle High German *rot,* Gothic *rauths,* Gaelic *ruadh,* reddish, ruddy, red-haired, Latin *ruber, rufus,* red, Greek *erythos,* Sanskrit *rudhira, rohita*; + start Middle English *start, stert, sterten, stirte, stuarte, starte,* an animal's tail, Old English *steort,* tail, rump].

robin - refers to Robin, *Erithacus reubecula.* [from Middle English *Robin Redbreast,* Middle English *Robin,* Old French *Robin,* a nickname from *Robert,* a proper name, Old High German *Hruodperht,* Robert, fame-bright, bright with glory, from *hruod-, ruod-,* fame, glory + *berahr,* bright].

rook - refers to Rook, *Corvus frugilegus.* [Middle English *rok, roc, rook,* Old English *roc, hroc,* compare: Middle Dutch *roec, roek,* rook, Old Norse *hrokr,* rook, Old High German *hruoh,* crow, Danish *raage,* Latin *cornix,* crow, Greek *krozeir,* to croak, to caw; name reflective of bird's call].

ruff - refers to Ruff, *Philomachus pugnax.* [ruff, ruffle Middle English *ruffe,* Middle English *ruffelen,* to wrinkle, compare: Early Frisian *ruffeln,* Old Norse *rjufa,* to break, Low German *ruffelen,* to wrinkle, curl; a reference to its puffed-out neck feathers].

sanderling, refers to Sanderling, *Calidris alba.* [Old English *sandyroling,* sand Middle English *sand, sond,* Old English *sond, sand,* compare: Old Saxon *sand,* Old Norse *sandr,* Danish *sand,* Old Frisian *sond,* Frisian *san,* sand, Middle Dutch *sant, sand*; Dutch *zand,* Middle High German *sant,* Old High German *sant,* German *sand*; + -er, Old English *-ere,* suffix + *-ling* Old English *-ling,* Old Norse *-lingr,* small].

sandgrouse - refers to Black-bellied Sandgrouse, *Pterocles orientalis*, or Pin-tailed Sandgrouse, *Pterocles alchata*. [sand Middle English *sand*, *sond*, Old English *sond*, *sand*, compare: Old Saxon *sand*, Old Norse *sandr*, Danish *sand*, Old Frisian *sond*, Frisian *san*, sand, Middle Dutch *sant*, *sand*, Dutch *zand*, Middle High German *sant*, Old High German *sant*, German *sand*; + grouse Early Modern English *grewes*, *grows*, *grous*, possibly from *gorse*, heath or from Latin *grus*, a crane, or from another origin, inhabits arid, sandy areas of Eurasia].

sandpiper - example: Common Sandpiper, *Actitis hypoleucos*, or Purple Sandpiper, *Calidris maritima*. [sand Middle English *sand*, *sond*, Old English *sond*, *sand*, compare: Old Saxon *sand*, Old Norse *sandr*, Danish *sand*, Old Frisian *sond*, Frisian *san*, sand, Middle Dutch *sant*, *sand*, Dutch *zand*, Middle High German *sant*, Old High German *sant*, German *sand*; + piper Middle English *pipere*, Old English *pipere*, Latin *pipiare*, a pipe, a wind instrument].

scaup - refers to Scaup, *Aythya marila*. [Scottish *scalp*, *scaup*, a bed of mussels, named for its eating habits].

scoter - refers to Common Scoter, *Melanitta nigra*. [English dialect *scote*, shoot, scoot, to squirt, compare: Old Norse *skoti*, a shooter, Old Norse *skjota*, to shoot out; named for its swift movements].

shag - refers to Shag, *Phalacrocorax aristotelis*. [shag Middle English *shagge*, Old English *sceacga*, hair or rough hair, compare: Old Norse *skegg*, beard, Danish *skjæg*, Swedish *skägg*; name refers to bird's rough crest].

shearwater - example: Manx Shearwater, *Puffinus puffinus*.
[shear Middle English *scheren*, *sheren*, to shear, cut, shave, Old
English *sceran*, *scieran*, *scyran*,to cut, shear, compare: Old Frisian *skera*, Frisian *skeare*, shave, Old High German *sceran*,
Middle High German *scheren*, to shear, Dutch *scheren*, Old
Norse *skera*; + water Middle English *water*, *wæter*, *weter*, Old
English *wæter*, compare Old Saxon *watar*, Old Frisian *wetir*,
weter, Low German *water*, Danish *vand*, Swedish *vatten*, Greek
hydor, Sanskrit *udan*, water, Hittite *watar*, water;].

shrike - refers to Great Grey Shrike, *Lanius excubitor*, or Red-
backed Shrike, *Lanius collurio*.[Old English *scric*, *screc*, thrush
or shrike, compare: Middle Low German *schrik*, corncrake,
Swedish *shrika*, jay, Icelandic *skrikja*, shrike, Icelandic *skrikja*,
the shrike, to titter, Norwegian *shrike*, jay; from bird's cry].

siskin - refers to Siskin, *Carduelis spinus*. [siskin Middle Dutch
siseken, *sijskijn*, Early Flemish *sijsken*, Middle Low German
sisek, *csitze*, diminutive of *zeisig*, siskin, canary, of Slavic origin, compare: Polish *czyz*; + kin Middle Dutch *-kin*, *-kijn*, *-ken*,
Middle Low German *-kin*, small, little, of imitative origin].

skua - refers to Great Skua, *Stercorarius skua*. [Modern Latin,
Faeroese *skugvur*, *skugver*, Old Norse *skufr*, *skumr*, the skua or
brown gull, compare: Icelandic *skumi*, dusk, Swedish *skum*,
dusky, Old Norse *skufr*, tassel, tuft; unknown origin, possibly
named for color].

skylark - refers to Skylark, *Alauda arvensis*. [sky Middle
English *skye*, *skie*, sky, cloud, Old Norse *sky*, cloud, cloudy sky,
compare: Old Saxon *scio*, cloud; + lark Middle English
laverock, lark, *laverke*, Old English *laferce*, *læwerce*, *lauricæ*,
unknown origin].

snipe - refers to Snipe, *Gallinago gallinago*. [snipe, Scandinavian origin, Middle English *snipe, snype*, Old English *snite*, Old Norse *snipa, snipe*, compare: Danish *sneppe*, snipe, Dutch *snip*, German *schnepfe*, snipe, snite, Old Saxon *sneppa*, Middle Dutch *snippe, sneppe*, Old High German *snepfa, schnepfe*, from German *schneppe*, bill; named after its long beak].

sparrow - refers to House Sparrow, *Passer domesticus*, or Tree Sparrow, *Passer montanus*. [Middle English *sparowe, sparwa, sparewe, sparwe*, Old English *spearwa*, sparrow, compare: Middle High German *sparwe*, Old High German *sparo*, German *sperling*, Gothic *sparwa*, Old Norse *spörr*, Danish *spurv, spurre*, Frisian *sparreg*;].

spoonbill - refers to Spoonbill, *Platalea leucorodia*. [spoon Middle English *spoon, spon, spone*, spoon, chip, Old English *spon*, wood chip, compare: Old Norse *sponn, spann*, chip, spoon, Dutch *spaan*, spoon, Danish *spaan*, Middle Dutch *spaen*, Old High German *span*, Middle High German *span*; + bill Middle English *bil, bile*, Old English *bill, bil, bile*, to strike, compare: Old Saxon *bil*, sword, Old High German *bill*, pickax, Old Norse *bildr*, Old Slavic *biti*, to strike; named for unique spoon-like shape of bill].

starling - refers to Starling, *Sturnus vulgaris*. [Early Modern English *sterlyng*, proper surname *Starling*, Middle English *sterling, sterlyng*, Old English *stærling, stæline*, a diminutive of *stær*, starling, *sterlyng*, Latin *sturnus*, starling, star, compare: Old Norse *stari*, Danish *stær*, Swedish *stare*, Old High German *stard*, Middle High German *star*; + *-ling* Old English *-ling*, Old Norse *-lingr*, small].

stilt - refers to Black-winged Stilt, *Himantopus himantopus*. [Middle English *stilte*, Middle Low German *stilte*, Flemish *stilte*, compare: Danish *stylte*, stilt, Dutch *stelt*, German *stelze*, stilt, Swedish *styla*, Old High German *stelza*; named for its extra-long legs].

stork - refers to White Stork, *Ciconia ciconia*. [Middle English, Old English *storc*, compare: Old Norse *storkr*, Old Saxon *stork*; Dutch *stork*, Danish *stork*, Swedish *stork*, Old High German *storah*, German *storch*, Middle High German *storch*, stork; according to an old legend, a stork passes over a house where a baby is about to be born, hence, the stork's connection to the bringing of a child into the world, refers to bird's stiff-legged walk or its stiff stance].

swallow - refers to Swallow, *Hirundo rustica*. [Early Modern English *swallowe, swallow*, Middle English *swalwe, swalu, swalowe, swalewe*, Old English *swalewe, swalewe, swealwe*, swallow, compare: Old Frisian *swale*, Old High German *swalawa, swalwa*, Old Saxon *swala*, Middle Dutch *swalu*, Dutch *zwaluw*, German *schwalbe*, Old Norse *svala*;].

swan - example: Mute Swan, *Cygnus olor*. [Middle English *swan*, Old English *swan*, compare: Dutch *zwaan*, Icelandic *svanr*, Old Saxon *swan, suan*, Old High German *swan, swan(a), swon*, German *schwan*, Swedish *svan*, Danish *svane*, Latin *sonare*, to sound, Sanskrit *svan*, to resound, to sound, to sing; possibly echoic from sounds of singing swan].

swift - refers to Swift, *Apus apus*. [Middle English, Old English *swift*, Old English *swifan*, to move in a course, sweep, move quickly, compare: Old English *swapan*, to sweep, Old English *swipu*, a whip, Old Norse *svifa*, to rove, to turn, to sweep, Old Frisian *swivia*, Old High German *sweibon*, to move or turn quickly, Middle High German *sweifen*, to swing; refers to bird's rapid flight].

teal - refers to Teal, *Anas crecca*. [Early Modern English *tele, teale*, Middle English *tele*, compare: Middle Dutch *teelingh, teiling, teling*, teal, Dutch *teling, taling*; unknown origin].

tern - example: Common Tern, *Sterna hirundo*. [of Scandinavian origin, compare: Danish *terne, tærene*, Swedish *tarna*, Faroese *terna*; Old Norse *therna*, tern].

thrush - refers to Song Thrush, *Turdus philomelos*, or Mistle Thrush, *Turdus viscivorus*. [Middle English *thrusch, thrusche*, Old English *thrysce, thrysee, thryssce, thruesce*, a thrush, Latin *turdus*, thrush].

tit - example: Great Tit, *Parus major*. [shortened form of *titmouse*, Middle English *tit*, Icelandic *tittr*, titmouse, a bird, a small plug or pin, literally, anything small, Old Norse *titlingr*, little bird].

turnstone - refers to Turnstone, *Arenaria interpres*. [turn Middle English *turnen*, *tournen*, Old English *turnian, tyrnan*, Old French *turner, tourner, torner*, to turn, Latin *tornare*, to round off, to turn on a lathe, from Latin *tornus*, a lathe, Greek *tornos*, a (turner's) lathe, a turner's chisel, a carpenter's tool for drawing circles + stone Middle English *ston*, Old English *stan*, named for bird's food gathering technique which involves turning over small stones].

vulture - example: Black Vulture, *Aegypius monaehus*. [Middle English *vulture, vultur, voltur, voltor*, Anglo-Norman *vultur*, Old French *voultour, voltour, vautour, voltor*, Latin *vulturius, vultur*, a vulture, Old Latin *uolturus*, a tearer].

wagtail - refers to Grey Wagtail, *Motacilla cinerea*. [wagtail, wagstert, wagsterd, wagstyrt, wag Middle English *wagge*, *waggen*, Old English *wagian*, to move, wag, totter, sway, Old Norse *vagga, vaga*, a cradle, compare: Swedish *vagga*, to wag, to sway, to rock (a cradle), Middle Dutch vagen, Middle High German *wacken*, to totter, shake; + *stert*, a tail, named for the bird's continual wagging of its tail].

warbler - example: Grasshopper Warbler, *Locustella naevia*. [warble Middle English *werble, werblen, werbelen, werbeln, werblen*, Norman French *werbler, werble*,to sing, trill, play on a musical instrument, Middle High German *werbelen, wirbeln*, to warble, to roll, to rotate, to turn, compare: Old Frankish *wirbil*, whirlwind;].

waxwing - refers to Waxwing, *Bombycilla garrulus*. [wax Middle English *wax*, *wex*, Old English *wæx*, *weax*, beeswax, wax, compare: Old Frisian *wax*, Frisian *waaks*, wax, Dutch *was*, German *wachs*, Old High German *wahs*, Old Norse *vax*, Swedish *vax*, Danish *vox*; + wing Middle English *winge*, *wenge*, *whing*, *weng*, Old Norse *vængir*, *vængr*, a wing, compare: Dutch *wagien*, to fly, to blow; named for red spots resembling flattened tips of red sealing wax on wings].

weaver finch - a genus of Old World birds, example: House Sparrow, *Passer domesticus*. [weaver, weave, Middle English *weuen*, *weven*, Old English *wefan*, to weave, compare: Old High German *weban*, Old Norse *vefa*, Dutch *weven*, German *weben*, Danish *væve;* + finch Middle English *fincq*, *finch*, *fynch*, Old English *finc*, so called for their elaborate woven nests].

wheatear - refers to Wheatear, *Oenathe oenanthe*. - [Early Modern English *wheatear*, *wheatears*, *wheat*, *whiteass*, *white rump*, *whitetail*, *wheat*, white + *ers*, *eeres*, arse, Old English *hwit*, white + *ærs*, rump, in reference to its white rump].

whimbrel - refers to Whimbrel, *Numenius phaeopus*. [*whympernell*, *whimrel*, from *whimp*, + *-rel*, Old French *-erel*, named after its cry].

wigeon - refers to Wigeon, *Anas penelope*. [wigeon, widgeon Early Modern English *wigene*, *widgeon*, *wigeon* Middle French *vigeon*, a kind of duck, Old French *vigeon*, Latin *vipio*, a kind of small crane].

woodcock - refers to Woodcock, *Scolopax rusticola*. [Middle English *wodekoc*, Old English *wude-coco*, *wuducoc*, from Old English *wudu*, *widu*, *wude*, *wiodu*, wood + *cocc*, *coce*, cock].

woodpecker -example: Great Spotted Woodpecker, *Dendrocopos major*. [wood Middle English *wode*, *wude*, Old English *wudu*, *wude*, *widu*, *wiodu*, wood, forest, compare: Old High German *wit*, Old Norse *vithr*, Danish *ved*, wood, Swedish *ved*, wood, Gaelic *fiodh*, Old Irish *fid*, Welsh *gwydd*, trees, shrubs; + peck Middle English *pecken*, a variant of *picken*, pick, Old English *pycan*, to pick or peck, Middle Low German *pekken*, to peck with beak + *-er*, Old English *-ere*, suffix].

wren - refers to Wren, *Troglodytes troglodytes*. [Middle English *wren*, *wrenne*, Old English *werna*, *wrenna*, *wærna*, *wrænna*, a wren, compare: Old Norse *rindill*, Old High German *wrendo*, *wrendilo*].

yellowhammer - refers to Yellowhammer, *Emberiza citrinella*. [yellowhammer, yellow-ham, yelamire, yelambre, yellowammer, Old English *geolu*, yellow +*hama*, covering, i.e., yellow-feathered bird, compare: German *Ammer*, bunting; (yelamire Old English *geolu*, yellow + *amore*, a kind of bird, a small bird, akin to Old High German *amaro*, a kind of finch that fed on emmer), compare: Middle Dutch *emmerick*, a yellowammer, German *gelbammer*, *goldammer*, yellow-ammer, goldammer;].

yellowlegs - refers to Greater Yellowlegs, *Tringa melanoleuca*, or Lesser Yellowlegs, *Tringa flavipes*. [yellow Middle English *yelow*, *yelwe*, *yelu*, *yelowe*, Old English *geolu, geolo, geolwe*, compare: Dutch *geel*, Old Saxon *gelo*, Old High German *gelo*, German *gelb*, Old Norse *gulr*; + leg Middle English, Old Norse *legge*, *leggr*, leg, bone, named for its yellow-colored legs].

North American Bird Name Origins

Bird names that were created by the colonial immigrants from England had linguistic roots that came from English bird names, Native American names, Spanish names, Portuguese names, French-canadian names, bird calls, bird habits, and bird colors. The following is a listing of common American bird names, with etymology enclosed within brackets. Scientific names and roots are italicized. These species were the first ones to be encountered by the English colonists settling in the Northeast and Mid-Atlantic areas. When possible, individual species referred to by the generic name are listed. If many birds have the same root name, then an example is selected. The scientific names, root words, word of the same meaning in other languages amd cognates are all shown in italics. All spelling variations for the italicized root words are listed. With the exception of Scandinavian words with umlauts, diacritical marks for pronunciation have been omitted for ease of reading. Alternative etymologies are listed within parentheses. [Barnhart][Fowler][Newfeldt][Onions][Soukhanov] [Skeat][Weekley].

albatross - refers to Black-footed Albatross, *Diomedea nigripes*, or Laysan Albatross, *Diomedea immutabilis*. [Latin *albus*, white, + Early Modern English *alcatras*, alcatraz, frigatebird, pelican, Portuguese *algratross*, *alcatra*, Portuguese *akatraz*, cormorant, albatross, (from Portuguese *alcatraz*, bucket, water jar, *alcatruz*, bucket of a water wheel), Spanish *alcatraz*, *alcatra*, pelican, Arabic *al-qadus*, machine for drawing water, jar, pitcher, Arabic *al*, the + *ghattas*, a sea eagle, Greek *kados*, jar, water vessel, Hebrew *kad*, *kadh*, water jar, bucket, named for the size and shape of the bird's pouch, based on the old tale that the pelican carried water to its young in its pouch].

anhinga - refers to Anhinga, *Anhinga anhinga*. [Portuguese, Tupi *ayinga*].

ani - refers to Smooth-billed Ani, *Crotophaga ani,* or Groove-billed Ani, *Crotophaga sulcirostris.* [South American Spanish *ani,* Portuguese, Brazilian, Tupi *ani*].

auklet - example: Crested Auklet, *Aethia cristatella.* [auklet, auk from Scandinavian, Old Norse *alka,* auk, compare: Danish *alke,* Swedish *alka,* auk; + diminutive suffix, *-let,* small].

avocet - refers to American Avocet, *Recurvirostra americana.* [avocet, avoset, French *avocette,* Italian *avocetta, avosetta,* Ferrarese *avosetta, avocetta,* literally, "graceful bird," diminutive, Latin *avis,* bird, unknown origin].

bald eagle - refers to Bald Eagle, *Haliaeetus leucocephalus.* [bald Middle English *balled, ballede,* shining, white, from obs. *bal,* white spot, Celtic *bal,* a white mark, + *-ed,* adjectival suffix, compare: Breton *bal,* a white mark on an animal's face, Welsh *bal,* having a white spot on the forehead, Danish *bældet,* bald, Gothic *bala,* white-faced horse, Lithuanian *baltus,* white; + eagle Middle English *egle,* Anglo-Norman *egle,* Old French *egle, aigle,* Old Provencal *aigla,* Latin *aquila,* black eagle, Latin *aquilus,* dark-colored, blackish].

baldpate - refers to Baldpate, or American Widgeon, *Mareca americana.* [bald Middle English *balled, ballede,* shining, white, from obs. *bal,* white spot, Celtic *bal,* a white mark, + *-ed,* adjectival suffix, compare: Breton *bal,* a white mark on an animal's face, Welsh *bal,* having a white spot on the forehead, Danish *bældet,* bald, Gothic *bala,* white-faced horse, Lithuanian *baltus,* white; + pate Middle English *pate,* the head, origin unknown, so called because of white markings on its head].

baltimore oriole - refers to Baltimore Oriole, *Icterus galbula*, now named Northern Oriole. [baltimore, so named for having the same colors, black and orange, as the coat of arms and livery of Lord Baltimore, the son of the founder of the State of Maryland] + [oriole French *oriol*, Old French *oriol*, Middle Latin *auerolus*, golden, Latin *aureus*, golden, Latin *aurum*, gold].

bananaquit - refers to Bananaquit, or Bahama Honeycreeper, *Coereba flaveola*. [banana Portuguese, Spanish, Wolof (a West African language), *banana*. + quit, Jamaican suffix for small birds, compare: John-chewit; echoic origin, named after its call].

barn swallow - refers to Barn Swallow, *Hirundo rustica*. [barn Middle English *bern*, Old English *bern*, *beren*, from *bere-ern*, *bere*, barley + *ærn*, a place, a building, + swallow Early Modern English *swallowe*, *swallow*, Middle English *swalwe*, *swalu*, *swalowe*, *swalewe*, Old English *swalewe*, *swalewe*, *swealwe*, swallow, compare: Old Frisian *swale*, Old High German *swalawa*, *swalwa*, Old Saxon *swala*, Middle Dutch *swalu*, Old Norse *svala*; from bird's predilication for barns and other old buildings].

becasse - folkname for American Woodcock and Black-necked Stilt. [French *becasse*, woodcock].

becassine - folkname for American Avocet, American Woodcock, Black-necked Stilt, Common Snipe, Short-billed Dowitcher and Solitary Sandpiper. [French *becassine*, snipe].

becard - refers to Rose-throated Becard, *Platypsaris aglaiae*. [French *becard*, *beccard*, a merganser with a prominant beak, French *bec*, beak, + French *-ard*, a depreciative suffix, compare: French *becarde*, shrike; refers to its large, hooked beak].

bittern - refers to American Bittern, *Botaurus lentiginosus*, or Least Bittern, *Ixobrychus exilis*. [Middle English *bitor, bitore, bitour, bittour, bitoure, botor*, Old English *bitoure, bittour, bittourn, butoure, botor, botour, buttour, bytoure, buttoure*, Old French *butor*, Anglo-Latin *bitorius, butorius,*Vulgar Latin *butitaurus*, Latin *butio*, bittern + *taurus*, bull, Pliny said that in Gaul the bittern was called *taurus*, i.e., "ox" because its voice resembled the bellowing of oxen, named for its cry].

blackbird - refers to Red-winged Blackbird, *Agelaius tricolor*, or Rusty Blackbird, *Euphagus carolinus*. [black Middle English *blak, blakke*, Old English *blac, blæc, blacc*, dark, black, ink, compare: Old Saxon *blac*, ink, Old Norse *blakkr*, black, dark, swarthy, Old High German *blah*, black, Swedish *black*, ink, Dutch *blaken*, to burn with a black smoke, Latin *flagro*, to blaze, burn, glow, flame, Greek *phlegein*; + bird Middle English *bird, brid, bred*, Old English *bridd, brid*, bird, young bird, from Old English *bredan*, to breed, so called because of its black color].

bluebird - refers to Eastern Bluebird, *Sialia sialis*. [blue Middle English *blue, bleu, blew, blew(e)*, Old English *blaw*, Old French *bleu, blo* + bird Middle English *bird, brid* Old English *bridd*, bird, young bird, unknown origin, so called because of its blue back].

bluethroat - refers to Bluethroat, *Lusinia svecica*. [blue Middle English *blue, bleu, blew, blew(e)*, Old English *blaw*, Old French *bleu, blo* + throat Middle English *throte*, throat, Old English *throte, throta, throtu*, throat, compare: Icelandic *throti*, swelling, Dutch *strot*, Middle Dutch *stroot*, the throat, gullet, Swedish *strupe*, the throat, Danish *strube*, the throat; so called because of the blue markings on its throat].

bobolink - refers to Bobolink, *Dolichonyx oryzivorus*. [*boblincoln, Bob Lincoln, Bob o' Lincoln, bob-a-lincum*, named after its call].

bobwhite - refers to Bobwhite, *Colinus virginianus.* [reflective of its call].

booby - example: Brown Booby, *Sula leucogaster.* [Spanish *bobo*, stupid, silly, fool, seabird, Old French *baube*, a stammerer, Latin *balbus*, stammering, stuttering].

brant - refers to Brant, *Branta bernicla.* [Scandinavian, from *brand*, burnt, dark, named for dark color of bird].

bufflehead - refers to Bufflehead, Bucephala albeola. [buffle Obsolete English *buffle*, buffalo, fool, Old French, Late Latin *bufalus*, Greek *boubalos*, antelope + head Middle English *hede*, *heved*, *he(f)d*, Old English *heafod*, compare: Dutch *hoofd*, Swedish *hufvud*, Danish *hoved*, Old Saxon *hobid*, Old High German *houbit*, Old Norse *haufuth*, Gothic *haubith*, *houbith*, head; so called for the bird's large head, like a buffalo's].

bulbul - refers to Red-whiskered Bulbul, *Pycnonotus jocosus.* [Persian *bulbul*, nightingale, Arabic *bulbul*, probably reflection of bird's call].

bullfinch - folkname for Pyrrhuyloxia, Pine Grosbeak, and Rufous-sided Towhee. [bull Middle English *bul*, *bule*, *bole*, Old English *bula*, bull, Old Norse *boli*, *bole*, bull, compare: Dutch *bol*, *bul*, German *bulle*, Middle Dutch *bulle*, *bolle*, Middle Low German *bulle*; + finch Middle English *finch*, *fynch*, *fincq*, Old English *finc*, finch, compare: Dutch *vink*, Old High German *fincho*, *finco*, Middle High German *vinke*, German *fink*; refers to birds' large head and stout beak].

bunting - refers to Indigo Bunting, *Passerina cyanea.* [Scottish *buntlin*, *corn buntlin*, Middle English *bunting*, *buntyle*, *bountyng*, plump, name may reflect bird's plumpness].

bushtit - refers to Common Bushtit, *Psaltriparus minimus*.
[bush Middle English *bush*, *busch*, *busk*, *bussh*, Old English
busk, *bosk*, *busc*, Old French *bois*, *bos*, wood, Old Norse *bushr*,
busk, Medieval Latin *boscum*, *boscus*, *buscus* + tit shortened
form of *titmouse*, Middle English *tit*, Icelandic *tittr*, a bird, Old
Norse *titlingr*, little bird].

canary - refers to Common Canary, *Serinus canaria*. Also, a
folkname for American Goldfinch, Evening Grosbeak, Indigo
Bunting, Lesser Goldfinch, Painted Bunting, Pine Siskin and
Yellow Warbler. [French *canari*, *Canarie*, Spanish *canario*,
meaning of Islas Canarias, the Canary Islands, Latin *Canaria
Insula*, Isle of Dogs, so called from its large dogs, Latin *canis*, a
dog].

canvasback, refers to Canvasback, *Aythya valisineria*. [canvas
Middle English *canevas*, Old French *canevas*, *chanevaz*, Old
French *caneve*, hemp, Italian *canavaccio*, Medieval Latin *cane-
bacium*, *canavasium*, Vulgar Latin *cannapaceum*, hempen
cloth, Late Latin *camabacius*, hempen cloth, canvas, Latin *can-
nabis*, hemp, Greek *kannabis*, hemp + back Middle English
bac, *bak*, Old English *bæc*, back, Old Saxon, Old Norse bak,
named for the canvas-like appearance of bird's back].

caracara - refers to Caracara, *Caracara cheriway* - [Spanish
caracara, Portuguese *caracara*, Tupi *caracara*, named in imita-
tion of its cry].

cardinal - refers to Cardinal, *Cardinalis cardinalis*. [Middle
English, Old French *cardinal*, Italian *cardinale*, Medieval Latin
Cardinalis, a cardinal, Late Latin *cardinalis*, a cardinal, Latin
cardinalis, principal, essential, chief, Latin *cardo*, a door hinge,
axis, named for red color, similar to color of church official's
robes].

catbird - refers to Catbird, *Dumetella carolinensis.* [cat Middle English, Old English *cat, catte, catt,* Anglo-Norman *cat,* Old French *chat,* Late Latin *cattus, catus, catta,* cat, Latin *catta,* Hindi *katas,* Turkish *qadi,* cat + bird Middle English *bird, brid,* Old English *bridd,* bird, young bird, named for its mew-like alarm call].

chachalaca - refers to Chachalaca, *Ortalis vetula.* [Spanish, native Mexican Indian Nahuati, imitative of bird's call].

chat - refers to Yellow-breasted Chat, *Icteria virens.* [chat, chatter Middle English *chatten, chateren, chiteren,* to jabber, from its chattering calls].

chickadee - refers to Black-capped Chickadee, *Parus atricapillus.* [named for its call, which sounds like "chicka-dee-dee-dee"].

chuck-will's-widow - refers to Chuck-will's-widow, *Caprimulgus carolinensis.* [named for its call].

chukar - refers to Chukar, *Alectoris graeca.* chukar. [Hindi *cakor,* Sanskrit *cakora, cakorah*].

condor - refers to California Condor, *Gymnogyps californianus.* [Spanish *condor,* Peruvian Quechuan *condor, cuntur,* condor].

coot - refers to American coot, *Fulica americana.* [Middle English *coot, cout, cote, coote,* Welsh *cwta-air,* literally, short-tailed hen, compare: Dutch *koet,* Middle Dutch *cuut, coet;* unknown origin, possibly echoic of bird's cry].

cormorant - refers to Double-crested Cormorant, *Phalacrocorax auritus.* [Middle English *cormoraunt, cormeraunt,* Old French *cormoran, cormaran, cormarent, cormareng,* raven of the sea, Latin *corvus,* raven, crow + *marenc,* marine, of the sea].

corn crake - refers Corncrake, *Crex crex*. [corn Middle English *corn*, grain, Old English corn, compare: Dutch *koren*, Old Saxon *korn*, Icelandic *korn*, Old High German *korn*, Gothic *kaurn*, Old Slavic *zruno*, grain, Latin *granum*, grain, seed,Greek *geras*, old age, Sanskrit *jirna*, old, worn out, withered, Sanskrit *jir*, grain; + crake Middle English *crak*, Old Norse *kraka*, crow, *krakr*, raven; corn, refers to bird's habit of raiding grain fields, crake, probably reflective of bird's cry].

cowbird - refers to Brown-headed Cowbird, *Molthrus ater*. [cow Middle English *cow*, *cou*, *cu*, *ku*, Old English *cu*, *cy*, compare: Old Frisian *ku*, Frisian *ko*, cow, Old Norse *kyr*, Old Saxon *ko*; Latin bos, cow, Greek *bous*, Sanskrit *gaus* + bird Middle English *bird*, *brid*, Old English *bridd*, bird, young bird, named for its association with cows].

crane - refers to Sandhill Crane, *Grus canadensis*, or Whooping Crane, *Grus americana*. [Middle English, Old English *cran*, crane, Old German *kraen*, compare: Dutch *krann*, Old German *kraen*, Low German *kraan*, Welsh *garan*, Old Norse *trana*, Latin *grus*, Greek *geranos*; name may be reflective of bird's cry].

creeper - refers to Brown Creeper, *Certhia familiaris*. [creeper, creep Middle English *crepen*, *creopen*, Old English *creopan*, to creep, to go bent down, to crawl, compare: Dutch *kruipen*, Old Norse *krjupa*, to creep, Greek *grypos*, curved; + *-er*, Old English *-ere*, suffix].

crossbill - refers to Red Crossbill, *Loxia curvirostra*, or White-winged Crossbill, *Loxia leucoptera*. [cross Middle English *cros*, *crois*, Old English *cros*, Old Irish *cross*, Old Norse *kross*, Latin *crux*, a cross + bill Middle English *bille*, *bile*, Old English *bile*, beak, bird's bill, *bil*, to strike, in old legend, the bird twisted its bill trying to draw out the nails that held Christ to the Cross].

crow - refers to Common Crow, *Corvus brachyrhynchos.* [Middle English *croue, crowe,* Old English *craw, crawe, crawa,* a crow, Old English *crawan,* to crow, compare: Middle Dutch *crayen,* Dutch *kraai,* German *kruähe,* Old Icelandic *kraka,* crow; reflective of bird's hoarse cry].

cuckoo - refers to Yellow-billed Cuckoo, *Coccyzus americanus,* or Black-billed Cuckoo, *Coccyzus erythropthalmus.* [Early Modern English *cuckow,* Middle English *cuccu, coccou, cukkow,* Old English *coccou, cuccu, cukkow, cocow, cuckow,* Old French *coucou, cucu,* Latin *cuculus,* Greek *kokkux, kokkyx,* Sanskrit *kokilas, kokila,* from the bird's cry].

curlew - refers to Long-billed Curlew, *Numenius americanus.* [Middle English *curleu,* Middle French *corlieu, courlieu,* Old French *corlieu, corlue, courlis,* from the bird's cry, which sounds like "cur-lew"].

darter - refers to American Darter, or Anhinga, *Anhinga anhinga.* [darter, dart Middle English *dart,* Old French *dart,* of Teutonic origin, compare: Swedish *dart,* dagger, Icelandic *darraor,* dart, Old High German *tart,* javelin, dart; + *-er,* suffix, name a reference to bird's rapid motion, diving in water to spear and catch a fish].

dickcissel - refers to Dickcissel, *Spiza americana.* [named for its call].

dipper - refers to Dipper, *Cinclus mexicanus.* [dipper, dip Middle English *dippen, duppen,* to baptize, *dipen,* to immerse, Old English *dyppan,* dip, baptize, to plunge in, *dippan, duppan* to immerse, compare: Old Norse *depa,* Swedish *doppa,* Old Saxon *dopian,* Dutch *doopen;* Gothic *daupain;* + *-er,* Old English *-ere,* suffix, refers to its habit of dipping under water in search of food].

dotterel - refers to Dotterel, *Eudromias morinellus*. [dotterel Middle English *doterel*, *dotterel*, dote Middle English *dotien*, *doten*, to be foolish, Middle Dutch *doten*, to be silly or crazy, to dote, Old Dutch *doten*, to be silly, compare: Dutch *dutten*, doze, dote, Icelandic *dotta*, to nod from sleep; + diminitive suffix -*erel*, bird named for its supposed stupidity in being easily captured].

dove - refers to Mourning Dove, *Zenaidura macroura*. [Middle English *dove*, *duve*, *dofe*, *douve*, Old English *dufe*, *dufa*, *dufan*, dark-colored, obscured, compare: Old Saxon *duba*, Dutch *durf*, Danish *due*, Gothic *dubo*, Old Swedish *duva*, Old Norse *dufa*, Old Irish *dub*, black;].

dovekie - refers to Dovekie, *Alle alle*. [dovekie, a nickname of *dove*].

dowitcher -refers to Short-billed Dowitcher, *Limnodromus griseus*, or Long-billed Dowitcher, *Limnodromus scolopacaus*. [Native American, Iroquois name].

duck - refers to Black Duck, *Anas rubripes*. [Middle English *doke*, *douke*, *duke*, *duk*, Old English *duce*, a duck, a diver, literally, a ducker, compare: Dutch *duiken*; named for its habit of diving under water while feeding].

dunlin - refers to Dunlin, *Erolia alpina*. [from *dunling*, dun Middle English *dunn*, dark or obscure, gray-brown, Old English *dunn*, dun, dark brown, Old Saxon *dun*, brown, compare: Gaelic *donn*, *duinne*, brown, Welsh *dwn*, dusky; + -*ling*, Common Germanic, diminutive -*ling*, small].

eagle - refers to Bald Eagle, *Haliaeetus leucocephalus*, or Golden Eagle, *Aquila chrysaëtos*. [Middle English *egle*, Anglo-Norman *egle*, Old French *egle*, *aigle*, Old Provencal *aigla*, Latin *aquila*, black eagle, Latin *aquilus*, dark-colored, blackish].

egret - refers to Common Egret, *Casmerodius albus*, or Snowy Egret, *Leucophoyx thula*. [Middle English *egrete*, Anglo-Norman *egrette*, Old French *egrette*, *aigrette*, egret, tuft of feathers, Old Provencal *aigreta*, heron, *aigron*, Old High German *aigron*, *heigir*, heron, from Teutonic source].

eider - refers to Common Eider, *Somateria mollissima*. [eider Old Norse *œdur*, *œthar*, *aethr*, eider, compare: Danish *edder*, *eder*, Norwegian *ejdar*, Swedish *eider*, Dutch *eider*, German *eider*, Sanskrit *atris*, water bird;].

falcon - refers to Peregrine Falcon, *Falco peregrinus*. [Middle English *faucon*, *facon*, Old French *faucon*, *falcun*, *faulcon*, Late Latin *falco*, *falcon*, *falconem*, (named for its curved, sickle-shaped talons), Latin *falx*, *falcis*, sickle, hook-shaped, compare: Old High German *falcho*, Old Norse *falki*;].

finch - refers to Purple Finch, *Carpodacus purpureus*. [Middle English *finch*, *fynch*, *fincq*, Old English *finc*, finch, compare: Dutch *vink*, Old High German *fincho*, *finco*, Middle High German *vinke*, German *fink*;].

flamingo - refers to American Flamingo, *Phoenicopterus ruber*. [Portuguese *flamengo*, flamingo, Portuguese *flamma*, flame, Spanish *flamenco*, a Fleming, flamingo, Spanish *Fleming*, Old Provencal *flamenc*, flamingo, Old Provencal *flama*, flame, Latin *flamma*, flame, + Germanic suffix -*ing*, named for its bright colors].

flicker - refers to Common Flicker, *Colaptes auratus*. [flicker Middle English *flikeren*, behave frivolously, trifle, Old English *flicorian*, *flycerian*, *flicerian*, to flutter, compare: Old Norse *flokrea*; may be named for its motion flying from tree to tree, showing white wing spots, which present a flickering effect].

flycatcher - example: Least Flycatcher, *Empidonax minimus*. [fly Middle English *flye, flie, fleen, flien, fleyen*, Old English *flyge, flege, fleoge*, Old English *fleogan*, to fly, move quickly, flee, Old Saxon *flioga*, fly, compare: Old High German *fliogan*, Old Norse *fljuga*, Dutch *vliegen*; + catch Middle English *cachen, cacchen*, Anglo-English *cachier*, Old French *chacier*, Late Latin *captiare, capteare, capere*, to take, Vulgar Latin *captiare*, Latin *captara*, to catch (an animal) + *-er*, Old English *-ere*, suffix].

frigatebird - refers to Magnificent Frigatebird, *Fregata magnificens*. [frigate French *fregate*, Italian *fregata*, (unknown origin) + bird Middle English *bird, brid*, Old English *bridd*, bird, young bird].

fulmar - refers to Fulmar, *Fulmarus glacialis*. [Hebrides dialect, Old Norse *full, ful*, foul, unpleasant, + *mar*, sea mew, gull, named for unpleasant odor, from its own oil glands and from its food].

gadwall - refers to Gadwall, *Anas strepera*. [Origin unknown].

gallinule - refers to Common Gallinule, *Gallinula chloropus*. [Modern Latin, Latin *gallinula*, a pullet, a chicken, Latin *gallina*, hen].

gannet - refers to Gannet, *Sula bassanus*. [Middle English *gant, ganat, gante, ganot*, gannet, seabird, Old English *ganot, ganote, ganet*, gannet, solon goose, sea fowl, fen duck, sea bird, compare: Dutch *gent*, Old High German *gannazza, ganzo*, gander;].

gaulin - example, Green Gaulin, folkname for Little Green Heron. [gaulin, term used in Jamaica and other Caribbean islands for certain herons, egrets and related birds, possibly from Scottish *gawlin*].

gnatcatcher - refers to Blue-gray Gnatcatcher, *Polioptila caerulea*. [gnat, gnatt Middle English *gnatt*, Old English *gnaet*, *gnætt*, *gnæt*, compare: Old Norse *gnit*, Low German *gnatte*, a gnat, Old English *gnidan*, to rub; + catch Middle English *cachen*, *cahten*, *cacchen*, capture, ensnare, Anglo-Norman *cachier*, Old French *chacier*, Latin *captara*, to catch (an animal) + *-er*, Old English *-ere*, suffix].

goatsucker - folkname for Common Night Hawk. [goat: Middle English *got*, *geat*, *gote*, *goot*, *gat*, Old English *gat*, she-goat + suck Middle English *suche*, *suken*, to draw into the mouth, Old English *sucan*, *sugan*, *swilc*, *swelc* + *-er*, Old English *-ere*, suffix, from myth that birds suckled from a goat, and thereby made the goat go blind].

godwit - refers to Marbled Godwit, *Limosa fedoa*, or Hudsonian Godwit, *Limosa haemastica*. [Old English *god*, good + Old English *wihta*, *wiht*, an animal, literally, good eating].

goldeneye - refers to Common Goldeneye, *Bucephala clangula*. [golden Middle English *gilden*, Old English *gylden*, gold(en); gold Middle English *gold*, Old English *gold*, gold, to gleam or shine, compare: Old Norse *gull*, German *gold*, Dutch *goud*, Old Saxon *gold*, Gothic *gulth*, Sanskrit *hiranya*, gold, *hari*, yellow; + *-en*, suffix + eye Middle English *eye*, *eie*, *ege*, *eige*, Old English *ege*, *eage*, *eag*, eye, eye of needle, compare: Old Saxon *oga*, Old Frisian *age*, Frisian *each*, eye, Old High German *ouga*, German *auge*, Dutch *oog*, Old Norse *auga*, Latin *oculus*, eye, Greek *okkos*, eye, Sanskrit *aksi*; named for its gold-colored eye].

goldfinch - refers to American Goldfinch, *Spinus tristis*. [gold Middle English *gold*, Old English *gold*, gold, to gleam or shine, compare: Old Norse *gull*, German *gold*, Dutch *goud*, Old Saxon *gold*, Gothic *gulth*, Sanskrit *hiranya*, gold, *hari*, yellow; + finch Middle English *finch*, *fynch*, *fincq*, Old English *finc*, finch, compare: Dutch *vink*, Old High German *fincho*, *finco*, Middle High German *vinke*, German *fink*;].

48

goose - example: Canadian Goose, *Branta canadensis*. [Middle English *gos, gose, goos*, Old English *gos*, goose, compare: Dutch *gans*, goose, Old Frisian *gos*, Frisian *goes*, goose, Middle High German *gans*, goose, Old High German *gans*, goose, Irish-Gaelic *geis*, swan, Old Norse *gas*, Latin *anser*, Greek *chen*, Sanskrit *hamsa*;].

goshawk - refers to Goshawk, *Accipiter gentilis*. [Middle English *goshauk*, Old English *goshafuc, goshafoc, gos-hafoc*, from *gos*, goose + *hafoc*, hawk].

grackle - refers to Common Grackle, *Quiscalus quiscula*. [Modern English *gracule, gracula, grakle*, Latin *graculus*, jackdaw, name echoic of bird's call].

grebe - refers to Least Grebe, *Podiceps dominicus*. [French *grebe*, unknown origin].

grosbeak - refers to Evening Grosbeak, *Hesperiphona vespertina*, or Rose-breasted Grosbeak, *Pheucticus ludovicianus*. [French *grosbec*, from *gros*, large, thick + *bec*, beak].

ground-chat - refers to Ground-chat, *Chamaethlypis poliocephala*. [ground Middle English *ground, grund*, Old English *grund*, ground, bottom, foundation, compare: Old Frisian *grund*, Frisian *grun*, soil, ground, bottom, Old Saxon *grund*, Old Norse *grunner*; + chat, from chatter Middle English *chatten, chateren, chiteren*, to jabber, from its chattering calls].

grouse - refers to Ruffed Grouse, *Banasa umbellus*. [Early Modern English *grewes, grows, grous*, possibly from *gorse*, heath (or from Latin *grus*, a crane), or from another origin].

guillemot - refers to Black Guillemot, *Cepphus grylle*. [French *guillemot*, diminutive of *Guillaume. Guilaume*, William, a proper name].

gull - example: Herring Gull, *Larus argentatus*. [Middle English *gull*, of Celtic origin, Cornish *gullan, guilan, gwilan*, gull, (Old English *gul*, yellow, literally, a yellow bird, from prominent yellowness of gull chicks, compare: Icelandic *gulr*, yellow, Danish *gul, gaul*, yellow;) compare: Welsh *gwylan*, seagull, *gilbin*, to weep, wail, Breton *gwelan, goelann*, gull, Old Norse *gulr*, Cornish *gullan*, gull; named for its cry].

gyrfalcon - refers to Gyrfalcon, *Falco rusticolus*. [Middle English *gerfaucoun, gerfaucon, girfaucoun*, Old French *gerfaucon, girfaucon, gerfauc*, Old Norse *geirfalki*, falcon, spear, Late Latin *gyrofalco*, from *gyros*, a circle, so called from its flight, compare: Old High German *gir*, vulture; + falcon Middle English *faucon, facon*, Old French *faucon, falcun, faulcon*, falcon, Late Latin *falconem*, Latin *falco*].

harrier - refers to: Northern Harrier, *Circus cyaneus*. [harry Middle English *hergien, haryen, herien, harien*, Old English *hergian*, to make war, to ravage, to lay waste, to plunder, make raid, Old English *here*, an army, predatory troop, band of thieves, compare: Old High German *herion*, Middle High German *hern*, to ravage, to plunder, Old Norse *herja*, to plunder, to make a raid; + -ier, French -ier, suffix].

hawk - example: Red-tailed Hawk, *Buteo jamaicensis*. [Middle English *hauk, hauek, havek, havec*, Old English *hafoc, heafoc, heafuc, habuc, hebuc*, Old Norse *haukr*, compare: Swedish *hök*, Danish *høg*, Middle Low German *havec*, Middle Dutch *havik*, Dutch *havik*, Old High German *habuh*, German *Habicht*, hawk;].

heron - example: Great Blue Heron, *Ardea herodias*. [Middle English *heron, heroun, heiron, hern, heyrun, heyroun, hayroun, heiroun*, Old French *heron, hairon, haigron, hegron*, heron, compare: Old High German *heigir, heiger, heigara, heigir*, heron, Old Norse *hegri, heri*, heron, of Teutonic origin; from bird's cry].

honeycreeper - refers to Bahama Honeycreeper, *Coereba fla-veola*. [honey Middle English *huni*, *honi*, *hunig*, Old English *huneg*, *hunig*, compare: Old Frisian *hunig*, Frisian *huning*, *hunich*, honey, Old Saxon *honeg*, *hunig*, Old Norse *hunang*; + creeper Middle English *crepen*, Old English *creopan*, to creep].

hummingbird - refers to Ruby-throated Hummingbird, *Archilochus colubris*. [hum Middle English *hommen*, *hummen*, of echoic origin + -ing Old English *-ing*, *-ung*, suffix, + bird Middle English *bird*, *brid* , Old English *bridd*, bird, young bird, name from sound bird's wings make during flight].

ibis - example: Glossy Ibis, *Plegadis falcinellus*. [Middle English *ibin*, *ybyn*, Latin *ibis*, Greek *ibis*, ibis, Egyptian *hb*, *hbj*, *heb*, *hib*, *hab*, a sacred bird of Egypt + Greek suffix *-is*].

iiwi - refers to Iiwi, *Vestariaa coccinea*. [native Hawai'ian].

jacana - refers to Jacana, *Jacana spinosa*. [Portuguese *jacana*, Brazilian, Tupi-Guarani, *jacanam*, *jascanam*, *jasana*].

jaeger - example: Pomarine Jaeger, *Stercorarius pomarinus*. [German *jagen*, to hunt, Middle High German *jeger*, hunter, Old High German *jagon*, to hunt].

jay - refers to Blue Jay, *Cyanocitta cristata*. [Middle English *jay*, Old French *jay*, *gai*, *geai*, *iay*, *gay*, jay, (possibly from Old French *gai*, gay, so called from its gay plumage), Late Latin *gaius*, a jay, Vulgar Latin *gaius*, Latin *Gaius*, a proper name, Latin root name imitative of bird's call].

junco - refers to Slate-colored Junco, *Junco hyemalis*. [Modern Latin, Spanish *junco*, reed, Latin *juncus*, a rush].

kestrel - refers to American Kestrel or Sparrow Hawk, *Falco sparverius*.[Early Modern English *castrel, kistrell, kestril,* Middle English *castrel, castrell,* Old French *cresserelle, cresserele, quercerelle,* kestrel, clacker,Vulgar Latin *crepicella,* a rattle, Latin *crepitaculum,* a rattle, Latin *crista,* crest, name reflects bird's cry].

killdeer - refers to Killdeer, *Charadrius vociferus.* [killdeer, killdee, named for bird's cry].

kingbird - refers to Eastern Kingbird, *Tyrannus tyrannus.* [king Middle English *king,* monarch, chief ruler, Old English *cing, cyng, cyning, cynn,* king + bird Middle English *bird, brid,* Old English *bridd,* bird, young bird].

kingfisher - refers to Belted Kingfisher, *Megaceryle alcyan.* [Middle English *kyngys fyschare,* king's fisher, Old English *cyng,* king + *fiscere,* fisher].

kinglet - refers to Golden-crowned Kinglet, *Regulus satrapa,* or Ruby-crowned Kinglet, *Regulus calendula.* [kinglet, king Middle English *king,* monarch, chief ruler, Old English *cing, cyng, cyning, cynn,* king, a tribe, compare: Old Saxon *kuning,* Dutch *koning,* Old High German *kuning,* German *könig,* Old Norse *konungr,* Danish *konge*; + *-let* Middle English, Middle French -*el,* (Old French *-elet,* Latin *-ellus*) +*et* Old French *-et,* suffix, named for red or gold "crown" on top of head, hence kinglet, or little king].

kite - example: Swallow-tailed Kite, *Elanoides forficatus.* [Middle English *kite, kyte,* Old English *cyta, kyte,* kite, bittern, compare: Welsh *cud,* Breton *kidel,* a hawk; name reflects bird's cry].

kittewake - refers to Black-tailed Kittewake, *Rissa tridactyla.* [kittewake, cattiwake, name from bird's cry].

knot - refers to Knot, *Calidris canutus*. [Middle English *knot*, *knotte*, Old English *cnotta*, compare: German *knoten*, Danish *knude*, Latin *nodus*, a knot, unknown origin].

lapwing - refers to Lapwing, *Vanellus vanellus*. [Middle English *lappewinke*, *lapwinge*, *lap wynke*, *leepwynke*, lapwink, Old English *læpwince*, *hlæpewince*, *hleapewince*, *hleapan*, *hledpewince*, lapwing, one who turns about in flight or running, literally, 'a wavering leap,' Old English *hleapan*, to leap, jump, + Old English *wincian*, to wink, compare: *wancol*, wavering; present form uses: + wing Middle English *winge*, *wenge*, *weng*, Old Norse *vænht*, *væner*, *væner*, bird's wing, compare: Swedish *vinge*; refers to bird's slow irregular flapping flight].

lark - refers to: Horned Lark, *Eremophila alpestris*. [Middle English *lark*, *laverke*, *laverock*, *larke*, Old English *laferce*, *læwerce*, *lauricæ*, *lawerce*, *lauerce*, lark, compare: Danish *lerke*, Dutch *leeuwerik*, Old Swedish *lærikia*, Low German *lewerke*, Old High German *lerahha*, Old Norse *laevirki*, *lævirki*, German, *Lerche*, lark; unknown origin, possibly echoic].

limpkin - refers to Limpkin, *Aramus guarauna*. [limp Middle English *lympen*, Old English *limpan*, *limphin*, to limp, Old English *lemphealt* + -kin, Middle English, Middle Dutch *-ken*, *-kijn*, small, named for its walk].

linnet - folkname for Common Redpoll, House Finch, Pine Siskin, Purple Finch, Rose-breasted Grosbeak, and Wood Thrush. [Middle English *linet*, Old English *linete*, *linece*, from *linetwige*, linnet, Old French *linette*, *linot*, *linotte*, from *lin*, flax, + -ottus, Roman diminutive suffix, Latin *linum*, flax, so called from its habit of feeding on the seeds of flax and hemp].

longspur - refers to: Lapland Longspur, *Calcarius lapponicus.* [long Middle English *lang, long,* Old English *long, lang,* Latin *longus,* long, compare: Old Frisian *lang, long,* Frisian *lang,* long, Old Saxon *lang, long,* Old High German *lang,* Old Norse *langr*; + spur Middle English *spure,* Old English *spura, spora, sporu,* a spur, name a reference to long rear toes, used for scratching ground for seeds].

loon - refers to Common Loon, *Gavia immer.* [from *loom,* of Scandinavian origin, Shetland *loom,* Old Norse *lomr,* compare: Danish *lom,* Swedish *lom*;].

magpie - refers to Black-billed Magpie, *Pica pica.* or Yellow-billed Magpie, *Pica nutalli.* [magpie, Middle English *magpye, magot, magot pie* (from bird's habit of picking maggots from the backs of sheep), *mag,* nickname of *Margaret,* French *Margot,* a magpie, diminutive of French *Marguerite,* Latin *margarita,* a pearl + pie Middle English *pie,* Old French *pie,* Latin *pica,* magpie].

mallard - refers to Mallard, *Anas platyrnchos.* This is the ancestor of the domesticated white duck. [Middle English *malarde,* Old French *mallart, malart,* a wild drake, Old French *male,* male, Flemish *maskelaar*].

man-o'-war bird - refers to Man-o'-war Bird, Magnificant Frigatebird, *Fregata magnificens.* man-o'-war [man-of-war Late Middle English, a fighting man, a heavily armed warship, bird named because of its large size, superior navigating, and-flying ability, as well as its predatory habits].

martin - refers to Purple Martin, *Progne subis.* [Middle English *martoune,* from the proper name *Martin,* Middle French *martin, Martin,* Latin *Martinus,* Latin *Mars,* god of war].

meadowlark - refers to Eastern Meadowlark, *Sturnella magna*. [meadow Middle English *medewe, medow, medwe, medoue,* Old English *mædwe, mæd,* meadow (mowed land) + lark Middle English *lark, laverke, laverock,* Old English *laferce, læwerce, lauricæ, lawerce,* lark, unknown origin].

merganser - example: Red-breasted Merganser, *Mergus serrator*. [Modern Latin *merganser,* Latin *mergus,* diver, gull, a kind of diving duck + Latin *anser,* goose, duck].

merlin - refers to Merlin, *Falco columbarius*. [Middle English *merlion, meriloun,* Old English *marlin, marlion,* Anglo-French *merilun,* Old French *esmerillon,* diminutive of *esmeril,* merlin].

mockingbird - refers to Mockingbird, *Mimus polyglottos*. [mock Middle English *mokken, mokke, mocque,* Middle French *mocquer,* Old French *mocquer, moquer,* to mock, Greek *mokos,* a mocker + bird Middle English *bird, brid,* Old English *bridd,* bird, young bird].

murre - refers to Common Murre, *Uria aalge,* or Thick-billed Murre, *Uria lomvia*. [unknown origin].

murrelet - example: Marbled Murrelet, *Brachyramphus marmoratum*. [*murre* + *-let,* Middle English, Middle French *-el,* Old French *-elet,* Latin *-ellus,* unknown origin].

myna - refers to Crested Myna, *Acridotheres cristatellus*. [myna, mynah, mina Hindi *maina,* Sanskrit *madana-s, madanah*].

nighthawk - refers to Common Nighthawk, *Chordeiles minor*. [night Middle English *night, niht,* Old English *niht, næht,* night + hawk [Middle English *hauk, hauek, havek,* Old English *hafoc, heafoc, habuc, hebuc,* named for its evening flights and hawk-like appearance].

night heron - refers to Black-crowned Night Heron, *Nycticorax nycticorax*, or Yellow-crowned Night Heron, *Nycticorax violaceus*. [night Middle English *night, niht*, Old English *niht, næht, neaht*, night, compare: Old Saxon naht, Old High German naht, Old Norse nott, natt, Gothic nahts, Old Slavic nosti, German *nacht*, Latin *nox*, night, Greek *nyx, nyktos*, Sanskrit *nakta, nakti*; + Middle English *heron, heroun, heiron, hern, heyrun, heyroun, hayroun, heiroun*, Old French *heron, hairon, haigron, hegron*, heron, compare: Old High German *heigir, heiger, heigara, heigir*, heron, Old Norse *hegri, heri*, heron, of Teutonic origin; from bird's cry].

nightjar - refers to Buff-colored Nightjar, *Caprimulgus ridgwayi*. [night Middle English *night, niht*, Old English *niht, næht, neaht*, night, compare: Old Saxon naht, Old High German naht, Old Norse nott, natt, Gothic nahts, Old Slavic nosti, German *nacht*, Latin *nox*, night, Greek *nyx, nyktos*, Sanskrit *nakta, nakti*; + jar, *jar, chirr, gerre, ier, charre*, harsh sounds, Middle English *charken*, to creak, Old English *cearcian*, to gnash, named for sounds made by bird].

noddy - example: Brown Noddy, *Anous stolidus*. Also a folkname for Black Noddy Tern, Common Murre, Dovekie, Noddy Tern, Razorbill, Ruddy Duck, Thick-billed Murre and White Tern. [from obsolete Early Modern English *noddy*, foolish, silly, from bird's tameness, interpreted as foolish].

nutcracker - refers to Clark's Nutcracker, *Corvus columbiana*. [nut Middle English *nutte, nute, note*, Old English *hnutu*, compare: Old Norse *hnot*, Old High German *nuz*, Old Irish *enu*, Welsh *eneuen*, Dutch *noot*, German *nuss*, Latin *nux, nucis*; + crack Middle English *craken, craken*, to crack, to crash, to break, Old English *cracian*, to crack, Old English *cracina*, to resound, compare: Gaelic *crac, cnac*, crack, break, crash, German *kracken*, Dutch *kraken*; + -er, Old English -ere, suffix].

nuthatch - example: White-breasted Nuthatch, *Sitta carolinensis*. [Middle English *notehach, notehak, notehagge, nuthake, notehache, nuthak*, literally, nut-hacker, nut Middle English *nutte, nute*, Old English *hnutu,* compare: Old Norse *hnot*, Dutch *noot*, German *nuss*; + hatch Late Middle English *hache*, Medieval French *hach(er)*, to cut up, from *hache*, ax, or from hack Old English *hacke(n)*, Old English (to) *haccian*, to hack to pieces, an allusion to bird's ability to crack nuts].

oldsquaw - refers to Oldsquaw, *Clangula hyemalis*. [old Middle English *old, ald*, Old English *eald, aid*, compare: West Saxon *eald*, Old Saxon *ald*, Medieval Dutch *alt, aot, oul*; + squaw Native American, Algonquian, (Massachuset) *squa, eshqua*, woman, Narragansett *squaw, esquaw*].

oriole - refers to Baltimore Oriole, now Northern Oriole, *Icterus bullockii*. [oriole French *oriol*, Old French *oriol*, Middle Latin *auerolus*, golden, Latin *aureus*, golden, Latin *aurum*, gold, originally named after Lord Baltimore, whose colors were orange and black].

osprey - refers to Osprey, *Pandion haliaetus*. [Late Middle English *ospray*, Old French *ospres, ospreit*, Latin *ossifraga*, the osprey or bone-breaker].

ouzel - refers to Water Ouzel, *Cinclus mexicanus*, also called Dipper. [ouzel, ousel Middle English *ouzel, osul, osel, ouizle, uzzle, ousel*, Old English *osle*, blackbird, compare: Old High German *amsala*, German *amsel*;].

ovenbird - refers to Ovenbird, *Seiurus aurocapillus*. [oven Middle English *ouen*, oven, Old English *ofen, ofn*, compare: Old Norse *ofn*, Old Frisian *oven*, Frisian *un(e)*, oven, Medieval Dutch *aven*, Dutch *oven*, Danish *ovn*, German *ofen*; + bird Middle English *bird, brid* , Old English *bridd*, bird, young bird, name refers to bird's domed oven-like nest].

owl - example: Screech Owl, *Otus asio.* [Middle English *ule, owle, oule,* Old English *ule,* compare: Dutch *uil,* Old High German *uwila,* Middle High German *iuwel, iule,* Old Saxon *uwila,* German *eule,* Danish *ugle,* Old Norse *ugla,* Latin *ulula,* screech owl, Latin *ululare,* to howl, the owl's call was considered similar to a wolf's howl; reflective of bird's call,].

oystercatcher - refers to American Oystercatcher, *Haematopus palliatus.* [oyster Middle English *oistre,* Old French *oistre, uistre,* Latin *ostrea, ostreum,* oyster, Greek *ostreon,* oyster, Greek *osteron,* bone, *ostrakon,* hard shell + catch Middle English *cacchen,* Anglo-English *cachier,* Old French *chacier,* Latin *captare,* to seize + *-er,* Old English *-ere,* suffix].

partridge - refers to Gray Partridge, *Perdix perdix.* It is also part of several folknames for members of the grouse family. [Early Modern English *pertridge,* Middle English *pertrich, partrich, partriche, pertriche,* Scottish *partrick,* Old English *pertriche,* Old French *perdriz, perdix, pertris, perdrix,* Latin *perdix,* partridge, Greek *perdix,* from flight sounds].

parrot - refers to Thick-billed Parrot, *Rhynchopsitta pachyrhyncha.* [Early Modern English *parrot,* Middle English *perrot, parrot,* French *Perrot, Pierrot,* French *Pierre,* Peter].

pauraque - refers to Pauraque, *Nyctidromus albicollis.* [Mexican Spanish, Native Mexican Indian, echoic of its call].

pelican - refers to White Pelican, *Pelecanus erythrorhynchos,* or Brown Pelican, *Pelecanus occidentalis.* [pelican, pelecan Middle English *pelican, pellican,* Old English *pellican, pellicane,* Old French *pelican,* Late Latin *pelicanus,* Latin *pelicanus, pelecanus,* pelican, Greek *pelekan,* Greek *pelekus, pelekys,* axe, Sanskrit *parasus,* axe, Assyro-Babylonian *piliqqu,* axe, Sumerian *balaq,* name reflecting bird's bill shape].

peregrine - refers to Peregrine Falcon, *Falco peregrinus*. [Middle English *pelegrim*, Old French *pelegrin*, Late Latin *pelegrinus*, travelling abroad, Latin *peregrinis*, foreign, Latin *peregrinus*, foreigner, *per*, through + *ager*, territory, country, field, so called because of its long migrations].

petrel - refers to Wilson's Petrel, *Oceanites oceanicus*. [petrel French *petrel*, Late Latin *Petrus*, Peter, Latin *Petrus*, Peter, Greek *Petros*, Peter, reference to St. Peter's walking upon the Lake of Gennesareth, from the bird's seeming ability to walk on water (feeding on surface swimming organisms)].

pewee - refers to Eastern Wood Pewee, *Contopus virens*. [pewee, peewee, name reflective of bird's call].

phainopepla - refers to Phainopepla, Phainopepla nitens. [New Latin, Greek *phaeinos*, shining, *phaein*, to shine + *peptos*, robe].

phalarope - example: Northern Phalarope, *Lobipes lobatus*. [French, Modern Latin *phalaropus*, Greek *phalaris*, a coot + *pous*, a foot].

pheasant - refers to Ring-necked Pheasant, *Phasianus colchicus*. It is also part of several folknames for members of the grouse family. [Middle English *fesan*, *fesant*, *fesaunt*, *faisant*, Anglo-Norman *fesaunt*, Old French *faisan*, *fesan*, *fesant*, *faisant*, Provencal *faisan*, Latin *phasianus*, Latin *Phasianus*, the Phasian Bird, Greek *phasaianos*, the Phasian bird, after *Phasis*, river of Colchis, where birds collected at the river's mouth, on the Black Sea, in what is now Georgia].

phoebe - refers to Eastern Phoebe, *Sayornis phoebe*. [from proper name, *Phoebe*, from Greek mythology, Artemis, goddess of the moon, from its call, "fee-bee"].

pigeon - refers to Domestic Pigeon, *Columba livia*, known scientifically as Rock Dove. [Middle English *pigeon, pejon, peion, pyion, pegeon, pygeon, pichon, pijon*, pigeon, dove, Middle French *pigeon, pijon*, Old French *pijon, pyjoun, pipion*, young bird, young dove, Late Latin *pipo, pipio, pipire*, chirping bird, Latin *pipio*, squab, young bird, Latin *pipire*, to peep, of imitative origin].

pileated woodpecker - refers to Pileated Woodpecker, *Dryocopus pileatus*. [pileated (having a pileate or cap), pileate Latin pileatus, from Latin *pileus*, felt cap + **woodpecker** - wood Middle English *wode, wude*, Old English *wudu, wude, widu, wiodu*, wood, forest, compare: Old High German *wit*, Old Norse *vithr*, Danish *ved*, wood, Swedish *ved*, wood, Gaelic *fiodh*, timber, wood, tree, wilderness, Old Irish *fid*, Welsh *gwydd*, trees, shrubs; + peck Middle English *pecken*, a variant of *picken*, pick, Old English *pycan*, to pick or peck, Middle Low German *pekken*, to peck with beak + *-er*, Old English *-ere*, suffix].

pintail - refers to Pintail, *Anas acuta*. [Middle English *pinne, pyn*, Old English *pinn*, a pin, a peg, Latin *pinna*, wing, feather, compare: German *pinne*, Dutch *pin*, Middle Low German *pinne*, Old Norse *pinni*; + tail Middle English *tail, tayl*, Old English *tægel, tægl*, tail, compare: Old Norse *tayl*, Old High German *zagal*, Swedish *tagel*, Gothic *tagl*, hair; named for its long central tail feathers].

pipit - example: Water Pipit, *Anthus spinoletta*. [Early Modern English *pipit, pippit*, name is probably a reflection of the bird's call].

plover - example: American Golden Plover, *Pluvialis dominica*. [Middle English *plover, pluver*, Anglo-Norman *plover*, Old French *plovier, pluvier, plevier*, rain bird, Vulgar Latin *pluviarius*, Latin *pluvia*, rain, named because flocks usually arrived in rainy season].

pochard - refers to Common Pochard, *Aythya ferina*, or Red-crested Pochard, *Netta rufina*. [unknown origin].

poor-will - refers to Poor-will, *Phalaenoptilus nuttalis*. [named for bird's call].

prairie chicken - refers to Greater Prairie Chicken, *Tympanuchus cupido* or Lesser Prairie Chicken, *Tympanuchus pallidicinctus*. [so called, when seen by westward migrating explorers and pioneers, it seemed to be a chicken of the prairies].

ptarmigan - example: Willow Ptarmigan, *Lagopus lagopus*. [Greek *pteron*, wing + Scottish-Gaelic *tarmigan, tarmachan, termigan, termagant, tormichan, termigant*, ptarmigan, unknown origin].

puffin - refers to Common Puffin, *Fratercula arctica*. [Middle English *poffin, pophyn, puffon, puffoun, pofin*, Cornish, possibly from Middle English *puf*, puff, reflecting bird's plump appearance or large beak].

pyrrhuloxia - refers to Pyrrhuloxia, *Cardinalis sinuatus*. [Modern Latin *Pyrrhula*, Greek *pyrrhoulas, purrhoulas*, a red-colored bird, *pyrrhos, purros*, red, *pur*, fire + *loxia*, crossbill genus, Greek *loxos*, oblique].

quail - example: Gambel's Quail, *Lophortyx gambelli*. [Middle English *quaille, quayle, quaile*, Old French *quaille, caille*, Medieval Latin *quaccula, coacula*, Middle Latin *quaccola, cuacula*, compare: Dutch *kwakkel*, Old High German *quahtela*, name is a reflection of the bird's cry].

rail - refers to Virginia Rail, *Rallus limicola*. [Middle English *raile, rayle, rale, rayl*, Anglo-Norman *radle*, Middle French *rale, raale, raaler*, to rattle or screech, Old French *raille, raale, raalle*, Vulgar Latin *rasclare, rascula*, to grate, reflective of bird's call].

raven - refers to Common Raven, *Corvus corax*. [Middle English *raven*, *reven*, *reaven*, Old English *hrefn*, *hræfn*, Old Norse *hrafn*, compare: Middle Dutch *raven*, Dutch *raaf*, Danish *ravn*, Middle Low German *rave*, Old High German *hraban*, *rabo*, Middle High German *raben*, *rabe*, German *rabe*, Latin *cornix*, a crow, Greek *korax*; name reflective of bird's harsh call].

razorbill - refers to Razorbill, or Razor-billed Auk, *Alca torda*. [razor Middle English *rasoure*, *rasor*, *rasour*, Old French *rasor*, *raser*, *rasour*, to scape, Vulgar Latin *rasdre*, Late Latin *rasorium*, a scraper, Latin *radere*, scrape, to shave + bill Middle English *bil*, *bile*, *bille*, Old English *bile*, beak of a bird, named for its rather short, sharp bill].

redhead - refers to Redhead, Aythya americana. [red Middle English *red*, *reed*, *read*, Old English *read*, red, compare: Old Saxon *rod*, Old Norse *rathr*, *rjothr*, *rauor*, *rjoor*, Danish *rød*, Old Frisian *rad*, Frisian *rea(d)*, red, Middle Dutch *root*, *rood*, Old High German *rot*, Middle High German *rot*, Gothic *rauths*, Gaelic *ruadh*, reddish, ruddy, red-haired, Latin *ruber*, *rufus*, red, Greek *erythos*, Sanskrit *rudhira*, *rohita*; + head Middle English *hede*, *heved*, *he(f)d*, Old English *heafod*, compare: Dutch *hoofd*, Swedish *hufvud*, Danish *hoved*, Old Saxon *hobid*, Old High German *houbit*, Old Norse *haufuth*, Gothic *haubith*, *houbith*, head; so called for the bird's reddish-colored head].

redpoll - refers to Common Redpoll, *Acanthis flammea*. [red Middle English *red*, *reed*, *read*, Old English *read*, red, compare: Old Saxon *rod*, Old Norse *rathr*, *rjothr*, *rauor*, *rjoor*, Danish *rød*, Old Frisian *rad*, Frisian *rea(d)*, red, Middle Dutch *root*, *rood*, Old High German *rot*, Middle High German *rot*, Gothic *rauths*, Gaelic *ruadh*, reddish, ruddy, red-haired, Latin *ruber*, *rufus*, red, Greek *erythos*, Sanskrit *rudhira*, *rohita*; + poll Middle English *pol*, head, especially back portion].

redstart - refers to American Redstart, *Setophaga ruticilla*. [red Middle English *reed*, Old English *read*, red, compare: Old Saxon *rod*, Old Norse *rathr*, *rjothr*, *rauor*, *rjoor*, Danish *rød*, Old Frisian *rad*, Frisian *rea(d)*, red, Middle Dutch *root*, *rood*, Old High German *rot*, Middle High German *rot*, Gothic *rauths*, Gaelic *ruadh*, reddish, ruddy, red-haired, Latin *ruber*, *rufus*, red, Greek *erythos*, Sanskrit *rudhira*, *rohita*; + start Middle English *start*, *stert*, *sterten*, *stirte*, *stuarte*, *starte*, an animal's tail, Old English *steort*, tail, rump].

roadrunner - refers to Roadrunner, *Geococcyx californianus*. [road Middle English *rode*, *rade*, a riding, Old English *rade*, *rad*, a ride, a passing or travelling on horseback, a way, a road, from *ridan*, to ride, Scottish *raid*, a riding, especially hostile + run Middle English *runnen*, *rinnen*, *rennen*, *renne*, *runen*, *irnen*, Old English *rinnan*, *eornan*, *earnan*, *irnan*, compare: Old Norse *rinna*, Old Frisian *renna*, *rinna*, *runna*, to run, to flow, Frisian *rinne*, to walk, to flow; + -er, Old English -*ere*, suffix, named for habit of running, often along roads].

robin - refers to Robin, *Turdus migratorius*. [from Middle English *Robin Redbreast*, Middle English *Robin*, Old French *Robin*, a nickname from *Robert*, a proper name, Old High German *Hruodperht*, Robert, fame-bright, bright with glory, from *hruod*-, *ruod*-, fame, glory + *berahr*, bright].

rook - folkname for American Crow, Common Crow and Ruddy Duck. [Middle English *rok*, *roc*, *rook*, Old English *roc*, *hroc*, compare: Middle Dutch *roec*, *roek*, rook, Old Norse *hrokr*, rook, Old High German *hruoh*, crow, Danish *raage*, Latin *cornix*, crow, Greek *krozeir*, to croak, to caw; name reflective of bird's call].

ruff - refers to Ruff, *Philomachus pugnax*. [ruff, ruffle Middle English *ruffe*, Middle English *ruffelen*, to wrinkle, compare: Early Frisian *ruffeln*, Old Norse *rjufa*, to break, Low German *ruffelen*, to wrinkle, curl; a reference to its puffed-out neck feathers].

sanderling, refers to Sanderling, *Croethia alba*. [Old English *sandyroling*, sand Middle English *sand, sond*, Old English *sond, sand*, compare: Old Saxon *sand*, Old Norse *sandr*, Danish *sand*, Old Frisian *sond*, Frisian *san*, sand, Middle Dutch *sant, sand*; Dutch *zand*, Middle High German *sant*, Old High German *sant*, German *sand*; + *-er*, Old English *-ere*, suffix + *-ling* Old English *-ling*, Old Norse *-lingr*, small].

sandgrouse - refers to Chestnut-bellied Sandgrouse, *Pterocles exustus*. [sand Middle English *sand, sond*, Old English *sond, sand*, compare: Old Saxon *sand*, Old Norse *sandr*, Danish *sand*, Old Frisian *sond*, Frisian *san*, sand, Middle Dutch *sant, sand*, Dutch *zand*, Middle High German *sant*, Old High German *sant*, German *sand*; + grouse Early Modern English *grewes, grows, grous*, possibly from *gorse*, heath or from Latin *grus*, a crane, or from another origin, inhabits arid, sandy areas of Eurasia].

sandpiper - example: Spotted Sandpiper, *Actitis macularia*. [sand Middle English *sand, sond*, Old English *sond, sand*, compare: Old Saxon *sand*, Old Norse *sandr*, Danish *sand*, Old Frisian *sond*, Frisian *san*, sand, Middle Dutch *sant, sand*, Dutch *zand*, Middle High German *sant*, Old High German *sant*, German *sand*; + piper Middle English *pipere*, Old English *pipere*, Latin *pipiare*, a pipe, a wind instrument].

sapsucker, refers to Yellow-bellied Sapsucker, *Sphyrapicus varius*. [sap Middle English *sap, zep*, Old English *saep, sæp*, + suck Middle English *suken, souken*, Old English *sucan* + *-er*, Old English *-ere*, suffix, from its habits of drilling holes in trees for the sap and insects attracted to sapflow].

scaup - refers to Greater Scaup, *Aythya marila*, or Lesser Scaup, *Aythya affinis*.[Scottish *scalp, scaup*, a bed of mussels, named for its eating habits].

scoter - example: Black Scoter, *Melanitta nigra*, also called Common Scoter. [English dialect *scote*, shoot, scoot, to squirt, compare: Old Norse *skoti*, a shooter, Old Norse *skjota*, to shoot out; named for its swift movements].

seedeater - refers to White-collared Seedeater, *Sporophila torqueola.* [seed Middle English *sede, sed, seed*, Old English *sæd, sed*, seed + eat Middle English *eten*, Old English *etan*, + *-er*, Old English *-ere*, suffix, named for its habit of feeding upon seeds].

shag - folkname for Great Cormorant, *Phalacrocorax carbo*, Brandt's Cormorant, *Phalacrocorax penicillatus*, and Double-crested Cormorant, *Phalacrocorax auritus*. [shag Middle English *shagge*, Old English *sceacga*, hair or rough hair, compare: Old Norse *skegg*, beard, Danish *skjæg*, Swedish *skägg*; name refers to bird's rough crest].

shearwater - example: Greater Shearwater, *Puffinus gravis*. [shear Middle English *scheren, sheren*, to shear, cut, shave, Old English *sceran, scieran, scyran*, to cut, shear, compare: Old Frisian *skera*, Frisian *skeare*, to shave, Old High German *sceran*, Middle High German *scheren*, to shear, Dutch *scheren*, Old Norse *skera*; + water Middle English *water, wæter, weter*, Old English *wæter*, compare Old Saxon *watar*, Old Frisian *wetir, weter*, Frisian *wetter*, water, rain, urine, Frisian *wiet*, water, Low German *water*, Danish *vand*, Swedish *vatten*, Greek *hydor*, Sanskrit *udan*, water, Hittite *watar*, water;].

shoveler - refers to Shoveler, *Spatula clypeata*. [shovel Middle English *schovele*, Old English *sceofl, scofl*, a shovel + *-er*, Old English *-ere*, suffix, named for its shovel-like bill].

shrike - refers to Northern Shrike, *Lanius excubitor*, or Logger-head Shrike, *Lanius ludovicanus*.[Old English *scric, screc*, thrush or shrike, compare: Middle Low German *schrik*, corn-crake, Swedish *shrika*, jay, Icelandic *skrikja*, shrike, Icelandic *skrikja*, the shrike, to titter, Norwegian *shrike*, jay; from bird's cry].

silky flycatcher - folkname for Phainopepla. [silky, silk Middle English *silke, seolke, selk, silk*, Old English *seoluc, sioloc, seole, seoloc, seolc*, silk, Latin *sericum*, Seric cloth, so called from Serica, ancient name of China, compare: Old Norse *silki*, Old Slavic *shelku*; Chinese *se, si*, silk, from apparent silkiness of bird's feathers] + flycatcher.

siskin - refers to Pine Siskin, *Carduelis pinus.* [siskin Middle Dutch *siseken, sijskijn*, Early Flemish *sijsken*, Middle Low German *sisek, csitze*, diminutive of *zeisig*, siskin, canary, of Slavic origin, compare: Polish *czyz*; + kin Middle Dutch *-kin, -kijn, -ken*, Middle Low German *-kin*, small, little, of imitative origin].

skimmer - refers to Black Skimmer, *Rynchops nigra* - [skim Middle English *skimen, skimmen, skymen,* to remove floating material from liquid, to froth, Old French *escumer, escumoir*, to remove scum, German *escume*, scum + *-er*, Old English *-ere*, suffix, from bird's habit of skimming surface of water in search of small fish].

skua - refers to Great Skua, *Catharacta skua*. [Modern Latin, Faeroese *skugvur, skugver*, Old Norse *skufr, skumr*, the skua or brown gull, compare: Icelandic *skumi*, dusk, Swedish *skum*, dusky, Old Norse *skufr*, tassel, tuft; unknown origin, possibly named for color].

skylark - refers to Eurasian Skylark, *Alauda arvensis*, also called Skylark, Common Skylark, and European Skylark. Folkname for Horned Lark and Sprague's Pipit. [sky Middle English *skye*, *skie*, sky, cloud, Old Norse *sky*, cloud, cloudy sky, compare: Old Saxon *scio*, cloud; + lark Middle English *laverock*, *lark*, *laverke*, Old English *laferce*, *lœwerce*, *lauricœ*, unknown origin].

snipe - refers to Common Snipe, *Gallinago gallinago*. [snipe, Scandinavian origin, Middle English *snipe*, *snype*, Old English *snite*, Old Norse *snipa*, *snipe*, compare: Danish *sneppe*, snipe, Dutch *snip*, German *schnepfe*, snipe, snite, Old Saxon *sneppa*, Middle Dutch *snippe*, *sneppe*, Old High German *snepfa*, *schnepfe*, from German *schneppe*, bill; named after its long beak].

snow bunting - refers to Snow Bunting, *Plectrophenax nivalis*. [snow Middle English *snow*, *snaw*, Old English *snaw*, compare: Old Frisian *sne*, Frisian *snee*, *snie*, snow, Dutch *sneeuw*, Low German *snee*, Old Saxon *sneo*, *sneu*, Danish *snee*, Swedish *snö*, Icelandic *snjor*, *snœr*, *snaer*, *snjar*, German *schnee*, Gothic *snaivs*, *snaiws*, Irish *snechd*, Gaelic *snechd*, Welsh *nyf*, *nuf*, Lithuanian *snégas*, Russian *snieg*, *snyeg*, Latin *nix*, *nivis*, snow, Greek *niphas*, *nipha*, (*neiphei*, it snows); + bunting Scottish *buntlin*, *corn buntlin*, Middle English *bunting*, *buntyle*, *bountyng*, plump, name may reflect bird's plumpness].

solitaire - refers to Townsend's Solitaire, *Myadestes townsendi*. [French *solitaire*, *solitary*, Old French, Latin *solitarius*, solitary].

sora - refers to Sora, *Porzana carolina*. [Native American name].

sparrow - example: House Sparrow, *Passer domesticus*, or Song Sparrow, *Melospiza melodia*. [Middle English *sparowe*, *sparwa*, *sparewe*, *sparwe*, Old English *spearwa*, sparrow, compare: Middle High German *sparwe*, Old High German *sparo*, German *sperling*, Gothic *sparwa*, Old Norse *spörr*, Danish *spurv*, *spurre*, Frisian *sparreg*;].

sparrow hawk - refers to Sparrow Hawk or American Kestrel, *Falco sparverius*. [Early Modern English *sparhawk*, Middle English *sparhauk*, Old English *spearhofoc*].

spoonbill - refers to Roseate Spoonbill, *Ajaia ajaja*. [spoon Middle English *spoon*, *spon*, *spone*, spoon, chip, Old English *spon*, wood chip, compare: Old Norse *sponn*, *spann*, chip, spoon, Dutch *spaan*, spoon, Danish *spaan*, Middle Dutch *spaen*, Old High German *span*, Middle High German *span*; + bill Middle English *bil*, *bile*, Old English *bill*, *bil*, *bile*, to strike, compare: Old Saxon *bil*, sword, Old High German *bill*, pickax, Old Norse *bildr*, Old Slavic *biti*, to strike; named for unique spoon-like shape of bill].

starling - refers to Starling, *Sturnus vulgaris*. [Early Modern English *sterlyng*, proper surname *Starling*, Middle English *sterling*, *sterlyng*, Old English *stærling*, *stæline*, a diminutive of *stær*, starling, *sterlyng*, Latin *sturnus*, starling, star, compare: Old Norse *stari*, Danish *stær*, Swedish *stare*, Old High German *stard*, Middle High German *star*; + -*ling* Old English -*ling*, Old Norse -*lingr*, small].

stilt - refers to Black-necked Stilt, *Himantopus mexicanus*. [Middle English *stilte*, Middle Low German *stilte*, Flemish *stilte*, compare: Danish *stylte*, stilt, Dutch *stelt*, German *stelze*, stilt, Swedish *styla*, Old High German *stelza*; named for its extra-long legs].

stork - refers to Wood Stork, *Mycteria americana*, also known as Wood Ibis. [Middle English, Old English *storc*, compare: Old Norse *storkr*, Old Saxon *stork*; Dutch *stork*, Danish *stork*, Swedish *stork*, Old High German *storah*, German *storch*, Middle High German *storch*, stork; according to an old legend, a stork passes over a house where a baby is about to be born, hence, the stork's connection to the bringing of a child into the world, refers to bird's stiff-legged walk or its stiff stance].

storm-petrel - refers to members of Family Hydrobatidae, example: Wilson's Petrel, *Oceanites oceanicus*. [storm Middle English *storm*, Old English *storm*, compare: Old Saxon *storm*, Old Norse *stormr*, a storm, German *storm*, storm, attack, Medieval Dutch *storem*, *stoorm*; + petrel Late Latin *Petrus*, Peter, Latin *Petrus*, Peter, Greek *Petros*, Peter, reference to St. Peter's walking upon the Lake of Gennesareth, from the bird's seeming ability to walk on water (flying just above surface)].

surfbird - refers to Surfbird, Aphriza virgata. [surf Early Modern English *surf*, *suff*, *suffe*, *sough*, + bird Middle English *bird*, *brid*, Old English *bridd*, bird, young bird, named for its habit of feeding along the surfline of a beach].

swallow - example: Barn Swallow, *Hirundo rustica*. [Early Modern English *swallowe*, *swallow*, Middle English *swalwe*, *swalu*, *swalowe*, *swalewe*, Old English *swalewe*, *swalewe*, *swealwe*, swallow, compare: Old Frisian *swale*, Old High German *swalawa*, *swalwa*, Old Saxon *swala*, Middle Dutch *swalu*, Dutch *zwaluw*, German *schwalbe*, Old Norse *svala*;].

swan - example: Whistling Swan, *Cygnus columbianus*. [Middle English *swan*, Old English *swan*, compare: Dutch *zwaan*, Icelandic *svanr*, Old Saxon *swan*, *suan*, Old High German *swan*, *swan(a)*, *swon*, German *schwan*, Swedish *svan*, Danish *svane*, Latin *sonare*, to sound, Sanskrit *svan*, to resound, to sound, to sing; possibly echoic from sounds of singing swan].

swift - refers to Chimney Swift, *Chaetura pelagica*. [Middle English, Old English *swift*, Old English *swifan*, to move in a course, sweep, move quickly, compare: Old English *swapan*, to sweep, Old English *swipu*, a whip, Old Norse *svifa*, to rove, to turn, to sweep, Old Frisian *swivia*, Old High German *sweibon*, to move or turn quickly, Middle High German *sweifen*, to swing; refers to bird's rapid flight].

tanager - refers to Scarlet Tanager, *Piranga olivacea* and Summer Tanager, *Piranga rubra*. [Modern Latin, *tanagra*, Portugaese *tanagara*, Brazilian, Tupi *tangara*, *tangora*, tanager].

tattler - refers to Wandering Tattler, *Heteroscelus incanus*. [tattler, tattle, Middle English *tatelen*, *totelen*, *tateren*, to tattle, prattle, Middle Dutch *tateren*, *tatelen* to stammer, of imitative origin, compare: Low German *tateln*, to gabble, cackle, quack, German *tattern*, to prattle, Dutch *tateren*, to stammer; named for its loud cry].

teal - refers to Blue-winged Teal, *Anas discors*, or Green-winged Teal, *Anas carolinensis*. [Early Modern English *tele*, *teale*, Middle English *tele*, compare: Middle Dutch *teelingh*, *teiling*, *teling*, teal, Dutch *teling*, *taling*; unknown origin].

tern - example: Common Tern, *Sterna hirundo*. [of Scandinavian origin, compare: Danish *terne*, *tærene*, Swedish *tarna*, Faroese *terna*; Old Norse *therna*, tern].

thrasher - refers to Brown Thrasher, *Toxostoma rufum*. [thrash, from thresh Middle English *threschen*, Old English *threscan*, *therscan*, to tread, to thresh, to beat grain + *-er*, Old English *-ere*, suffix, a possible variation of thrush or a reflection of active movement of bird's tail].

thrush - refers to Hermit Thrush, *Hylocichla guttata*, or Wood Thrush, *Hylocichla mustelina*. [Middle English *thrusch*, *thrusche*, Old English *thrysce*, *thrysee*, *thryssce*, *thruesce*, a thrush, Latin *turdus*, thrush].

tit - folkname for some chickadees and nuthatches, example: Black-capped Tit, or Black-capped Chickadee. [shortened form of *titmouse*, Middle English *tit*, Icelandic *tittr*, titmouse, a bird, a small plug or pin, literally, anything small, Old Norse *titlingr*, little bird].

titmouse - refers to Tufted Titmouse, *Parus bicolor*. [tit- shortened form of *titmouse*, Middle English *tit*, Icelandic *tittr*, a bird or literally, anything small, Old Norse *titlingr*, little bird + mose Middle English *mose*, Old English *mase*, titmouse, or any small bird].

towhee - refers to Rufous-sided Towhee, *Pipilo erythrophthalmus*. [name is reflective of bird's call].

trogon - refers to Elegant Trogon, *Trogon elegans* - [Modern Latin, Greek *trogon*, to gnaw].

tropic bird - refers to White-tailed Tropic Bird, *Phaethon lepturus*. [tropic Middle English *tropik*, *tripik*, Old French *tropique*, Late Latin *tropicus*, Latin *tropicus*, pertaining to a turn, Greek *tropikos*, belonging to a turn (of the sun at the solstice) Greek *trope*, a turning + bird Middle English *bird*, *brid*, Old English *bridd*, bird, young bird, named for its habitat in the tropical regions of the world].

turkey - refers to Turkey, *Meleagris gallopavo*. [French *turquie*, turkey, French *Turc*, a Turk, Tatar, *Turk*, a Turk, originally referred to the domesticated Guinea Fowl, *Numida meleagris*, which was imported to Europe from Guinea, Africa through Turkey, name is sonic; the birds call sounds like, "turk, turk"].

turnstone - refers to Ruddy Turnstone, *Arenaria interpres*. [turn Middle English *turnen*, *tournen*, Old English *turnian*, *tyrnan*, Old French *turner*, *tourner*, *torner*, to turn, Latin *tornare*, to round off, to turn on a lathe, from Latin *tornus*, a lathe, Greek *tornos*, a (turner's) lathe, a turner's chisel, a carpenter's tool for drawing circles + stone Middle English *ston*, Old English *stan*, named for bird's food gathering technique which involves turning over small stones].

veery - refers to Veery, *Hylocichla fuscenscens*. [name reflects bird's call].

verdin - refers to Verdin, *Auriparus flaviceps* - [French bunting, *vert*, green, Old French *verd*].

vireo - refers to Red-eyed Vireo, *Vireo olivaceus*. [Latin *vireo*, a type of bird, green].

vulture - example: Black Vulture, *Coraagyps atratus*, or Turkey Vulture, *Cathartes aura*. [Middle English *vulture*, *vultur*, *voltur*, *voltor*, Anglo-Norman *vultur*, Old French *voultour*, *voltour*, *vautour*, *voltor*, Latin *vulturius*, *vultur*, a vulture, Old Latin *uolturus*, a tearer].

wagtail - refers to Yellow Wagtail, *Motacilla flava*. [wagtail, wagstert, wagsterd, wagstyrt, wag Middle English *wagge*, *waggen*, Old English *wagian*, to move, wag, totter, sway, Old Norse *vagga*, *vaga*, a cradle, compare: Swedish *vagga*, to wag, to sway, to rock (a cradle), Middle Dutch vagen, Middle High German *wacken*, to totter, shake; + *stert*, a tail, named for the bird's continual wagging of its tail].

warbler - example: Yellow Warbler, *Dendroica petechia*. [warble Middle English *werble*, *werblen*, *werbelen*, *werbeln*, *werblen*, Norman French *werbler*, *werble*,to sing, trill, play on a musical instrument, Middle High German *werbelen*, *wirbeln*, to warble, to roll, to rotate, to turn, compare: Old Frankish *wirbil*, whirlwind;].

waterthrush - refers to Northern Waterthrush, *Seiursu noveboracensis*. [water Middle English *water*, *wæter*, *weter*, Old English *wæter*, compare Old Saxon *watar*, Old Frisian *wetir*, *weter*, Frisian *wetter*, *wiet*, water, Low German *water*, Danish *vand*, Swedish *vatten*, Greek *hydor*, Sanskrit *udan*, water, Hittite *watar*, water; + thrush Middle English *thrusch*, *thrusche*, Old English *thrysce*, *thrysee*, *thryssce*, *thruesce*, a thrush, Latin *turdus*, thrush].

waxwing - refers to Cedar Waxwing, *Bombycilla cedrorum*. [wax Middle English *wax*, *wex*, Old English *wæx*, *weax*, beeswax, wax, compare: Old Frisian *wax*, Frisian *waaks*, wax, Dutch *was*, German *wachs*, Old High German *wahs*, Old Norse *vax*, Swedish *vax*, Danish *vox*; + wing Middle English *winge*, *wenge*, *whing*, *weng*, Old Norse *væng1ir*, *væng1r*, a wing, compare: Dutch *wagien*, to fly, to blow; named for red spots resembling flattened tips of red sealing wax on wings].

weaver finch - a genus of Old World birds, example: House Sparrow, *Passer domesticus*. [weaver, weave, Middle English *weuen*, *weven*, Old English *wefan*, to weave, compare: Old High German *weban*, Old Norse *vefa*, Dutch *weven*, German *weben*, Danish *væve;* + finch Middle English *fincq*, *finch*, *fynch*, Old English *finc*, so called for their elaborate woven nests].

wheatear - refers to Wheatear, *Oenathe oenanthe*. - [Early Modern English *wheatear*, *wheatears*, *wheat*, *whiteass*, *white rump*, *whitetail*, *wheat*, white + *ers*, *eeres*, arse, Old English *hwit*, white + *ærs*, rump, in reference to its white rump].

whimbrel - refers to Whimbrel, *Numenius phaeopus*. [whimbrel, *whympernell*, *whimrel*, from *whimp*, + *-rel*, Old French *-erel*, compare: *whimper*; named after its cry].

whip-poor-will - refers to Whip-poor-will, *Caprimulgus vociferus*. [*whip* + *poor* + *Will*, a proper name, named for bird's call. which sounds like, "whip-poor-will"].

whiskey-jack - refers to Gray Jay, *Perisoreus canadensis* and Clark's Nutcracker, *Nucifraga columbiana*. [Modern English *whiskie, whisky, whiskey-john*, Scottish *whiskybea*, Gaelic *uisge beatha*, (*uisge*, water, shower, rain + *beatha*, life, victuals, food, livelihood, welcome, literally, 'water of life'), Native North American Cree *wiiskachaan, wiskatjan*, Montagnais *wishkuts-han* + jack, familiar form of *John*, Middle English *Jacke, Jakke*, John, a form representing everyman, Old French *Jacques*, James, Late Latin *Jacobus*, Latin *Jacobus*, Greek *Iakodus*, Hebrew *Ya'aqob, Ya'aqobh*, Jacob, the supplanter].

wigeon - refers to American Wigeon, *Anas americana*. [wigeon, widgeon Early Modern English *wigene, widgeon, wigeon* Middle French *vigeon*, a kind of duck, Old French *vigeon*, Latin *vipio*, a kind of small crane].

willet - refers to Willet, *Catoptrophorus semipalmalus*. [name reflects bird's call].

woodcock - refers to Amercian Woodcock, *Scolopax minor*. [Middle English *wodekoc*, Old English *wude-coco, wuducoc*, from Old English *wudu, widu, wude, wiodu*, wood + *cocc, coce*, cock].

woodpecker - example: Hairy Woodpecker, *Dendrocopos villosus*. [wood Middle English *wode, wude*, Old English *wudu, wude, widu, wiodu*, wood, forest, compare: Old High German *wit*, Old Norse *vithr*, Danish *ved*, wood, Swedish *ved*, wood, Gaelic *fiodh*, Old Irish *fid*, Welsh *gwydd*, trees, shrubs; + peck Middle English *pecken*, a variant of *picken*, pick, Old English *pycan*, to pick or peck, Middle Low German *pekken*, to peck with beak + -er, Old English *-ere*, suffix].

wren - refers to House Wren, *Troglodytes aedon*. [Middle English *wren, wrenne*, Old English *werna, wrenna, wœrna, wrœnna*, a wren, compare: Old Norse *rindill*, Old High German *wrendo, wrendilo*].

wrentit - refers to Wrentit, *Chamaea fasciata*. [wren Middle English wren, *wrenne*, Old English *wrenna*, *wrænna*, wren + tit Middle English *tit*, Icelandic *tittr*, a bird, Old Norse *titlingr*, little bird].

yellowhammer - a folkname for the Northern Flicker, *Colaptes auratus*. [yellowhammer, yellow-ham, yelamire, yelambre, yellowammer, Old English *geolu*, yellow +*hama*, covering, i.e., yellow-feathered bird, compare: German *Ammer*, bunting; (yelamire Old English *geolu*, yellow + *amore*, a kind of bird, a small bird, akin to Old High German *amaro*, a kind of finch that fed on emmer), compare: Middle Dutch *emmerick*, a yellowammer, German *gelbammer*, *goldammer*, yellow-ammer, goldammer;].

yellowlegs - refers to Greater Yellowlegs, *Tringa melanoleuca*, or Lesser Yellowlegs, *Tringa flavipes*. [yellow Middle English *yelow*, *yelwe*, *yelu*, *yelowe*, Old English *geolu*, *geolo*, *geolwe*, compare: Dutch *geel*, Old Saxon *gelo*, Old High German *gelo*, German *gelb*, Old Norse *gulr*; + leg Middle English, Old Norse *legge*, *leggr*, leg, bone, named for its prominent yellow-colored legs].

yellowthroat - refers to Yellowthroat, Geothlypis trichas. [yellow, Middle English *yelow*, *yelwe*, *yelu*, Old English *geolu*, *geolo* + throat Middle English throte, Old English, named for its prominent yellow throat].

Domestic North American Bird Name Origins

Names for domestic birds that were brought over to America from England and Europe have their linguistic roots that trace back into Middle English and earlier. The following is a listing of common North American domestic bird names, with etymology enclosed within brackets. The scientific names and root words are shown in italics. All spelling variations for the italicized root words are listed. Diacritical marks for pronunciation have been omitted for ease of reading. [Dodge][Flexner] [Hoffmeister][Hvass][Lewis][Neufeldt][Onions] [Soukhanov] [Skeat][Vriends].

Domestic Poultry terms:

bird - [Middle English *bird, brid,* bird, Old English *brid, bridd,* bird, young bird, unknown origin].

cock - [Middle English *cok,* Old English *coc, cocc, kok,* Old French *coc, coq,* compare: Danish *kok,* Old Norse *kokkr, kokr,* cock, Old Slavic *kokotu*; Medieval Latin *coccus,* from *coco, coco coco,* the cock's cry, a cackling, Sanskrit *kukkuuta-s,* cock, of echoic origin].

fowl - [Middle English *fowel, foul, foule, foghel, fuwel, fugel,* Old English *fugel, fugol,* a bird, Old English *flug,* flight, compare: Old Frisian *fugel,* a bird, Frisian *fugel,* bird, Frisian *fugelt,* fowl, Old Saxon *fugal,* Middle Dutch *voghel,* Danish *fugl,* Old High German *fogal,* Middle High German *vogel,* Old Icelandic *fugl,* Gothic *fugls,* bird, fowl;].

game - [starting around A.D. 1300, the term was used to refer the catching of wild animals for sport. Middle English *game, gamen,* gome, Old English *gamen, gomen,* joy, mirth, fun, sport, amusement, *gamenian,* to play, compare: Old Frisian *game,* joy, glee, Old Saxon *gamen,* game, sport, Icelandic *gaman,* game, sport, merriment, Danish *gammen,* Old High

German *gaman*, joy, mirth; of unknown origin.].

hen - [Middle English hen, Old English *hen, henn, hæn, hana*, a hen, from Old English *hana*, a cock, literally, 'a singer', compare: Old Frisian *henn*, hen, Frisian *hin*, hen, Old High German *henna*, Middle High German *henne*, Dutch *hen*, Middle Dutch *henne*, German *henne*, Icelandic *hæna*, Danish *hone*;].

poultry - [Middle English *pultrie, pultry, pulterie*, Old French *pouletrie*, domestic fowl, *pouletier*, dealer in domestic fowl, *poulet*, young fowl, *poule*, hen, Latin *pullus*, young animal]

rooster - [rooster, roost Early Modern English *roost*, cock, Middle English *rooste*, a perch for fowls, Old English *hrost*, wooden framework of a roof, perch, a roost, compare: Middle Dutch *roest*, a hen-roost, Old Saxon *hrost*, spars of a roof, Old Norse *hrot*, Gothic *hrot*, roof; + suffix, *-er*].

Traditional Domestic Poultry:

chicken - refers to Domestic Chicken, *gallus domesticus*, (descended from Red Jungle Fowl, *Gallas gallas*). [Middle English *chicken, chiken, chikene, cheken, chyken, chekin*, chicken, young chicken, Old English *cycen, cicen*, diminutive of *coc*, a cock, compare: Middle Dutch kieken, kiekijen, kuken, chicken, young fowl; root name imitative of bird's sound].

duck, refers to Domestic Duck, *Anas platyrhynchos*, (descended from Mallard, *Anas platyrhynchos*). [Middle English *duk, doke, douke, duke*, a duck, Old English *duce*, diver, ducker].

goose - refers to Domestic Goose, *Anser anser*, descended from Gray Lag goose, *Anser anser* or refers to Muscovy Duck, *Cairina moschata*, from Tropical America. [Middle English *gose*, Old English *gos*, compare: Old Frisian *gos, goz*, goose, Frisian *goes*, goose, Middle Dutch *gans*, Old Icelandic *gas*, Irish-Gaelic *geis*, swan].

guinea fowl - refers to domesticated Guinea Fowl, *Numida meleagris*, [guinea, from *Guinea*, name of country of origin of bird in West Africa].

turkey - refers to Turkey, *Meleagris gallopavo*, from North America. [French *turquie*, *turkey*, *Turkey*, French *Turc*, a Turk, Tatar, *Turk*, a Turk, originally referred to a Guinea-fowl which was imported to Europe from Turkey and the East].

Other Poultry:

ostrich - refers to Ostrich, *Struthio camelus*. [Middle English *ostrice*, *oystryche*, *ostriche*, Old French *ostrice*, *ostrusce*, Medieval Latin *ostrica*, *ostrigius*, Latin *avis*, bird + *struthio*, ostrich-bird, Greek *strouthion*, ostrich, from *strouthes megale*, great sparrow].

pigeon - refers to Pigeon, *Columba livia*. [Middle English *pejon*, *peion*, *pyion*, *pegeon*, *pygeon*, *pichon*, pigeon, dove, Middle French *pijon*, young bird, Old French *pijon*, *pyjoun*, young bird, young dove, Late Latin *pipo*, *pipio*, *pipire*, Latin *pipio*, squab, young bird].

Ornamentals:

flamingo - refers to Greater Flamingo, *Phoenicopterus ruber*. [Portuguese *flamengo*, flamingo, Spanish *flamenco*, *Fleming*, Old Provencal *flamenc*, *flama*, flame, Latin *flamma*, flame, named for its bright colors].

peacock - refers to Peacock, *Pavo cristatus*. [Middle English *pecoc*, *pacok*, *pocok*, *pecok*, male peafowl, *po*, peacock + *coc*, cock, Old English *pawa*, *pea*, peafowl + *cok*, cock, male bird, male fowl, Latin *pavo*, peafowl, peacock, Persian *tawus*, *taus*, a peacock, Old Tamil *tokei*, *togei*, a peacock].

pheasant, refers to Golden Pheasant, Chysolophus pictus, from China. [Middle English *fesan*, *fesant*, *fesaunt*, *faisant*, Anglo-Norman *fesaunt*, Old French *faisan*, *fesan*, *fesant*, *faisant*, Provencal *faisan*, Latin *phasianus*, Latin *Phasianus*, the Phasian Bird, Greek *phasaianos*, the Phasian bird, after *Phasis*, river of Colchis, where birds collected at the river's mouth, on the Black Sea, in what is now Georgia].

swan - refers to Mute Swan, *Cygnus olor*. [swan Middle English *swan*, Old English *swan*, compare: Dutch *zwaan*, Icelandic *svanr*, Old Saxon *swan*, *suan*, Old High German *swan*, *swan(a)*, *swon*, Latin *sonare*, to sound, Sanskrit *svan* to resound, to sound, to sing; possibly echoic from sounds of singing swan].

Cage and Pet birds:

amazon - refers to genus Amazona, a type of tropical American parrot, example: Blue-fronted Amazon, *Amazona aestiva*. [amazon Spanish, from the river Amazon, named for native female warriors encountered there, Latin *Amazon*, Greek *Amazon*, of unknown origin, but derived by folk etymology *a*-, without + *mazos*, breast, a race of Scythian women warriors, referring to tale that the Amazon women cut off their right breast to facilitate archery].

budgerigar, budgereegah - refers to Budgerigar, *Melopsittacus undulatus*. [Aboriginal Australian name, *budgeri*, good + *gar*, cockatoo].

bulbul - example: Red-bellied Bulbul, *Pycnonotus fuscus*. [Persian *bulbul*, a nightingale, Arabic *bulbul*, probably reflection of bird's call].

canary - refers to Canary, *Serinus canaria*. [French *canari*, *Canarie*, Spanish *canario*, meaning of Islas Canarias, the Canary Islands, Latin *Canaria Insula*, Isle of Dogs, so called from its large dogs, Latin *canis*, a dog].

cockatiel - refers to Cockatiel, *Nymphicus hollandicus*. [Dutch *kaketielje*, Malay *kakatua*].

cockatoo - [Early Modern English *cacatoe*, Dutch *kaketoe*, *kakatoe*, Hindi *kakatua*, a cockatoo, Malay *kakatua*, *kakatuwa*, a cockatoo, probably a contraction of *kakak tuwa*, 'old sister,' name echoic of bird's call].

conure - example: Nanday Conure, *Nandayus nenday*. [New Latin *conurus*, Greek *konos*, cone + *oura*, tail].

cordon bleu - example: Red-cheeked Cordon Bleu, *Uraeginthus bengalus*. [French *cordon*, ribbon + *bleu*, blue, originally referred to a blue ribbon, worn as a scarf or badge, of the Order of the Holy Ghost, the highest order of the old French chivalry under the Bourbon monarchy, so called from the sash-like blue breast of the bird].

finch - example: Red-headed Finch, *Amadina erythrocephala*. [finch Middle English *finch*, *fynch*, *fincq*, Old English *finc*, finch, compare: Dutch *vink*, Old High German *fincho*, *finco*, Middle High German *vinke*, German *fink*;].

galah - refers to Galah Cockatoo, *Eolphus roseicapillus*. [Australian Aboriginal name].

leafbird - example: Golden-fronted Leafbird, *Chloropsis aurifrons*. [leaf Middle English *lef*, *leef*, *lefe*, Old English *leaf*, compare: Gothic *laufs*, leaf, Old Saxon *lof*, Old Frisian *laf*, Dutch *loof*, foliage, Icelandic *lauf*, Old Norse *lauf*, Swedish *löf*, Danish *löv*, Old High German *loub*, leaf, foliage, Gothic *lauf*, *laufs*, foliage; + bird Middle English *bird*, *brid*, *bred*, Old English *bridd*, *brid*, bird, young bird, from Old English *bredan*, to breed].

lorikeet - example: Rainbow Lorikeet, *Trichoglassus haematodus*. [lorikeet, diminutive of *lori* + (para)*keet*].

lory - refers to parrots of subfamily Loriinæ, of Southeast Asia and Australia, example: Chattering Lory, *Lorius garrulus*. [lory Malay *luri, nuri*, a lory, a kind of parrot].

lovebird - refers to African genus, *Agapornis*. [lovebird love Middle English *love, luve*, Old English *lufu, lufan*, love, affection, compare: Old Frisian *luve*, Frisian *leafde*, love, Old High German *luba*, Old Norse *lof, ljufr*, Obs. Dutch *lieven*, to love, Dutch *lief*, Old Frisian *liaf*, German *liebe*, Gothic liufLatin *lubet, libet*, it pleases, Sanskrit *lubh*, to desire; + bird Middle English *bird, brid*, bird, Old English *brid, bridd*, bird, young bird, unknown origin, so-called because they are very attached to their mates].

macaw - [Portuguese *macao, macau*, from *macauba*, macaw palm, Tupi *macavuana*, from Tupi *macauba*, the macaw palm, bird's name is from the macaw palm, whose fruits it feeds upon].

manakin - example: Golden-headed Manakin, *Pipra erythocephala*. [mannikin, manikan, Dutch *maneken, man*, man +diminutive suffix *-ken*, name originally applied to a bird with beard-like feathers on its chin].

mesia - example: Silver-eared Mesia, *Leiothrix argentauris*. [origin unknown].

munia - example: White-headed Munia, *Lonchura maja*. [origin unknown].

myna - refers to Crested Myna, *Acridotheres cristatellus*. [myna, mynah, mina Hindi *maina*, Sanskrit *madana-s, madanah*].

parakeet - [Early Modern English *parakeete*, Spanish *periquito, perico*, Pedro, a proper name, Middle French *paroquet, perrot, perroquet*, a parakeet, Old French *Pierre*, Peter].

parrot - [Early Modern English *parrot*, Middle English *perrot*, *parrot*, French *Perrot*, *Pierrot*, French *Pierre*, Peter].

red bishop - refers to Red Bishop, *Euplectes orix*. [red Middle English *red*, *reed*, *read*, Old English *read*, red, compare: Old Saxon *rod*, Old Norse *rathr*, *rjothr*, *rauor*, *rjoor*, Danish *rød*, Old Frisian *rad*, Frisian *rea(d)*, red, Middle Dutch *root*, *rood*, Old High German *rot*, Middle High German *rot*, Gothic *rauths*, Gaelic *ruadh*, reddish, ruddy, red-haired, Latin *ruber*, *rufus*, red, Greek *erythos*, Sanskrit *rudhira*, *rohita*; + bishop Middle English *bischop*, *biscop*, *bisceop*, Old English *biscop*, *bisceop*, *bisceope*, Vulgar Latin *ebiscopus*, Late Latin *episcopus*, an overseer, Latin *episcopus*, overseer, bishop, Greek *episkopos*, overseer, Greek *epi*, upon + *skopos*, inspector, watcher, *skopcin*, *skopein*, to look, compare: Old Frisian *biskop*, Frisian *biskop*, bishop, Old Saxon *biskop*, Middle Dutch *bisschop*, Old Norse *biskup*, Old High German *biscof*; so called from the bird's red and black bishop-like colors, also named Grenadier Weaver and Orange Bishop].

rosella - example: Crimson Rosella, Platycercus elegans. [rosella, New Latin, diminutive of Latin *rosa*, rose, corruption of *Rose-hiller*, from *Rose Hill*, name of the governor's residence at Parramatta, near Sydney, New South Wales, Australia].

shama - example: Shama, *Copsychus malbaricus*. [Hindi *shama*, *sama*, Old Indian *syamah*, black, dark-colored].

toucan - example: Cuvier's Toucan, *Ramphastos cuvieri*. [French *toucan*, Brazilian Portuguese *tucano*, Tupi *tucano*, *tucan*, *tuca*, *tucana*, from the cry of the bird].

waxbill - example: Common Waxbill or St. Helena Waxbill, *Estrilda astrild*. [wax Middle English *wax*, *wex*, Old English *wæx*, *weax*, beeswax, wax, compare: Old Frisian *wax*, Frisian *waaks*, wax, Dutch *was*, German *wachs*, Old High German *wahs*, Middle High German *wahs*, Old Saxon *wahs*, Old Norse *vax*, Swedish *vax*, Danish *vox*; + bill Middle English *bille, bile*, Old English *bile*, beak of a bird, *bil*, to strike, named for the wax-like appearance of its bill].

weaver - example: Grenadier Weaver, *Euplectes orix*. [weaver, weave, Middle English *weuen, weven*, Old English *wefan*, to weave, compare: Old High German *weban*, Old Norse *vefa*, Middle Low German *weven*, Middle Dutch *weven*, Dutch *weven*, German *weben*, Danish *væve*;].

white eye - example: Indian White Eye, *Zosterops palpebrosus*. [white Middle English *whit(e), whit*, Old English *hwit*, compare: Old Frisian *hwit*, Frisian *wyt*, white, Old Saxon *hwit*, Dutch *wit*, German *weiss*, Old High German *wiz*, Old Norse *hvitr*, Swedish *hvit, vit*, Norwegian *kvit*, Danish *hvid*, Gothic *hweits*, Sanskrit *sveta*, white; + eye Middle English *eye, eie, ege, eige*, Old English *ege, eage*, eye, compare: Old Saxon *oga*, Old Frisian *age*, Frisian *each*, eye, Old High German *ouga*, German *auge*, Dutch *oog*, Old Norse *auga*, Latin *oculus*, eye, Greek *okkos*, eye, Sanskrit *aksi*; named for the ring of white feathers around its eye].

whydah - refers to Paradise Whydah, *Vidua paradisea* or *Steganura paradisea*. [whydah, whidah, whidah finch, whydah bird, vida finch, widoo bird, widowbird, alternation after widow(bird), to make name agree with name of West African seaport town in Dahomey, *Whidah*, (present name, Ouidah) where the bird resides].

zebra finch - refers to Zebra Finch, *Poephila cstanotis*, *Poephila guttata* or *Taeniopygia guttata*. [zebra Early Modern English *zebra*, Italian *zebra*, Spanish *zebra, zebro*, Portuguese *zebra*, Old Portuguese *zevro, zevra*, originally, a wild ass, Congolese, Amharic *zebra*, + finch Middle English *finch, fynch, fincq*, Old English *finc*, finch, compare: Dutch *vink*, Old High German *fincho, finco*, Middle High German *vinke*, German *fink*; named for its black and white striped tail].

Birds seen in zoos:

bird of paradise - example: Superb Bird of Paradise, *Lophorina superba*. [bird Middle English *bird*, *brid*, *bred*, Old English *bridd*, *brid*, bird, young bird, from Old English *bredan*, to breed, + of Middle English *of*, Old English *of*, *off*, *af*, æf, compare: Old Saxon *af*, Old Norse *af*, Gothic *af*, Swedish *af*, Danish *af*, Old High German *aba*, German *ab*, Latin *ab*, Greek *apo*, Sanskrit *apa*, away; + paradise Middle English *paradis*, Old English *paradis*, Old French, Late Latin *paradisus*, heaven, abode of the blessed, Latin *paradicus*, Greek *paradeisos*, garden, enclosed park, paradise, pleasure-grounds, royal park, enclosure, Old Persian (Avestan)(Zend) *pairi-daeza*, enclosure, park, from *pairi-*, around + *daeza-*, wall, (*diz*, to mould form), so called for their beautifully colored feathers].

bower bird - [bower Middle English *bour*, *bur*, *boure*, small room, chamber, Old English *bur*, *bar*, a dwelling, room, chamber, from *buan*, to build, Icelandic *bua*, to dwell, compare: Old Saxon *bur*, Old High German *bur*, dwelling, Middle High German *bur*, chamber, cage, Old Norse *bur*, *bar*, chamber, storehouse, Gothic *bauan*, dwell, inhabit, live, Swedish *bur*, cage, German *bauer*, birdcage; + bird Middle English *bird*, *brid*, *bred*, Old English *bridd*, *brid*, bird, young bird, from Old English *bredan*, to breed]

bustard - refers to Great Bustard, *Otis tarda*. [Late Middle English, Old French *bistard*, *oustarde*, Provencal *aus tarda*, Latin *avis tarda*, literally, 'slow bird', compare: Old Irish *bistarda*, Spanish *avertarda*, bustard; named for its slow and stately gait].

cacique - example: Great Crested Cacique, *Ostinops decumanus*. [French or Spanish, Arawakan or Taino (Hispaniola)].

cariama - example: Crested Cariama, *Cariama cristata*. [carima, seriema New Latin, Portuguese].

cassowary - example: Common Cassowary, *Casuarius casuarius*. [cassowary Central Moluccan *kasuwari*, *kasuwali* or Malay *kesuari*].

cock-of-the-rock - refers to Cock-of-the-rock, *Rupicola rupicola*. [named for its rooster-like looks with its large crest].

cotinga - [New Latin, French *cotinga*, Tupi *cotinga*, *cutinga*, Tupi *coting*, to wash, + *tinga*, white].

drongo - example: Drongo, *Dicurus adsimilis*. [Madagascaran, native Malagasy].

emu - refers to Emu, *Dromiceius novae-hollandiae*. [emu, emeu, emia, eme, Portuguese *ema*, ostrich, rhea, originally, a crane, shortened from Portuguese *ema di gei*, crane of the ground, Moluccan *emeu*, *eme*].

great curassow - refers to Great Curasso. [great Middle English *gret*, *greet*, *grete*, Old English *great*, thick, coarse, compare: Dutch *groot*, Ols Saxon *grot*, Old High German *gros*, German *gross*; + curassow, phonetic spelling of *Curaco*, named after island of its original habitat, *Curacao*, in the Caribbean].

hornbill - [horn Middle English *horn*, Old English *horn*, compare: Old Saxon *horn*, Dutch *horen*, *hoorn*, Old Norse *horn*, Old High German *horn*, German *horn*, Welsh *corn*, Gaelic *corn*, drinking horn or cup, trumpet, Irish *corn*, Gothic *haurn*, horn, Greek *keras*, horn; + bill Middle English *bille*, *bile*, Old English *bile*, beak of a bird, *bil*, to strike, so called from the size and character of its bill].

jacamar - example: Rufous-tailed Jacamar, *Galbula ruficanda*. [French, Tupi-Guarani *jacamaciri*].

jacana - example: South American Jacana, *Jacana spinosa jacana*. [Portuguese *jacana*, Tupi *jacanam*, *jassanam*, Guarani *jasana*].

kea - refers to Kea, *Nestor notabilis*. [New Zealand Maori *kea*, imitative of its cry].

kiwi - refers to Kiwi, *Apteryx australis*. [New Zealand native-Maori *kiwi*, imitative of its cry].

kookaburra - example: Laughing Kookaburra, *Dacelo novae-guineae*. [native Australian aboriginal: Wiradjuri *guguburra*, imitiative of its cry].

mallee fowl - refers to Mallee Fowl, *Leipoa ocellata*. [so called after its habitat, mallee vegetation, scrub forms of eucalyptus found it drier parts of Australia + fowl [Middle English *fowel*, *foul*, *foule*, *foghel*, *fuwel*, *fugel*, Old English *fugel*, *fugol*, a bird, Old English *flug*, flight, compare: Old Frisian *fugel*, a bird, Frisian *fugel*, bird, Frisian *fugelt*, fowl, Old Saxon *fugal*, Middle Dutch *voghel*, Danish *fugl*, Old High German *fogal*, Middle High German *vogel*, Old Icelandic *fugl*, Gothic *fugls*, bird, fowl;].

motmot - example: Common Motmot, *Momotus momota*. [American Spanish *motmot*, name is echoic of the bird's note].

penguin - example: King Penguin. [name originally applied to the garefowl or Great Auk, now extinct (name referred to large white patch between bill and eye), Welsh *pen*, head, chief + *gwyn*, *gwynn*, white].

quetzal - refers to Quetzal, *Pharomachrus mocino*. [Spanish, native Central American Indian Nahuatl *quetzall*, large brilliant tail feather of quetzal, *quetzalli*, plumage of the quetzal bird, the national bird of Guatemala].

rhea - example: Rhea, *Rhea americana*. [New Latin, Greek *Rhea*, from Greek mythology, daughter of Uranus and Gaea, wife of Cronus and mother of Zeus].

scrub-bird - example: Noisy Scrub-bird, *Atrichornis clamosa*. [scrub + bird, scrub Middle English, Scandanivan, compare: Danish *skrub*, brushwood; + **bird** Middle English *bird*, *brid*, bird, Old English *brid*, *bridd*, bird, young bird, unknown origin, name refers to bird's use of dense underbrush as habitat in Western Australia].

secretary bird - refers to Secretary Bird, *Sagittarius serpentarius*. [secretary Middle English *secretarie*, person entrusted with secrets, Medieval Latin *secretarius*, clerk, notary, confidant, one entrusted with secrets, Latin *secretus*, separated, set apart, private, secret, Latin *secretum*, a secret + -*ary*, suffix, a person or thing that does, from Latin -*arius* (alternative etymology: French *secretaire*, by folk etymology from Sudanese Arabic *sagral-ter*, *sagr*, -hawk +*al*, the, + *ter*, bird (collective)) + bird Middle English *bird*, *brid*, bird, Old English *brid*, *bridd*, bird, young bird, unknown origin, named for the feathers of its crest, which resemble pens stuck over the ear].

takahe - refers to Takahe, *Notornis hochstetteri*. [New Zealand native Maori name].

tinamou - example: Rufous Tinamou, *Rhynchotus rufescens*. [French, French Guinean, Carib Galibi *tinamu*].

tui - refers to Tui, *Prosthemadera novaes-zeelandiae*. [New Zealand Maori name, echoic of its song].

turaco - [turaco, touraco, turakoo Early Modern English, French *touraco* or Dutch *toerako*, West African, origin obscure, named from a coppery-red pigment, turacin, a copper complex of a porphin derivative, found on their feathers; birds are also called banana-eaters].

wood-hewer - example: Red-billed Wood Hewer, *Campylorhampus trochilirostris.* [wood Middle English *wode*, *wude*, Old English *wudu*, *wude*, *widu*, *wiodu*, wood, forest, compare: Old High German *wit*, Old Norse *vithr*, Danish *ved*, wood, Swedish *ved*, wood, Gaelic *fiodh*, Old Irish *fid*, Welsh *gwydd*, trees, shrubs;] + hewer, hew [Middle English *hewan*, Old English *heawan*, compare: Dutch *houwen*, Old High German *houwan*, German *hauen*, Icelandic *höggva*, Swedish *hugga*, Danish *hugge*; named for their brown creeper-like habit of slowing climbing trees in search of insects and other prey].

88

Sample Format

Thrushes, Solitaires, and Bluebirds (Family Turdidae)

Modern Name: Hermit Thrush
Scientific Name: Hylocichla guttata
Folknames and Names: Swamp Angel, Little Thrush, American Nightingale, Rufous-tailed Thrush, Solitary Thrush, and Swamp Robin.

Gallinaceous Birds (Order Galliformes)

Partridges, Grouse, Turkeys and Quails (Family Phasianidae)

Modern Name: Chukar
Scientific Name: Alectoris chukar
Folknames and Names: Chuckar, Chukor, Gray Partridge, Indian Hill Partridge, Redleg, Red-legged Partridge, Rock Partridge.
* introduced into Hawai'ian Islands, (Kaua'i, Maui, Hawai'i).

Note: both the modern names and the Folknames and Names entries are listed with all capitalizations for each part of the name. This follows the convention established by the American Ornithologists' Union in their *Check-list of North American Birds, Sixth Edition.* Of course, the scientific names are listed in traditional format with the genus name capitalized followed by the specific epithet in lower-case.

Birds currently residing in the islands of **Hawai'i** have been listed with an asterisk (*) following the main listing. Their local names are included in the main listing.

The Flicker: the bird with the most names

The Flicker has the singular honor of having more folknames and names than any other bird that breeds in North America.

Modern Name: Flicker
Scientific Name: Colaptes auratus
Folknames and Names: Antbird, Ant Woodchuck, Big Sapsucker, Big Woodpecker, Black-heart Woodpecker, Boreal Flicker, Buid-heag Bhuachair, Carpintero, Carpintero Collrejo, Carpintero Escapulario, Carpintero Ribero, Cave-duc, Clape, Claype, Common Flicker, Cotton-backed Yellowhammer, Cotton-rump, Cotton-tail, Crescent-bird, Eastern flicker, English Woodpecker, Fiddler, Flicker, Flicker Woodpecker, Flitter, French Woodpecker, Gaffer Woodpecker, Gaffle Woodpecker, Gale Shbecht, Gallie, Gel Specht, Gelb Specht, Golden Sapsucker, Golden-shafted Flicker, Golden-shafted Woodpecker, Golden-wing, Golden-winged Flicker, Golden-winged Woodpecker, Gold-wing Woodpecker, Golden-wing Woodpecker, Gold-winged Woodpecker, Golden Woodpecker, Golden-winged Woodcock, Gold Woodpecker, Grasshopper Woodpecker, Gree Shbecht, Hairy-wicket, Harry-wicket, Hammerhead, He-hi-holder, Heigh-ho, Hexa Shbecht, Hick-wall, High-hole, High-holer, High-hold, High-holder, High-ho Woodpecker, Higholder, Hittock, Hittocks, Hittuck, Hivel, Hybrid Flicker, Jaune, Joune, Le pic aux ailes dores, Little Woodchuck, Meadow Partridge, Missouri Red-moustashed Woodpecker, Mo-ning-quana, Northern Flicker, O-hi-o, Ome-tuc, On-thee-quan-nor-ow, O-zaw-wan-day Paw-Paw-say, Partridge Woodpecker, Paw-Paw-say, Paw-Paw-say-og, Peckwood, Peckerwood, Peerit, Pee-ut, Pe-up, Pic-a-bois, Picque-bois-jaune, Pic Dore, Pie-bis, Pie-bris, Pigeon, Pigeon Woodpecker, Pink-throat, Pique-bois Dore, Picque-bois-jaune, Piut, Pi-ute, Pivart, Poule de Bois, Rain Bird, Rain Fowl, Rampike, Red-shafted Woodpecker, Sapsuck, Sapsucker, Shad-spirit, Sharp-billed Flicker, Silver Dollar Bird, Spotted Woodpecker, Sucker, Specht, Speckt, Speight, Spright, Southern Flicker, Southern Woodpecker, Talpa-na-ni, Taping-bird, Treepecker, Wa-cup, Wah-cup, Walk-up, Wake-up, Wa-wup, Weather Bird, Weather-hen, Wheeler, Whittaker, Wild Hen, Will Crisson, Winter Robin, Woodchuck, Woodcock, Wood-lark, Woodpeck, Woodpecker, Woodpicker, Woodpecker Lark, Wood Pigeon, Woodquoi, Wood-wall, Xebec, Yacker, Yecker, Yucker, Yaffle, Yallow Wheeler, Yallow Whicker, Yarrup, Yarup, Yar-rup, Yawker Bird, Yaw-up, Yellow Flicker, Yellowhammer, Yellow-hammer High-hole, Yellerhammer, Yallerhammer, Yellow-'ammer, Yellow Jay, Yellow-shafted Flicker, Yellow-shafted Woodpecker, Yellow-winged Woodpecker, Yellow Wing, Yellow-winged Sapsucker, Yel-

low-winged Woodcock, Yellow Woodpecker, Zebec.

An early ornithologist, Frank L. Burns, listed over one hundred and twenty names in his "The Monograph of the Flicker," which appeared in the April 1900 issue of the *Wilson Bulletin*, published in Oberlin, Ohio. In this list there are one hundred and sixty names. The flicker also holds the record in North America for the most single word (un-hyphenated) names: forty-one (41). To show some of the varied roots of bird names, the discussions by Frank Burns will be shown for some of the Flicker names [Burns].

Format: **Bird   Name.** State(s) or region used. Discussion.

Antbird: Minnesota. Derived from its taste for eating ants. **Big   Sapsucker:** Northern States. Misnomer. **Carpintero:** Spanish. (Carpenter), name applied to entire woodpecker family. **Cav-duc:** Maine. French-canadian name. **Clape:** Western New York. Of English colonial origin. **Common   Flicker:** East and West. Refers to Yellow-shafted race, especially in parts of Midwest where its range overlapped with Red-shafted race. **Cotton-rump:** Pennsylvania. From white patch on rump. **Crescent-bird:** West. Named for crescents near neck. **English   Woodpecker:** Long Island and Newfoundland. name by early settlers who thought that the Flicker was related to an English woodpecker. **Fiddler:** Cape Cod. Supposedly from odd motions of a courting male. **Flicker:** Possibly from seeing colored shafts on wings while bird was flying. **Flitter:** Eastern Pennsylvania. Corruption of Flicker. **French   Woodpecker:** New Hampshire. Possibly derived from the term, "French-pie," which was used in parts of England as a name for the Great Spotted Woodpecker. **Gelb   Specht, Gel Specht:** Pennsylvania. Pennsylvania Dutch (Yellow Woodpecker). **Grasshopper   Woodpecker:** Vermont. From feeding habit. **Hairy-wicket:** New England. Corruption of mating call. **High-holer:** Northern United States and Canada; From usual location of nest in tree. **Hybrid   Flicker:** West. Name refers to birds of a mixing of the red-shafted race and the yellow-shafted race. **Jaune:** Louisiana. French for (Yellow). **Meadow Partridge:** Wisconsin. Misnomer, referring to partridge-like flushing behavior when startled while feeding in grasslands. **Ome-tuc:** Maine. Indian name. **On-thee-quan-nor-ow:** Northern Canada. Indian name referring to colors on wings. **Peckerwood:** South. Humorous twist of Woodpecker. **Peerit:** New England. From shrill calls. **Sapsucker:** South. From mistaken belief that Flickers suck sap from trees. **Shadspirit:** New England Coast. From belief that Flickers preceeded shad fish in vernal migration north. **Silver   Dollar   Bird:** Pennsylvania. From white rump mark. **Specht:** Pennsylvania. German for (Woodpecker). **Talpa-na-ni:** Southern Florida. Seminole Indianname. **Wa-cup:** Connecticut. Name from song. **Weather-hen:** Vermont. Named because of vocalizations before storms. **Yacker:** New England. Onomatopoeic origin. **Yarup:** Midwest. From call. **Yellowhammer:** New England and Midwest. Colonial name from England.

Listings

Birds (Class Aves)
True Birds (Subclass Neornithes)
Typical Birds (Superorder Neognathae)
Loons (Order Gaviformes)
Loons (Family Gaviidae)

Modern Name: Common Loon
Scientific Name: Garia immer
Folknames and Names: Big Diver, Big Hell-diver, Big Loon, Black-billed Loon, Buna Chuachaill, Burbhuachaille, Call-up-a-storm, Ember Goose, Grand Plongeon, Grand Plongeur, Great Northern Diver, Greenhead, Grosa Wosser, Guinea Duck, Hell-diver, Huard, Huard a Collier, Huart, Hurleur, Imber Diver, Inland Loon, Loo, Loom, Loon, Plongeon, Plongeon a Collier, Plongeur a Collier, Pond Loon, Riche-poom, Ring-necked Loon, Salt-water Loon, Scaloighter, Sheep Loon, Spotted Loo, Toadlie, Walloon, War-loo, War-loon, White-throated Loo.

Modern Name: Yellow-billed Loon
Scientific Name: Gavia adamsii
Folknames and Names: Adam's Loon, White-billed Loon, White-billed Northern Diver.

Modern Name: Arctic Loon
Scientific Name: Gavia arctica
Folknames and Names: Arctic Diver, Black-throated Diver, Black-throated Loon, Grayback Loon, Green-throated Loon, Little Diver, Pacific Diver, Pacific Loon, White-headed Loon.

Modern Name: Red-throated Loon
Scientific Name: Gavia stellata
Folknames and Names: Capederace, Cape Drake, Cape Race, Cape Racer, Carbreast, Cobble, Corbrace, Cou-rouge, Huard, Little Loon, Longneck, Peggin'-awl, Peggin'-awl Loon, Pegging-owl Loon, Pegmonk, Pepper-shinned Loon, Quaker Loon, Rain-goose, Red-throated Diver, Scape-grace, Sprat Loon, Waby, Wabby, Whabby, Wobby.

Grebes (Order Podicipediformes)
Grebes (Family Podicipedidae)

Modern Name: Horned Grebe
Scientific Name: Podiceps auritur
Folknames and Names: Big Hell-diver, Devil Diver, Didapper,

Dipper, Dusty Grebe, Hell-Diver, Little White Diver, Pink-eyed Diver, Pipe-neck, Plongeur, Sea Hen, Spirit Duck, Duck, Sprawfoot, Thread-neck, Water Witch.

Modern Name: Eared Grebe
Scientific Name: Podiceps nigricollis
Folknames and Names: American Eared Grebe, Black-necked Grebe, Eared Diver, Hell-diver, Little Water-hen, Water-hen.

Modern Name: Least Grebe
Scientific Name: Podiceps dominicus
Folknames and Names: Chico, Duck-and-teal, Diver, Diving Dapper, Hell Diver, Mexican Grebe, Petit Plongeon, Plongeon, Tigua, Zaramagullon.

Modern Name: Pied-billed Grebe
Scientific Name: Podilymbus podiceps
Folknames and Names: American Dabchick, Carolina Grebe, Chien d'Eau, Culotte, Dabchick, Devi-diver, Devil-diver, Didapper, Di-dipper, Diedapper, Dive-dapper, Dipper, Dipper-duck, Diver, Diving Dapper, Drek Shlibber, Duck-and-teal, Grand Plongeon, Hell-diver, Moqucuse, Mud-hen, Parer-de-plomb, Pied-billed Dabchick, Plongeon, Plongeur, Poule d' Eau, Sac-a-plomb, Small Hell-diver, Tad, Thick-billed Grebe, Water Witch, Wosser Shlibber, Zaramago, Zaramagoullon, Zaramagoullon Grande, Zambullidor Piquigrueso.
*Native to the Hawai'ian Islands (Hawai'i)

Modern Name: Red-necked Grebe
Scientific Name: Podiceps grisegena
Folknames and Names: American Red-necked Grebe, Diver, Hell-diver, Holboell's Diver, Holboell's Grebe, Laughing Diver, Red-eyes, Wagtoe, Water-hen, Water-witch.

Modern Name: Western Grebe
Scientific Name: Aechmophorus occidentalis
Folknames and Names: Hell-diver, Silver Diver, Silver Loon, Siwash Goose, Swan Grebe, Swan-necked Grebe, Swan-necked Hell-diver, Western Dabchick.

Tubenoses (Order Procellariiformes)
Albatrosses (Family Doimedeidae)

Modern Name: Laysan Albatross
Scientific Name: Diomedea immutabilis
Folknames and Names: Gooney, Gooney Bird, Moli, White Albatross, White Gooney, White Gooney Bird.
*Native to Hawai'ian Islands (NW islands, O'ahu, Kaua'i, Molo-

ka'i, Lana'i, and Hawai'i)

Modern Name: Black-footed Albatross
Scientific Name: Diomedea nigripes
Folknames and Names: Black Albatross, Black Gooney, Brown Gooney, Gony, Gony Bird, Gooney Bird, Gooney, Goony, Goony Bird.
*Native to Hawai'ian Islands (NW islands).

Shearwaters and Petrels (Family Procellari-idae)

Modern Name: Northern Fulmar
Scientific Name: Fulmarus glacalis
Folknames and Names: Fulmar, Fulmar Petrel, John Down, Mallemok, Mallemoker, Mallemuck, Mallemuke, Marbleheader, Mollimoke, Molly, Molly Hawk, Mollymake, Mallemoke, Noddy, Oil-bird, Sea Horse, White Hagdon.

Modern Name: Pink-footed Shearwater
Scientific Name: Puffinus creatopus
Folknames and Names: Cooper's Shearwater, Coues' Shearwater, Red-footed Shearwater.

Modern Name: Cory's Shearwater
Scientific Name: Puffinus diomedea
Folknames and Names: Cape Verde Shearwater, Cinereous Shearwater, Mediterrean Shearwater, North Atlantic Shearwater.

Modern Name: Greater Shearwater
Scientific Name: Puffinus gravis
Folknames and Names: Balk, Bauk, Bawk, Cape Hen, Cinereous Puffin, Common Atlantic Shearwater, Eggdown, Great Shearwater, Hag, Hagden, Hagdon, Haglet, Haglin, Wandering Shearwater, White Bauk.

Modern Name: Audubon's Shearwater
Scientific Name: Puffinus lherminieri
Folknames and Names: Cahen, Diablotin, Dusky Shearwater, Pampero, Pimlico, Rie, Wedrego.
Modern Name: New Zealand Shearwater
Scientific Name: Puffinus bulleri
Folknames and Names: Buller's Shearwater, Gray-backed Shearwater.

Modern Name: Manx Shearwater
Scientific Name: Puffinus puffinus
Folknames and Names: Common Shearwater, Black-vented Shear-

water.

Modern Name: Sooty Shearwater
Scientific Name: Puffinus griseus
Folknames and Names: Black Bauk, Black Haddown, Black Hag, Black Hagden, Black Hagdon, Black Hagdown, Dark-bodied Shearwater, Hagdown.

Modern Name: Short-tailed Shearwater
Scientific Name: Puffinus tenuirostris
Folknames and Names: Muttonbird, Slender-billed Shearwater, Whalebird.

Modern Name: Flesh-footed Shearwater
Scientific Name: Puffinus carneipes
Folknames and Names: Pale-footed Shearwater.

Modern Name: Black-capped Petrel
Scientific Name: Pterodroma hasitata
Folknames and Names: Blue Mountain Duck, Brown Petril, Chathuant, Diablotin, Dry Land Booby, Little Devil, West Indian Petrel.

Modern Name: Scaled Petrel
Scientific Name: Pterodroma inexpectata
Folknames and Names: Peale's Petrel.

Modern Name: Dark-rumped Petrel
Scientific Name: Pterodroma phaeopygia sandwichensis
Folknames and Names: Ua'u, Uuau, Uwau.
*native to Hawai'ian Islands (Maui, Lana'i, Kaua'i, Hawai'i).

Modern Name: Bonin Petrel
Scientific Name: Pterodroma hypoleuca
Folknames and Names: Bonin Island Petrel, Salvin's Petrel, Small Moaning Petrel.
*native to Hawai'ian Islands (NW islands)

Modern Name: Bulwer's Petrel
Scientific Name: Bulweria bulwerii
Folknames and Names: Ou, Owow.
*native to Hawai'ian Islands (NW islands, islets off main islands)

Modern Name: Wedge-tailed Shearwater
Scientific Name: Puffinus pacificus
Folknames and Names: Hoio, Moaning Bird, 'Ua 'u kani, Wedge-tailed Puffin.
*native to Hawai'ian Islands (Maui, Lana'i, Kaua'i, Hawai'i, and NW islands)

Modern Name: Townsend's Shearwater
Scientific Name: Puffinus auricularis
Folknames and Names: A'o, Newell's Shearwater.
*native to Hawai'ian Islands (Kaua'i, Hawai'i, Moloka'i)

Modern Name: Christmas Shearwater
Scientific Name: Puffinus nativitatis
Folknames and Names: Black Shearwater, Christmas Shearwater.
*native to Hawai'ian Islands (NW islands, islets off main islands)

Storm-Petrels (Family Hydrobatidae)

Modern Name: Black Storm-Petrel.
Scientific Name: Oceanodroma melania
Folknames and Names: Black Petrel.

Modern Name: Ashy Storm-petrel
Scientific Name: Oceanodroma homochroa
Folknames and Names: Ashy Petrel, Coues' Petrel.

Modern Name: Fork-tailed Storm-petrel
Scientific Name: Oceanodroma furcata
Folknames and Names: Fork-tailed Petrel.

Modern Name: Leach's Storm-petrel
Scientific Name: Oceanodroma leucorhoa
Folknames and Names: Carey, Carey Chick, Chicken, Common
Fork-tailed Petrel, Golondrina de Mar, Kerry Chicken, Leach's
Fork-tailed Petrel, Leach's Petrel, Mother Carew's Chicken,
Mother Carey's Chick, Mother Carey's Chicken, Mother Cary's
Chicken, Pall Carey, Pamperito, Pamperito Rabo Horquillado,
White-rumped Petrel.

Modern Name: Wilson's Petrel
Scientific Name: Oceanites oceanicus
Folknames and Names: Carey, Carey's Chick, Common Stormy Pe-
trel, Devil's Bird, Golondrina de Mar, Long-legged Storm-petrel,
Mother Carey's Chicken, Pamperito, Pamperito Rabo Cundrado,
Skipjack, Stormy Petrel, Wilson's Petrel, Witch.

Modern Name: Band-rumped Storm-petrel
Scientific Name: Oceanodroma castro
Folknames and Names: Ake 'ake, Band-rumped Storm-petrel, Hawai'ian Petrel, Hawai'ian Storm Petrel, Harcourt's Petrel, Madei-
ran Petrel, Oeoe, Oweowe.
*native to Hawai'ian Islands (Kaua'i)

Modern Name: Least Petrel
Scientific Name: Halocyptena microsoma
Folknames and Names: Wedge-tailed Petrel.

Totipalmate Swimmers (Order Pelecaniformes)
Tropicbirds (Suborder Phaethontes)
Tropicbirds (Family Phaethontidae)

Modern Name: Red-billed Tropicbird
Scientific Name: Phaethon aethereus
Folknames and Names: Boatswain Bird, Bosun Bird, Fleche-en-cul, Koae, Koa 'e 'ula, Marlinspike, Paille-en-cul, Paille-en-queue, Rabijunco piquicolorado, Trophic, Truphit, White Bird.

Modern Name: White-tailed Tropicbird
Scientific Name: Phaethon lepturus
Folknames and Names: Boatswain, Boatswain-bird, Bo'sun Bird, Chirre, Chirre de cola blanca, Chitee-churo, Ciberou, Contramaestre, Fetu, Fleche-en-cul, Gaviota Caracolera, Koae, Koa'e kea, Longtail, Marlinspike, Paille-en-cul, Paille-en-queue, Rabijunco, Rabijunco coliblanco, Trophic, Truphit, White Bird, White-tailed Bos'n, Yellow-billed Tropicbird.
*native to Hawai'ian Islands (Hawai'i, Kaua'i, Lana'i, Maui, Moloka'i, O'ahu).

Modern Name: Red-tailed Tropicbird
Scientific Name: Phaethon rubricauda
Folknames and Names: Koa 'e 'ula.
*native to Hawai'ian Islands (Hawai'i, Kaua'i, Lana'i, Maui, Moloka'i, O'ahu).

Boobies, Pelicans, Cormorants and Darters (Suborder Pelecani)
Boobies and Gannets (Family Sulidae)

Modern Name: Gannet
Scientific Name: Morus bassanus
Folknames and Names: Common Gannet, Fou, Gaunt Grand Fou, Gran Fou, Jan van Gent, Margot, Northern Gannet, Solan Goose, Soland Goose, Solon Goose, Sulaire, White Gannet.

Modern Name: Blue-faced Booby
Scientific Name: Sula dactylatra
Folknames and Names: A, Blue-faced Booby, Boba Enmarscarada, Booby, Fou Blanc, Masked Booby, Whistling Booby, White Booby.
*native to Hawai'ian Islands (off main islands, NW islands)

Modern Name: Brown Booby

Scientific Name: Sula leucogastor
Folknames and Names: A, Alcatraz, Boba Prieta, Booby, Booby Gannet, Bubi Chaleco, Catesby's Booby, Common Booby, Fou Brun, Fou Noir, Pajaro Bobo, Pajaro Bobo Prieto, White-bellied Booby, Yellow-footed Booby, Pajara Bobo
*native to Hawai'ian Islands (off main islands, NW islands)

Modern Name: Red-footed Booby
Scientific Name: Sula sula
Folknames and Names: A, Boba Blanca, Boba Patirroja, Booby, Bubi Blanco, Fuo Blanc, Pajaro Bobo Blanco, Pajaro Booby, Red-faced Booby, Tree Booby, White Booby.
*native to Hawai'ian Islands (off main islands, NW islands)

Modern Name: Blue-footed Booby
Scientific Name: Sula nebouxii
Folknames and Names: Camanay.

Pelicans (Family Pelecanidae)

Modern Name: Brown Pelican
Scientific Name: Pelecanus occidentalis
Folknames and Names: Alcatraz, American Brown Pelican, California Brown Pelican, Common Pelican, Grand Gosier, Joe Bird, Old Joe, Old Tom, Pelican, Pelicano pardo.

Modern Name: White Pelican
Scientific Name: Pelicanus erythrorhychos
Folknames and Names: Alcatraz Blanco, American White Pelican, Common Pelican, Grand Gasier, Pelicano blanco, Rough-billed Pelican.

Cormorants (Family Phalacrocoracidae)

Modern Name: Great Cormorant
Scientific Name: Phalacrocorax carbo
Folknames and Names: Barneche, Common Cormorant, Cormoran, Cormorant, European Cormorant, Margot, Sgarbh, Shag.

Modern Name: Brandt's Cormorant
Scientific Name: Phalacrocorax penicillatus
Folknames and Names: Brown Cormorant, Penciled Cormorant, Shag, Townsend's Cormorant, Tufted Cormorant.

Modern Name: Double-crested Cormorant
Scientific Name: Phalacrocorax auritus
Folknames and Names: Barneche, Black Shag, Cormoran, Cormoran Crestado, Cormoran Ordinaire, Cormorant, Cormoril, Cormoroe, Corua, Corua de Mar, Crow-duck, Duck, Farallon

Cormorant, Fish Duck, Florida Cormorant, Lawyer, Margot, Nigger Goose, Queen Bird, Sgarbh, Shag, Shaig, Shill-bird, Soldier, Taunton Turkey, Water-turkey, White-crested Cormorant.

Modern Name: Pelagic Cormorant
Scientific Name: Phalacrocorax pelagicus
Folknames and Names: Baird's Cormorant

Modern Name: Olivaceous Cormorant
Scientific Name: Phalacrocorax olivaceus
Folknames and Names: Brazilian Cormorant, Cormoran Olivaceo, Cormorant, Cormoril, Corua, Corua de Agua Dulce, Mexican Cormorant, Neotropic Cormorant, Nigger Goose, Water Turkey.

Modern Name: Red-faced Cormorant
Scientific Name: Phalacrocorax urile
Folknames and Names: -

Darters (Family Anhingidae)

Modern Name: Anhinga
Scientific Name: Anhinga anhinga
Folknames and Names: American Darter, Bec-a-lancette, Bec-a-lancette-des-bois, Black Darter, Black-bellied Darter, Corua Real, Darter, Gannet, Marbella, Snakebird, Water Turkey, White-bellied Darter.

Frigatebird (Suborder Fregatae)
Frigatebird (Family Fregatidae)

Modern Name: Magnificent Frigatebird
Scientific Name: Fregata magnificens
Folknames and Names: Cobbler, Fregate, Frigate Bird, Frigate Pelican, Gull Hawk, Hurricane Bird, Man-o-war, Man-o'-warbird, Queue en-Cisseaux, Rabihorcado, Rabijorcado, Scissorstail, Spanish Man-of-war, Tijerilla, Tijereta, Weather Bird.

Modern Name: Great Frigatebird
Scientific Name: Fregata magnificens
Folknames and Names: Iwa.
*native to Hawai'ian Islands (NW islands)

Herons, Ibises, Storks and Allies (Order Ciconiiformes)
Bitterns, Herons and Allies (Suborder Ardeae)
Bitterns and Herons (Family Ardeidae)

Modern Name: Common Egret
Scientific Name: Casmerodius albus
Folknames and Names: American Egret, American Great White Heron, Angel Bird, Big Plume Bird, Common Egret, Crane, Florida Heron, Garza Real, Garzon Blanco, Great Egret, Grand Heron Blanc, Great Egret, Great White Egret, Greater Egret, Greater Heron, Great White Heron, Long White, Plume Bird, White Crane, White Egret, White Gaulin, White Heron, White Morgan.

Modern Name: Snowy Egret
Scientific Name: Egretta thula
Folknames and Names: Aigrette Blanche, Bonnet Martyr, Brewster's Egret, Common Egret, Crabier Blanc, Garza Blanca, Garza de Rizos, Garza Real, Golden Slippers, Heron Blanc, Lesser Egret, Little Egret, Little Plume Bird, Little Snowy, Little White Egret, Little White Heron, Poor Job, Small Plume Bird, Snowy Heron, White Crane, White Gaulin, Yaller-tail, Yellow-tail.

Modern Name: Cattle Egret
Scientific Name: Bubulcus ibis
Folknames and Names: Buff-backed Heron, Cattle Gaulin, Cattle Heron, Cowbird, Crabier Garde-boeuf, Garrapatosa, Garza Del Ganado, Garza Africana, Garza Ganadera, Tick Bird.
*introduced into Hawai'ian Islands (Hawai'i, Kaua'i, Lana'i, Maui, Moloka'i, O'ahu)

Modern Name: Great Blue Heron
Scientific Name: Ardea herodias
Folknames and Names: Ars-nicker, Big Cranky, Blue Crane, Blue Gaulin, Blue John, Butor, Common Blue Crane, Common Crane, Corr, Corra-ghritheach, Couac, Crabier Noir, Crane, Fish Crane, Garcilote, Garzon Azulado, Garzon Blanco, Garzon Ceniciento, Garzon Cenizo, Gironde, Gray Crane, Gray Gaulin, Great Heron Blue, Grey Gaulin, Grue, Guardacosta, Hamlet-bud Dem, Hamlin, Hern, Heron, Heron Bleu, Heron Brun, Jackerne, Long John, Long Tom, Major, Morgan, Northwestern Coast Heron, Po Job, Po Joe, Poor Joe, Preacher, Red-shouldered Heron, San Joie, The "Major", Treganza's Heron, Ward Heron, Water Crane

Modern Name: Reddish Heron
Scientific Name: Dichromanassa rufescens
Folknames and Names: Crabier, Garza, Garza Rojiza, Gaulin, Muffle-jawed Egret, Peale's Egret, Plume Bird, Reddish Egret.

Modern Name: Louisiana Heron
Scientific Name: Hydranassa tricolor
Folknames and Names: Aigrette Caille, Blue Crane, Crane, Demoiselle, Demonoiselle, Egrette Folle, Garza Perchiblanca, Gaulin, Heron Dos-blanc, Lady-of-the-waters, Louisiana Egret, Silver-

gray Heron, Scoggin, Skoggin, Switching-neck, Tricolored Heron.

Modern Name: Little Blue Heron
Scientific Name: Egretta caerulea
Folknames and Names: Aligrette Blanche, Aligrette Bleue, Blue Crane, Blue Egret, Blue Gaulin, Blue Scoggin, Calico Heron, Crabier Blanc, Crazy Heron, Egrette Bleue, Egrette Folle, Garza Azul, Garza Blanca, Garza Comun, Garza Pinta, Levee Walker, Little Blue Crane, Little White Crane, Skoggin, Spotted Crane, White Crane, White Gaulin.

Modern Name: Green Heron
Scientific Name: Butorides virescens
Folknames and Names: Aguaita Caiman, Anthony Green Heron, Bitlin, Blue Bittern, Caali, Caga-leche, Cagon, Chalk-line, Copcop, Crab-catcher, Crabier, Cra-cra, Cuaco, Fly-up-the-Creek, Frazar Green Heron, Gaulching, Gaulin, Green-backed Heron, Green Bittern, Green Gaulin, Heron, Heron Vert, Indian Heron, Indian Pullet, Kio, Least Pond Gaulin, Little Gaulin, Little Green Heron, Martinete, Petit Butor, Poke, Poor Joe, Rac-rac, Shitepoke, Skeow, Skow, Swamp Squaggin, Valet de Caiman, Water Witch.

Modern Name: Black-crowned Night Heron
Scientific Name: Nycticorax nycticorax
Folknames and Names: American Black-crowned Night Heron, American Night Heron, Auku'u, Coq d'Eau, Coq de Nuit, Couac, Crab Catcher, Crabier, Fox Bird, Gardenian Heron, Gallinaza, Gaulin, Gros-bec, Gros-bec Dos-soie, Guanaba de la Florida, Guanaba Lominegro, Indian Hen, Indian Pullet, Marsh Hen, Night Heron, Night Gaulin, Night Skoggins, Qua-bird, Quac, Quawk, Quok, Quwak, Red-eye, Rey Congo, Squaw Bird, Squawk, Velvet-backed Gros-bec, Winter Grosbec, Yaboa Real.
*native to Hawai'ian Islands (main islands)

Modern Name: Yellow-crowned Night Heron
Scientific Name: Nyctanassa violacea
Folknames and Names: Bald-headed Gros-bec, Crab-catcher, Crabeater, Fish Crane, Gray Gaulin, Gros-bec, Indian Hen, Indian Pullet, Night Gaulin, Night Skoggins, Qua-bird, Quawk, Quok, Quwak, Squark, Squawk, White-jaw Gros-bec, Yaboa Comun.

Modern Name: American Bittern
Scientific Name: Botaurus lentiginosus
Folknames and Names: Barrel-maker, Bill-gudgeon, Biorque, Bittern, Bog-bull, Bog Hen, Bog-pumping Hell-driver, Bog-trotter, Buncom, Butor, Butter-bird, Butterbump, Corker, Cou Long, Devil's Pump, Flying Fox, Fly-up-the-creek, Fool Fowl, Gardesoleil, Gros-bec-a-gilet, Indian Hen, Indian Pullet, Jack Grindle,

Jeune Grue, Look-up, Marsh Hen, Meadow Hen, Mire Drum, Mud Hen, Mud Pump, Mud Pumper, Oomptah, Pile-driver, Pine-knot, Plumgudgeon, Poke, Pond Guinea, Pump Bird, Pumper, Pump-thunder, Punkatunk, Quac, Rice Lake Bittern, Scoggin, Shitipoke, Sky-gazer, Slough Pump, Slough Punk, Stake-bird, Stake-driver, Sun-gazer, Thunder-pump, Thunder Pumper, Visionnaire, Water-belcher, Weed Hen, Yaboa Americana.

Modern Name: Least Bittern
Scientific Name: Ixobrychus exilis
Folknames and Names: Bitlin, Cop-cop Dore, Dwarf Bittern, Fly-up-the-creek, Garde Soleil, Gaulin, Jean Charlot, Kite, Least Heron, Little Heron, Martinetite, Strike-fire, Yeux Clairs.

Ibises and Spoonbills (Suborder Threskiornithes) Ibises and Spoonbills (Family Threskiornithidae)

Ibises (Subfamily Threskiornithinae)

Modern Name: White-faced Ibis
Scientific Name: Plegadis chihi
Folknames and Names: Black Curlew, White-faced Glossy Ibis.

Modern Name: Glossy Ibis
Scientific Name: Plegadis falcinellus
Folknames and Names: Bay Ibis, Black Bec-croche, Black Curlew, Ciguena, Coco Prieto, Curlew, Eastern Glossy Ibis, Green Ibis, Ibis Lustroso, Liver, Ord's Ibis.

Modern Name: White Ibis
Scientific Name: Eudocimus albus
Folknames and Names: Bec-croche, Brown Curlew, Curlew, Ibis Blanco, Spanish Curlew, Stone Curlew, White Curlew.

Modern Name: White-faced Ibis
Scientific Name: Plegadis chihi
Folknames and Names: White-faced Glossy Ibis.

Spoonbills (Subfamily Plaataleinae)

Modern Name: Roseate Spoonbill
Scientific Name: Ajaia ajaja
Folknames and Names: Espatula Rosada, Pink-bird, Pink Curlew, Pinkie, Rosy Spoonbill, Skatule.

Storks (Suborder Ciconiae)
Storks (Family Ciconiidae)

Modern Name: Wood Stork
Scientific Name: Mycteria americana
Folknames and Names: American Jabiru, American Wood Stork, Blue Charley, Colorado Turkey, Flamant, Flinthead, Gannet, Goard, Gourd, Gourdhead, Ironhead, Hammerhead, Ironhead, Plumber, Preacher, Spanish Buzzard, Wood Ibis.

Flamingos (Order Phoenicopteriformes)
Flamingos (Family Phoenicopteridae)

Modern Name: American Flamingo
Scientific Name: Phoenicopterus ruber
Folknames and Names: Caribbean Flamingo, Fillymingo, Flamenco Americano, Greater Flamingo, Roseate Flamingo, Scarlet Flamingo, West Indian Flamingo.

Screamers, Swans, Geese and Ducks (Order Anseriformes)
Swans, Geese and Ducks (Suborder Anseres)
Swans, Geese and Ducks (Family Anatidae)
Whistling-Ducks, Swans and Geese (Subfamily Anserinae)

Modern Name: Fulvous Whistling-duck
Scientific Name: Dendrocygna bicolor
Folknames and Names: -
*Introduced to the Hawai'ian Islands (O'ahu)

Modern Name: Mute Swan
Scientific Name: Cygnus olor
Folknames and Names: Common Swan, Domestic Swan.

Modern Name: Whistling Swan
Scientific Name: Olor columbianus
Folknames and Names: American Whistling Swan, Big Whistler, Cisne Silbador, Common Swan, Cygne, Hoopers, Swan, Tohwah, Whistler, White Swan, Wild Swan.

Modern Name: Trumpter Swan
Scientific Name: Olor buccinator
Folknames and Names: Bugler, Cygne, Swan, White Swan, Wild Swan.

Modern Name: Canada Goose
Scientific Name: Branta canadensis
Folknames and Names: Awicher Yager, Bay Goose, Bernache, Big Canada, Big Goose, Big Gray Brant, Big Gray Goose, Big Honker, Big Mexican Goose, Bisk-a-sish, Black Brandt, Black Head, Black-headed Goose, Blackie, Blackleg, Black-necked Goose, Brant, Brillard, Bullneck, Bustard, Cackler, Cackling Goose, California Goose, Calling Goose, Canada Brant, Canada Hooker, Canadian Goose, Common Canada Goose, China Goose, Chornie Goose, Common Wild Goose, Cravat Goose, Crow Goose, Crybaby, Eastern Brandt, Eskimo Goose, Fall Goose, Flight Goose, French Goose, Goose Brandt, Gray Goose, Great Basin Goose, Greaser, Grey, Grey-bellied Goose, Grey Goose, Grey Mud Goose, Giadh Fiadh, Gronker, Honker, Honker Goose, Hounds, Hunker, Hunter, Husky Goose, Hutchins's Goose, La Barnache, Labrador Goose, Lesser Canada Goose, Little Bustard, Little Canada, Little Grey Goose, Little Honker, Little Squeaking Goose, Little Wavey, Long-necked Goose, Mershon Goose, Mexican Goose, Mud Goose, Nigger Goose, Northern Goose, Oie Canadienne, Oie Sauvage, Old Honker, Outarde, Piron, Prairie Goose, Reef Goose, Richardson's Goose, Ring-neck, Ring-neck Goose, Schna Gons, Short-necked Goose, Small Goose, Southern Goose, Trader, Wavey, Western Canada Goose, Whistler, White Cheek, White-cheeked Goose, White-chin, Wild Goose, Wild Wavey, Wilte Gons, Winter Goose, Yelper.

Modern Name: Nene
Scientific Name: Nesochen sandvicensis
Folknames and Names: Hawai'ian Goose.
*Native to the Hawai'ian Islands (Hawai'i, Kaua'i, Maui)

Modern Name: Brant
Scientific Name: Branta bernicle
Folknames and Names: American Brant, Barneche, Black Brant, Black Goose, Black Wavey, Brant Goose, Brent Goose, Burnt Goose, Chickeny Goose, China Goose, Clatter Goose, Common Brant, Cravant, Crocker, Eastern Brant, Eskimo Goose, Husky Goose, Light-bellied Brant, Little Goose, Pacific Brant, Quink, Sea Brandt, Wavey, White-bellied Brant, White-breasted Goose.

Modern Name: Emperor Goose
Scientific Name: Chen canagica
Folknames and Names: Beach Goose, Painted Goose, White-headed Goose.
*native to Hawai'ian Islands (NW Islands, Kaua'i)

Modern Name: White-fronted Goose
Scientific Name: Anser albifrons
Folknames and Names: American White-fronted Goose, Barred Goose, Brandt, California Goose, Checkerbelly, Checkerbreast,

China Goose, Field Goose, Gray Brant, Grey Goose, Gray Wavey, Harlequin Brant, Laugher, Laughing Goose, Laughing Jack, Laughing Wavey, Marble-belly, Marbled-breast Mottled Brant, Mottled Goose, Oie Caille, Oie Nonette, Pied Brant, Prairie Brant, Speckle-belly, Speckle-belly Brant, Specklebreast, Speckle-breast Goose, Speckled Brant, Speckled Goose, Speckled Wavey, Spotted Brant, Spotted Goose, Texas Goose, Tule White-fronted Goose, White-front, Yellow-legged Goose, Yellowlegs.

Modern Name: Blue Goose
Scientific Name: Chen caerulescens caerulescens
Folknames and Names: Alaska Goose, Bald Brant, Bald-headed Brant, Black Wavey, Blue Brant, Blue Snow Goose, Blue Wavey, Blue-winged Goose, Eagle-headed Brant, Ganso Prieto, Gray Brant, Gray Wavey, Oie Aigle, Oie Sauvage, Silver Brant, Skillet-head, Wavey, White-headed Bald Brant, White-headed Brant, White-headed Goose, White-headed Wavey.

Modern Name: Snow Goose
Scientific Name: Chen caerulescens caerulescens
Folknames and Names: Alaska Goose, Arctic Goose, Barking Wavey, Brant, Common Snow Goose, Common Wavey, Galoot, Ganso Blanco, Gee, Greater Snow Goose, Greater Wavey, Lesser Snow Goose, Lesser Snow Goose, Lesser Wavey, Little Wavey, Mexican Goose, Oie Blanche, Oie Sauvage, Piron, Ross's Goose, Scabby-nose, Scabby-nosed Goose, Scabby-nosed Wavey, Wart-nosed Wavey, Wavey, Wavey Goose, White Brant, White Goose, White Jangler, White Wavey, White Way-way, Winter Goose.

Ducks (Subfamily Anatinae)

Modern Name: Wood Duck
Scientific Name: Aix sponsa
Folknames and Names: Acorn Duck, Branchier, Branchu, Bridal Duck, Bush Duck, Canard du Bois, Carolina Duck, Huyuyo, Plumer, Squealer, Summer Duck, Swamp Duck, The Bride, Tree Duck, Wood Duck, Wood Wigeon, Woody.

Modern Name: Mallard
Scientific Name: Anas platyhynchos
Folknames and Names: Black Duck, Canard Francais, Canard Gris, Canard Ordinaire, Canard Sauvage, Common Mallard, Common Wild Duck, Curly-tail, Domestic Duck, Duck-and-Teal, English Duck, French Duck, French Stock Duck, Frosty-beak, Gibier Gris, Gray Duck, Gray Mallard, Green Mallard, Greentop, Greenhead, Greenhead Mallard, Grey Stock Duck, Greenhead, Green-neck, Ice-breaker, Ice Duck, Ice Mallard, Irish Mallard, Mallard Duck, Northern Mallard, Pato de Collar, Pato Ingles, Prairie Mallard, Red-legged Mallard, Redlegs, Ringneck, Snow Mallard, Sookie,

Stock Duck, Stubble Duck, Susies, Twister, Whistler, Wild Drake, Wild Duck, Wild Mallard, Wilte Ent, Yellow-leg Duck, Yellow-legged Mallard, Yellowlegs.

Modern Name: Hawai'ian Duck
Scientific Name: Anas wyvilliana
Folknames and Names: Koloa, Koloa maoli.
*native to Hawai'ian Islands (Kaua'i, O'ahu, Hawai'i)

Modern Name: Laysan Duck
Scientific Name: Anas laysanensis
Folknames and Names: Laysan Teal.
*native to Hawai'ian Islands (Laysan Island).

Modern Name: Mexican Duck
Scientific Name: Anas diazi
Folknames and Names: New Mexican Duck

Modern Name: Black Duck
Scientific Name: Anas rubipes
Folknames and Names: American Black Duck, Arctic Blue-wing, Beach Duck, Black, Black Duck, Black English Duck, Blackie, Blackjack, Black Mallard, Blackstock Duck, Blackwood Duck, Blue-wing, Blue-winged Black Duck, Blue-winged Duck, Brown Duck, Brown Mallard, Canard Noir, Canard Noir d'Hiver, Canard Noir du Nord, Common Duck, Duck, Dusky Duck, Dusky Mallard, English Duck, Fish-eater, Florida Black Duck, Florida Duck, Grey Duck, Inside Duck, Laborador Duck, Lach-dubh, Ledge Duck, Mallard, Marsh Duck, Nigger Duck, Noir, Northern Black Mallard, Old Winter Duck, Outside Black Duck, Outside Duck, Pato Oscuro, Puddle Duck, Red-footed Black Duck, Redleg, Red-legged Black Duck, Red-legged Duck, Red-paddle, Sea-duck, Shwortsa Ent, Striped Mallard, Summer Black Duck, Summer Duck, Spring Black Duck, Stock Duck, Summer Duck, Summer Mallard, Tunnag, Velvet Duck, Wild Duck, Winter Black Duck, Yellow-beak, Yellow-pad.

Modern Name: Mottled Duck
Scientific Name: Anas fulvigula
Folknames and Names: Black Mallard, Canard d'Ete, Canard Noir d'Ete, Dusky Duck, Florida Duck, Louisiana Summer Mallard, Mexican Mallard, Summer Black Duck, Summer French Duck.

Modern Name: Pintail
Scientific Name: Anas acuta
Folknames and Names: American Pintail, Bahama Pintail, Canard Gris, Canard Pilet, Canard Pilier, Common Pintail, Courbeaux, Coy, Cracker, Fall Duck, Gray Duck, Grey Wigeon, Harlan, Kite-tail, Kitetail Widgeon, Lady-bird, Long-neck, Long-neck Duck,

Long-necked Cracker, Long-tail, Minf
olk, Northern Pintail, Paille-en-queue, Pato Pescuecilargo, Peak-
tail, Petit Gris, Pheasant Dock, Pheasant Duck, Picket Duck,
Picket-tail, Pied Duck, Pied Widgeon, Pigeon-tail, Pile-start,
Pile-starter, Pinnie, Sea Pheasant, Sharp-ended Duck, Sharp-
tail, Smee, Smethe, Smoker, Spike-tail, Spindle-tail, Split-tail,
Sprig, Sprig Duck, Sprig-tail, Springtail, Spring-tailed Duck,
Sprit-tail, Squaw Duck, Trilby Duck, Water Duck, Winter Duck,
Wood Duck.

Modern Name: Gadwall
Scientific Name: Anas strepera
Folknames and Names: Blarting Duck, Bleating Duck, Canard
Gris, Chickacock, Common Gadwall, Creek Duck, Courbeaux, Gad-
dy, Gadwell, Gray Duck, Gray Wigeon, Minik, Prairie Mallard,
Red-wing, Speckle-belly, Small Mallard, Trash Duck, Wigeon.

Modern Name: American Widgeon
Scientific Name: Anas americana
Folknames and Names: Bald-crown, Bald-faced Widgeon, Bald-
head, Baldpate, Bald Widgeon, Baldy, Ball-pate Widgeon, Blue-
bill, Bluebill Duck, Blue-billed Widgeon, Bluebill Widgeon, But-
terball, California Widgeon, Canvas-back, Cock Widgeon, Dia-
mond Duck, French Teal, Gray Duck, Green-headed Widgeon,
Little Grey Duck, Pato Cabeciblanco, Poacher, Redhead, Smoke
Duck, Smoker, Smoking Duck, Southern Widgeon, Specklehead,
Swede, Wheat Duck, Whistler, Whistling Dick, Whistling Duck,
White Belly, Whiteface, Widgeon, Zan Zan.

Modern Name: European Widgeon
Scientific Name: Anas penelope
Folknames and Names: Eurasian Widgeon, Whew, Whewer, Whim,
Whistler, Widgeon.

Modern Name: Shoveler
Scientific Name: Anas clypeata
Folknames and Names: Bechleur de Merde, Blue-winged Shoveler,
Broad-bill, Broad-faced Mallard, Broady, Butterduck, Canard
Souhet, Canard Spatule, Caouanne, Chipewyan Duck, Common
Shoveler, Cow-frog, French Teal, Long-neck, Mesquin, Moniac,
Mud-duck, Mud Lark, Mud-shoveler, Mule Duck, Northern Shov-
eler, Pato Cuchareta, Red-breasted Shoveler, Scooper, Shovel-
bill, Shovel-bill Duck, Shoveler, Shovelmouth, Shovel-nose,
Spoonbill, Spoon-bill Duck, Spoon-bill Teal, Spoonie, Spoony,
Swaddle-bill, Till Duck, Trash Duck.

Modern Name: Cinnamon Teal
Scientific Name: Anas cyanoptera
Folknames and Names: Bluewing, Red-bellied Teal, Red-breasted

Teal, Redhead, Red Teal, River Teal, Silver Teal, South American Teal, Teal, Texas Teal.

Modern Name: American Green-winged Teal
Scientific Name: Anas crecca carolinensis (A. c. crecca)
Folknames and Names: Breakfast Duck, Butterball, Common Teal, Congo, Duck-and-teal, European Common Teal, Eurasian Green-winged Teal, Fall Duck, Greased Lightning, Greenie, Green-wing, Green-winged Duck, Green-winged Teal, Lake Teal, Mud Teal, Pato Aliverde, Partridge Duck, Petit Canard, Red-headed Teal, Redhead Teal, Teal, Sarcelle ail Verte, Sarcelle d'hiver, Sarcelle du Norde, Teal, Teal Duck, Water Partridge, Wigeon, Winter Teal.

Modern Name: Blue-winged Teal
Scientific Name: Anas discors
Folknames and Names: Autumn Teal, Blue Teal, Blue-wing, Blue-wing Teal, Breakfast Duck, Butterball, Duck-and-teal, Fall Duck, Fall Teal, Necktie Teal, Pato De La Florida, Pato Zarcel, Petit Canard, Printanniere, Sarcelle ailes Bleues, Sarcelle Autonniere, Sarcelle d'ete, Sarcelle Printanniere, Southern Teal, Summer Teal, Teal, Teal Duck, White-faced Teal.

Modern Name: Baikal Teal
Scientific Name: Anas formosa
Folknames and Names: Clucking Teal, Spectacled Teal.

Modern Name: Fulvous Tree Duck
Scientific Name: Dendrocygna bicolor
Folknames and Names: Bicolored Tree Duck, Chiriria Amarillenta, Chiriria Dominicana, Cornfield Duck, Fulvous Whistling-duck, Long-legged Duck, Mexican Duck, Mexican Squealer, Mexican Wood Duck, Pato Silvon, Squealer, Summer Duck, Tee-kee, Whistling Teal, Wood Duck, Yanguaza Dominicana, Yankee Duck, Yellow-bellied Fiddler Duck.

Modern Name: Black-bellied Tree Duck
Scientific Name: Dendrocygna autumnalis
Folknames and Names: Autumnal Tree Duck, Black-bellied Whistling Duck, Chiriria Pinta, Cornfield Duck, Long-legged Duck, Red-bellied Whistling Duck, Summer Duck.

Modern Name: Redhead
Scientific Name: Aythya americana
Folknames and Names: American Pochard, Canard Mulet, Canard Ateterouge, Cou-rouge, Fiddler, Fiddler Duck, Fool Duck, Grayback, Mule Duck, Muskeg Duck, Pochard, Raft Duck, Redhead, Red-headed Broadbill, Red-headed Raft Duck, Violon.

Modern Name: Canvasback
Scientific Name: Aythya valisineria
Folknames and Names: Big Grey Duck, Black Duck, Bull Can, Bullneck, Can, Canny, Cans, Canard Cheval, Canny, Canvas, Canvas Duck, Copper-head, Fish Duck, Gray Duck, Hickory-quaker, Horse-duck, Pato Piquisesgado, Pochard, Redhead, Red-headed Bullneck, Sheldrake, Whiteback.

Modern Name: Ring-necked Duck
Scientific Name: Aythya collaris
Folknames and Names: American Tufted Duck, Bastard Broadbill, Bastard Redhead, Black Duck, Blackhead, Blackjack, Bluebill, Broadbill, Buckeye, Bullneck, Bunty, Butterball, Canard Noir, Creek Redhead, Diver, Dogy, Fall Duck, Marsh Bluebill, Moonbill, Muskeg Duck, Pato Del Medio, Pond Bluebill, Ringbill, Ringbilled Blackhead, Ringbill Duck, Ring-billed Duck, Ringneck, Ring-neck Duck, Ring-necked Scaup, Tufted Duck.

Modern Name: Greater Scaup
Scientific Name: Aythya marila
Folknames and Names: American Scaup Duck, Bay Blackhead, Bellarge, Big Bay Bluebill, Big Blackhead, Big Bluebill, Big Fall Duck, Blackhead, Blackjack, Black-neck, Bluebill, Blue-billed Wigeon, Broadbill, Broadie, Bullhead, Bullneck, Butterball, Butterball Duck, Call Duck, Canard Caille, Common Scaup, Dog, Dogs, Dos-gris, Dos-gris de 'Mer, Dummy, Fall Duck, Fishing Duck, Floating Fowl, Flock Duck, Grand Morillon, Grayback, Greater Bluebill, Greater Broadbill, Greenhead, Gros Canard D'automme, Lake Bluebill, Laker, Large Brownhead, Little Dos-gris, Little Gray-back, Milouin, Muskeg Duck, Mussel Duck, Plonger, Raft Duck, Saltwater Broadbill, Scaup, Sea Dos-gris, Shuffler, Troop Duck, Troop-fowl, Whistler, White-faced Duck, Widgeon, Winter Duck, Wood Duck.

Modern Name: Lesser Scaup
Scientific Name: Athya affinis
Folknames and Names: Bellarge, Black Duck, Blackhead, Blackjack, Bluebill, Bluebill Coot, Booby, Broadbill, Broadie, Brownhead, Bullhead, Bullneck, Butterball, Canard Caille, Canvasback, Creek Broadbill, Diver, Dummy, Fall Duck, Freshwater Broadbill, Gold-eye, Grayback, Howden, Lake Duck, Lesser Broadbill, Lesser Scaup Duck, Little Bay Bluebill, LIttle Blackhead, Little Bluebill, Little Greyback, Little Mud Broadbill, Marsh Bluebill, Milouin, Muskeg Duck, Pato Pechiblanco, Plongeur, Raft Duck, River Broadbill, River Bluebill, River Duck, She-whistler, Small Blue-bill Duck, Small Brownhead, Summer Duck, Whistler, White-winged Teal, Widgeon, Wood Duck.

Modern Name: Common Goldeneye

Scientific Name: Bucephala Clangula
Folknames and Names: American Goldeneye, Black Duck, Brass-eye, Brass-eyed Whistler, Bullhead, Butterball Duck, Caille, Canard a Grosse Tete, Canard Caille, Canard Canadien, Canard Yankee, Cobhead, Conjuring Duck, Copperhead, Cub-head, Cur, Diver, European Goldeneye, Fiddler Duck, Garrot, Gold-eye, Golden-eye, Goldeneyed Duck, Great-head, Iron-head, Jingler, Merry-wing, Oyster Duck, Pie Bird, Pie Duck, Pied Duck, Pied Whistler, Pisque, Pixe, Plongeon, Plongeur, Pork Duck, Smoky Pie, Smoky Pie Bird, Spirit Duck, Tree Duck, Whiffler, Whistle Diver, Whistle-duck, Whistler, Whistler Duck, Whistle-wing, Whistle-wing Duck, Widgeon, Wiffler, Winter Duck, Wood Duck.

Modern Name: Barrow's Goldeneye
Scientific Name: Bucephala islandica
Folknames and Names: Black and White Diver, Butterball Duck, Cockpyeduck, Pie-bird, Pie Duck, Pied Whistler, Pisque, Plongeur, Rocky Mountain Garrot, Rocky Mountain Goldeneye, Tete Marteau, Tree Duck, Whistle-diver, Whistler, Whistle-wing, Wood Duck.

Modern Name: Bufflehead
Scientific Name: Bucephala albeola
Folknames and Names: Bighead, Black and White, Buffalo-head, Buffalo-headed Duck, Buffle-headed Duck, Bumblebee Dipper, Bumble Bee Duck, Butterback, Butterball, Butterball Duck, Butter-box, Butter Duck, Conjuring Duck, Dapper, Dipper, Dipper-Duck, Diver, Dopper, Fall Duck, Fishing Bird, Hell-diver, Little Black and White Duck, Little Brown Duck, Marionette, Pato Pinto, Pinto Duck, Robin Dipper, Scotch Dipper, Scotch Teal, Shotbag, Shot-eater, Sleepy Diver, Spirit, Spirit Duck, Whistler, Wood Duck, Wool-head.

Modern Name: Harlequin Duck
Scientific Name: Histrionicus histrionicus
Folknames and Names: Blue-streak, Canard de Baie, Canard des Roches, Cane de Roche, Circus Duck, Hell-diver, Imp, Jenny, Lord-and-lady, Lord and Lady Bird, Lords and Ladies, Mountain Duck, Old Lord, Painted Duck, Pie Duck, Rock Duck, Sea Pheasant, Sea Mouse, Sea Pigeon, Squealer, Wood Duck.

Modern Name: Common Eider
Scientific Name: Somateria mollissima
Folknames and Names: American Eider, Big Salt-water Duck, Big Sea-duck, Black and White Coot, Canard de Mer, Canard Eider, Canvasback, Coot, Dresser's Eider, Eskimo Duck, Gambird, Gam Drake, Husky Duck, Isle of Shoals Duck, Laying Duck, Looby, Moiaque Blanche, Moignac, Mooyak, Mojak, Mouniac, Mourriac, Moyac, Moynak, Northern Eider, Pied Wamp, Sea Coot, Sea Duck,

Sea Ducks and Drakes, Shoal Duck, Shore Duck, Shoreyer, Siolta, Squam Duck, Wamp.

Modern Name: King Eider
Scientific Name: Somateria spectablilis
Folknames and Names: Bottle-nose Drake, Canvasback, Cousin, Eskimo Duck, Isle of Shoals Duck, King Bird, King Drake, King-duck, Mongrel, Mongrel Duck, Old King, Ouarnicouti, Passing Duck, Sea Duck, Wamp's Cousin, Warnecootai, White-head Coot.

Modern Name: Spectacled Eider
Scientific Name: Somateria fischeri
Folknames and Names: Fischeri's Eider.
Modern Name: Steller's Eider
Scientific Name: Polysticta stelleri
Folknames and Names: Lesser Eider Duck, Soldier Duck.

Modern Name: Oldsquaw
Scientific Name: Clangula hyemalis
Folknames and Names: Aleck, Alewife, Cacouy, Calloo, Canard a Longue Queue, Cockawee, Coween, Granny, Hell's Chicken, Hound, Indian Duck, Injun Duck, Jackowly, John Connolly, Kakawi, Kla-how-ya, Long-tail, Long-tailed Duck, Long-tailed Squaw, Old Bil-ly, Old Granny, Old Injun, Old Molly, Old Squaw, Old Wife, Organ Duck, Pigeon, Pine-knot, Pintail, Quandy, Scoldenore, Scolder, Singing Duck, Siwash, Siwash Duck, Scolder, Sou-easterly, South-southerly, Souwester, Squaw, Squaw Duck, Squeaking Duck, Swallow-tailed Duck, Uncle Huldy, Winter Duck.

Modern Name: Common Scoter
Scientific Name: Melanitta nigra
Folknames and Names: American Scoter, Bay Muscovie, Beach-comber, Bec Jaune, Black Butterbill, Black Coot, Black Duck, Black Scoter, Black Sea Coot, Black Sea Duck, Black Whistler, Boo-by, Broadbilled Coot, Brown Coot, Browny Coot, Butter-bill, But-ter-bill Coot, Butter-billed Coot, Butter-nose, Butter-nose Coot, Butter-nosed Diver, Coot, Copper-bill, Copper-nose, Courting Coot, Deaf Duck, Diver, Dumb Coot, Fizzy, Gibier Noir, Gray Duck, Grey Coot, Hollow-billed Coot, Indian Duck, Iron Pot, King Coot, Macreuse, Niggerhead, Petit Noir, Pumpkin-blossom Coot, Red-billed Coot, Rock Coot, Scooter, Scoter, Sea Coot, Sea Duck, Sif-fleur, Siwash, Siwash Duck, Sleepy Diver, Sleigh-bell Duck, Smutty, Smutty Coot, Squaw Duck, Tar Bucket, Whistling Coot, Whistling Diver, Whistling Duck, Willow-legs, Yellow-bill, Yel-low-billed Coot, Yellow-nose.

Modern Name: White-winged Scoter
Scientific Name: Melanitta fusca deglandi
Folknames and Names: American Velvet Scoter, Assemblyman,

Basque, Bay Coot, Bay Muscovie, Beachcomber, Bell Coot, Bell-tongue, Bell-tongue Coot, Big Black Duck, Big Widgeon, Black Coot, Black Surf Duck, Black Whistler, Black White-wing, Booby, Brant, Brant Coot, Brass-winged Diver, Brown Coot, Bull Coot, Bull White-wing, Canard d'Hiver, Canard Francais, Channel Duck, Coot, Crow Duck, Deaf Duck, Eastern White-wing, Fausse Moiaque, Fausse Moniac, Fish Duck, Gibier Noir, Gray Coot, Gray White-wing, Great May White-wing, Great White-wing, Half-moon-eye, Horse-head Duck, Ice Duck, Indian Duck, Iron-headed Coot, Iron Pot, Lake Huron Scoter, May White-wing, Niggerhead, Pied-wing Coot, Pied-winged Coot, Rock Coot, Salt-water Duck, Scooter, Scoter, Sea Brant, Sea Coot, Sea Cott, Sea Duck, Sea-horse, Siwash, Siwash Duck, Squaw Duck, Uncle Sam Coot, Velvet Duck, Velvet Duck, Velvet Scoter, Tar Bucket, White-eye, White-eyed Coot, White-wing, White-wing Coot, White-wing Duck, White-winged Diver, White-winged Surf Duck, White-winger, Winter Duck.

Modern Name: Surf Scoter
Scientific Name: Melanitta perspicillata
Folknames and Names: Bald Coot, Bald-headed Coot, Bald-headed Scoter, Baldpate, Bald-pated Coot, Basse, Bay Coot, Bay Muscovie, Beachcomber, Black Coot, Black Diver, Black Duck, Blossom-bill, Blossom-billed Coot, Booby, Bottle-nosed Diver, Box Coot, Brisseux de Mer, Brown Coot, Bunk-bill, Butter-billed Coot, Button-bill Coot, Coot, Deaf Duck, Diver, Gibier Noir, Goggle-nose, Gray Coot, Hollow-billed Coot, Horse-head, Horse-head Coot, Indian Duck, Iron Pot, King Coot, Little Gray Coot, Macreuse, Morocco Jaw, Mussel-bill, Niggerhead, Patch-bill, Patch-bill Coot, Patch-head, Patch-head Coot, Patch-poll, Patch-poll Coot, Patch-polled Coot, Petit Noir, Pictured-bill, Pied Duck, Pish-aug, Plaster-bill, River Coot, Rock Coot, Sac a Plomb, Scoter, Sea Coot, Sea Duck, Scooter, Siwash, Siwash Duck, Skunk-bill, Skunk-bill Coot, Skunk-bird, Skunk-duck, Skunk-head, Skunk-head Coot, Skunk-top, Sleepy Diver, Snuff-taker, Speckle-bill, Speckle-billed Coot, Speckled-bill Coot, Spectacle Coot, Spectacled Coot, Squaw-Duck, Surf Coot, Surf Duck, Surfer, Surf Scooter, Tar Bucket, Whistling Diver, White-head, White-head Coot, White Scop.

Modern Name: Ruddy Duck
Scientific Name: Oxyura jamaicensis
Folknames and Names: Batter-scoot, Biddy, Blackjack, Blathers-kite, Bluebill, Bobbler, Booby, Booby Coot, Bristle-tail, Broad-bill, Broad-billed Buzzer, Broad-billed Coot, Broad-billed Dipper, Brown Diving Teal, Brown Teal, Bullneck, Bumble-bee Buzzer, Bumblebee Coot, Bumblebee Duck, Butterball, Butter Bowl, Butter Duck, Chunk Duck, Cock-tail, Creek Coot, Dapper, Daub Duck, Deaf Duck, Dicky, Dinky, Dipper, Dipper Duck, Dip-tail, Dip-tailed Diver, Diver, Diving Teal, Dopper, Dumb-bird,

Dummy Duck, Dumpling Duck, Dunbird, Dun-diver, Fall Duck, Fool Duck, God-damn, Goose Teal, Goose Widgeon, Gray Teal, Greaser, Hard-head, Hard-headed Broadbill, Heavy-tailed Coot, Hickory-head, Leather-back, Leather Breeches, Light-wood Knot, Little Soldier, Marteau, Mud-dipper, Murre, Muskrat Chick, Noddy, Noddy Paddy, North American Ruddy Duck, Paddy, Paddy-whack, Pato Chorizo, Pintail, Pond Coot, Quill-tail, Quill-tail Coot, Quill-tailed Coot, Red-backed Duck, Red Diver, Rook, Roody, Rubber Duck, Rudder Bird, Ruddy Diver, Saltwater Teal, Shot-pouch, Sinker, Sleepy Brother, Sleepy Coot, Sleepy Dick, Sleepy Duck, Sleepyhead, Spatter, Spike-tail, Spine-tail, Spine-tail Duck, Spoonbill, Spoon-billed Butterball, Sprig-tail, Steel-head, Stick-tail, Stiff-tail, Stiff-tailed Wigeon, Stiffy, Stub-and-twist, Swamp Duck, Tough-head, Wire-tail, Water Partridge, Wigeon Coot.

Modern Name: Masked Duck
Scientific Name: Oxyura dominca
Folknames and Names: Duck-and-teal, Squat Duck.

Modern Name: Common Merganser
Scientific Name: Mergus merganser
Folknames and Names: American Goosander, American Merganser, American Sheldrake, Bec-scie, Big Bec-scie, Big Fish Duck, Big Sawbill, Big Sheldrake, Big Winter Duck, Break Horn, Buff-breasted Merganser, Buff-breasted Sheldrake, Diver, Diving Duck, Dun Diver, Fish-duck, Fishing Duck, Freshwater Sheldrake, Gaspard, Gony, Goosander, Gosset, Gossard, Greater Merganser, Harle, Morocco-head, Pond Sheldrake, Sawbill, Saw-bill Duck, Sheldrake, Shelduck, Shelhard, Shellbird, Skunk, Spike, Tweezer, Water Pheasant, Wilte Ent, Winter Pheasant, Winter Sheldrake, Winter Shell-duck, Wood Duck.

Modern Name: Red-breasted Merganser
Scientific Name: Mergus serrator
Folknames and Names: Bec-scie, Bec-scie de Mer, Betsy, Common Saw-bill, Diver, Diving Duck, Fish Duck, Fishing Duck, Fuzzy-head, Garbill, Gaspard, Hairycrown, Hairyhead, Harle, Hell-diver, Indian Sheldrake, Jack, Little Fish Duck, Long Island Sheldrake, Mergansa Pechirroja, Pheasant, Pied Sheldrake, Pond Sheldrake, Red-breasted Fish Duck, Red-breasted Goosander, Red-breasted Sheldrake, Red-headed Duck, Saltwater Sheldrake, Saw-bill, Saw-bill Duck, Scale Duck, Sea Bec-scie, Sea Robin, Shellbird, Sheldrake, Shelduck, Shelhard, Shell-bird, Skunk, Spanish Drake, Spring Sheldrake, Whistler, Wilte Ent, Wood Duck.

Modern Name: Hooded Merganser
Scientific Name: Lophodytes cucullatus

Folknames and Names: Bastard Teal, Beaver Duck, Bec-scie, Bec-scie de Cypriere, Bec-scie du Lac, California Fish Duck, Cock-robin Duck, Cottonhead, Cottontop, Crow Duck, Di-dapper, Diving Duck, Fan-crested Duck, Fanhead, Fish Duck, Frog Duck, Fuzzhead, Goosander, Hairy-crown, Hairyhead, Harle, Hell-diver, Hooded Sheldrake, Hooder, Hoodie, Lake Sawbill, Little Fish Duck, Little Fishing Duck, Little Sawbill, Little Saw-bill Duck, Little Sheldrake, Mergansa De Caperuza, Moss-head, Mud Sheldrake, Pickaxe, Pickax Sheldrake, Pied Duck, Pied Sheldrake, Plongeon, Plongeon Diver, Pond Sheldrake, Round-crested Duck, Sawbill, Saw-bill Diver, Saw-bill Duck, Sharpy, Sheldrake, Shelhard, Shell-bird, Shell-duck, Smew, Spike-bill, Strawbill, Summer Sheldrake, Swamp Sheldrake, Tadpole, Towhead, Tree Duck, Water Pheasant, Whistler, Wilte Ent, Wirecrown, Wood Duck, Wood Sheldrake.

Diurnal Birds of Prey (Order Falconiformes)
American Vultures (Suborder Cathartae)
American Vultures (Superfamily Cathartoidea)
American Vultures (Family Cathartidae)

Modern Name: Turkey Vulture
Scientific Name: Cathartes aura
Folknames and Names: Aura Comun, Aura Tinosa, Buzzard, Carencro Tete Rouge, Carrion Crow, Jamaica Turkey, John Crow, John Crow Headman, John Crow Vulture, King Crow, Luder Awdler, Luder Fogel, Luder Krop, Osa, Osfogel, Red-headed Turkey-buzzard, Red-necked Buzzard, Turkey Buzzard, Wild Turkey.

Modern Name: Black Vulture
Scientific Name: Coragups atratus
Folknames and Names: Black Buzzard, Black Scavenger, Buzzard, Carencro Noir, Carrion Crow, Jim Crow, John Crow.

Modern Name: California Condor
Scientific Name: Gymnogyps californianus
Folknames and Names: California Vulture, Queleli.

Secretary Birds, Kites, Eagles, Hawks and Allies (Suborder Accipitres)
Kites, Eagles, Hawks and Allies (Superfamily Accipitroidea)
Kites, Eagles, Hawks and Allies (Family Accipitridae)

Ospreys (Subfamily Pandioninae)

Modern Name: Osprey
Scientific Name: Pandion haliaetus
Folknames and Names: Aigle de Mer, Aigle Pecheur, American Osprey, Awdler, Common Brown Fishing Eagle, Eagle, Fish Awdler, Fish Eagle, Fish Hawk, Fishing Eagle, Fishing Hawk, Fishwoi, Grepe, Iolair Uisge, Orfraie, Pecheur, Sea Eagle, Sea Hawk.

Kites, Eagles, Hawks and Allies (Subfamily Acciptrinae)

Modern Name: White-tailed Kite
Scientific Name: Elanus lencurus
Folknames and Names: Black-shouldered Kite, Black-winged Hawk, White Hawk.

Modern Name: Mississippi Kite
Scientific Name: Ictinia mississippiensis
Folknames and Names: Blue Kite, Locust-eater, Louisiana Kite, Mosquito Hawk.

Modern Name: Swallow-tailed Kite
Scientific Name: Elanoides forficatus
Folknames and Names: American Swallow-tailed Kite, Fork-tailed Kite, Queue Fourchu, Snake Hawk, Swallow-tail, Swallow-tailed Hawk, Wasp Hawk.

Modern Name: Everglade Kite
Scientific Name: Rostrhamus sociabilis
Folknames and Names: Black Hawk, Black Kite, Hookbill Hawk, Snail Hawk, Snail Kite, Sociable Marsh Hawk.

Modern Name: Goshawk
Scientific Name: Accipiter gentilis
Folknames and Names: American Goshawk, Autour, Black Hawk, Blue Darter, Blue Hen Hawk, Blue Darter, Blue Swifter, Boy, Chicken Hawk, Cossard, Dove Hawk, Goose Hawk, Goshawk, Gosh Hawk, Gos-sheobhag, Grey Hawk, Hen Hawk, Hinkelwoi, Manageur de Poulets, Northern Goshawk, Partridge Hawk, Speckled Partridge Hawk, Western Goshawk, Winter Hawk, Woi.

Modern Name: Cooper's Hawk
Scientific Name: Accipiter cooperii
Folknames and Names: Aiglon, Ailerond, Big Blue Darter, Blue Darter, Bluetail, Boy, Chicken Hawk, Cooper Hawk, Hen Hawk, Hinkelwoi, Pigeon Hawk, Quail Hawk, Stanley Hawk, Striker, Swift Hawk, Woi.

Modern Name: Sharp-shinned Hawk
Scientific Name: Accipiter striatus
Folknames and Names: Bog-trotter, Bon Volee, Bird Hawk, Bullet
Hawk, Chicken Hawk, Clairhan Speireag, Dauwa Shdosser, Dauwa
Woi, Emerillon, Epervier, Falcon De Sierra, Gavilan De Sierra,
Hen Hawk, Little Blue Darter, Little Chicken Hawk, Pigeon Hawk,
Sharp-shin, Shdos Fogel, Shdos Woi, Slate-colored Hawk, Sparrow
Hawk.

Modern Name: Northern Harrier
Scientific Name: Circus cyaneus
Folknames and Names: Aguilucho Palido, Blue Harrier, Blue
Hawk, Boy, Brown Harrier, Busard, Chicken Hawk, Chocolatier,
Corsage, Cossade, Cossarde, Duck Hawk, Frog Hawk, Gavilan De
Cienaga, Grey Harrier, Harrier, Hen-harrier, Hinkelwoi, Kay-
cake, Mad Hawk, Mangepoule, Marsh Harrier, Marsh Hawk, Mouse
Hawk, Prairie Hawk, Rabbit Hawk, Swamp Hawk, Toad Hawk,
White-rumped Hawk, Woi.

Modern Name: Rough-legged Hawk
Scientific Name: Buteo lagopus
Folknames and Names: American Rough-legged Hawk, Black
Hawk, Boy, Chap-Hawk, Chicken Hawk, Hinkelwoi, Mouse Hawk,
Rough-leg, Rough-legged Buzzard, Rough-legged Falcon, Squall-
ing Hawk, Squealing Hawk, Woi.

Modern Name: Ferruginous Hawk
Scientific Name: Buteo regalis
Folknames and Names: Chap-hawk, Eagle Hawk, Ferruginous
Rough-leg, Ferruginous Rough-legged Hawk, Gopher Hawk, Prai-
rie Eagle, Squirrel Hawk.

Modern Name: Red-tailed Hawk
Scientific Name: Buteo jamaicensis
Folknames and Names: Aguililla Colirrufa, Alaska Red-tail,
Black Red-tail, Black Warrior, Boy, Buzzard, Buzzard Hawk,
Chicken Hawk, Clamhan, Eastern Redtail, Gopher Hawk, Guara-
guao Colirrojo, Harlan Hawk, Harlan's Buzzard, Harlan's Hawk,
Harlan's Red-tailed Hawk, Hen Hawk, Hinkelwoi, Krider Hawk,
Krider's Hawk, Lechuza, Mouse Hawk, Pee-ank, Red Hawk, Red-
tail, Red-tailed Buzzard, Sparrow Hawk, Squealer, Western Red-
tail, Western Red-tailed Buzzard, White-breasted Chicken Hawk,
Woi.

Modern Name: Red-shouldered Hawk
Scientific Name: Buteo lineatus
Folknames and Names: Big Chicken Hawk, Boy, Brown Hawk,
Chicken Hawk, Florida Red-shouldered Hawk, Hen Hawk, Hinkel-

woi, Mouse Hawk, Red-bellied Hawk, Red-shouldered Buzzard, Red-shouldered Hawk, Southern Red-shouldered Hawk, Winter Hawk, Woi.

Modern Name: Swainson's Hawk
Scientific Name: Buteo swainsoni
Folknames and Names: Black Hawk, Brown Hawk, Brown-throated Hawk, Common Buzzard, Common Hen Hawk, Gopher Hawk, Grasshopper Hawk, Hen Hawk, Telephone-pole Hawk.

Modern Name: Broad-winged Hawk
Scientific Name: Buteo platypterus
Folknames and Names: Boy, Broad-winged Buzzard, Chicken Hawk, Guaraguao De Bosque, Hinkelwoi, Marsh Hawk, Woi.

Modern Name: Harris' Hawk
Scientific Name: Parabuteo unicinctus
Folknames and Names: Bat-winged Hawk, Chestnut-thighed Buzzard, Harris' Buzzard, Louisiana Hawk.

Modern Name: Black Hawk
Scientific Name: Buteogallus anthricinus
Folknames and Names: Common Black Hawk, Crab Hawk, Lesser Black Hawk, Mexican Black Hawk.

Modern Name: Zone-tailed Hawk
Scientific Name: Buteo albonotatus
Folknames and Names: Bandtail, Band-tailed Hawk, Zone-tailed Buzzard.

Modern Name: White-tailed Hawk
Scientific Name: Buteo albicaudatus
Folknames and Names: Prairie Hawk, Sennet's White-tailed Hawk, White-tail, White-tailed Buzzard.

Modern Name: Short-tailed Hawk
Scientific Name: Buteo brachyurus
Folknames and Names: Little Black Hawk, Short-tailed Buzzard.

Modern Name: Gray Hawk
Scientific Name: Buteo nitidus
Folknames and Names: Mexican Goshawk, Shining Buzzard-hawk.

Modern Name: Io
Scientific Name: Buteo solitarius
Folknames and Names: Hawai'ian Hawk
*Native to Hawai'ian Islands (Hawai'i)

Modern Name: Golden Eagle

Scientific Name: Aquila chrysaetos
Folknames and Names: American War Bird, Awdler, Bird of Jupiter, Black Eagle, Brown Eagle, Calumet Bird, Calumet Eagle, Canadian Eagle, Dark Eagle, Gray Eagle, Iolair Dubh, Jackrabbit Eagle, King of Birds, Mountain Eagle, Ringtail, Ring-tailed Eagle, Royal Eagle, War Bird, War Eagle, White-tailed Eagle.

Modern Name: Bald Eagle
Scientific Name: Haliacetus leycocephalus
Folknames and Names: Aigle a Tete Blanche, Alaska Bald Eagle, American Eagle, Awdler, Bald-headed Eagle, Black Eagle, Brown Eagle, Common Eagle, Fior-eun, Fish Eagle, Fishing Eagle, Gray Eagle, Great American Sea Eagle, Grepe, Iolair, Nonne, Northern Bald Eagle, Old Patriarch, Sea Eagle, Washington Eagle, White-headed Eagle, White-headed Sea Eagle, Bird of Washington.

Caracaras and Falcons (Suborder Falcones)
Caracaras and Falcons (Family Falconidae)

Modern Name: Crested Caracara
Scientific Name: Polyborus plancus
Folknames and Names: Audubon's Caracara, Brazilian Caracara Eagle, Caracara, Caracara Eagle, Common Caracara, King Buzzard, King of Vultures, Mexican Eagle, Mexican Buzzard.

Modern Name: Gyrfalcon
Scientific Name: Falco rusticolus
Folknames and Names: Asiatic Gyrfalcon, Black Gyrfalcon, Cyrfalcon, Duck Hawk, Gray Gyrfalcon, Greenland Falcon, Gyrfalcon, Ice Falcon, Iceland Falcon, Jer Falcon, Killer Hawk, Labrador Jer Falcon, MacFarlane's Gyrfalcon, Partridge Hawk, Speckled Hawk, Speckled Partridge-hawk, White Gyrfalcon, White Hawk, Winterer, Winter Hawk.

Modern Name: Prairie Falcon
Scientific Name: Falco mexicanus
Folknames and Names: American Lanner, American Lanneret, Bullet Hawk.

Modern Name: Peregrine Falcon
Scientific Name: Falco peregrinus
Folknames and Names: Aile Pointue, American Peregrine, Batarde Aigle, Beau Voleur, Boy, Bullet Hawk, Duck Hawk, Eagle Hawk, Falcon, Faucon, Falcon Peregrino, Frappe Canard, Great-footed Hawk, Hinkelwoi, Mangeur de Canards, Mangeur de Poules, Peale's Falcon, Peregrine Hawk, Pinnacle Hawk, Rock Peregrine, Sea Hawk, Tercel, Wandering Falcon, Woi.

Modern Name: Merlin
Scientific Name: Falco columbarius
Folknames and Names: American Merlin, Bird Hawk, Black Merlin, Black Pigeon Hawk, Bullet Hawk, Chicken Hawk, Eastern Pigeon Hawk, Esmerejon, Falcon Migratorio, La Petit Caporal, Little Blue Corporal, Meirneal, Merlin, Pigeon Falcon, Pigeon Hawk, Richardson's Merlin, Richardson's Pigeon Hawk, Small Bird Hawk, Sparrow Hawk, Suckley's Pigeon Hawk, Western Pigeon Hawk.

Modern Name: American Kestrel
Scientific Name: Falco sparverius
Folknames and Names: American Sparrow Hawk, Bastard Hawk, Bullet Hawk, Chicken Hawk, Cleek Cleek, Cliff Hawk, Dauwa Shdosser, Dauwa Woi, Desert Sparrow Hawk, Emerillon, Falcon Comun, Grasshopper Hawk, Halcon Cernicalo, House Hawk, Kestrel, Killey Hawk, Killy Hawk, Killy-killy, Little Brown Hawk, Little Sparrow Hawk, Mangeur de Poule, Mangeur Poulets, Merieleon, Mouse Hawk, Peregreve, Rusty-crowned Falcon, Shdos Fogel, Shdos Woi, Sparrow Hawk, Speireag, Short-winged Hawk, Tilly, Windhover, Wood Bird.

Modern Name: Aplomado Falcon
Scientific Name: Falco femoralis
Folknames and Names: American Hobby, Fermoral Falcon, Orange-chested Hobby.

Gallinaceous Birds (Order Galliformes)

Megapodes, Curassows and Guans (Superfamily Cracoidea)

Curassows and Guans (Family Cracidae)

Modern Name: Chachalaca
Scientific Name: Ortalis vetula
Folknames and Names: Common Chachalaca, Mexican Chachalaca, Plain Chachalaca.

Partridges, Grouse, Turkeys and Quails (Superfamily Phasianoidea)

Partridges, Grouse, Turkeys and Quails (Family Phasianidae)

Partridges, Grouse, Turkeys and Quails (Subfamily Phasianinae)

Modern Name: Gray Partridge
Scientific Name: Perdix perdix
Folknames and Names: Bohemian Partridge, Common Partridge,
English Partridge, European Gray Partridge, European Partridge,
Gray Partridge, Hun, Hungarian Partridge, Hungy, Hunky, Partridge, Redtail, Small Partridge.

Modern Name: Black Francolin
Scientific Name: Francolinus francolinus
Folknames and Names: -
* introduced into Hawai'ian Islands (Kaua'i, Moloka'i, Maui, Hawai'i).

Modern Name: Gray Francolin
Scientific Name: Francolinus pondicerianus
Folknames and Names: -
* introduced into Hawai'ian Islands,(Moloka'i, Lana'i, Maui, Hawai'i).

Modern Name: Erckel's Francolin
Scientific Name: Francolinus erckelii
Folknames and Names: -
* introduced into Hawai'ian Islands,(Kaua'i, Maui, Hawai'i).

Modern Name: Chukar
Scientific Name: Alectoris chukar
Folknames and Names: Chuckar, Gray Partridge, Indian Hill Partridge, Redleg, Red-legged Partridge, Rock Partridge.
* introduced into Hawai'ian Islands,(Kaua'i, Moloka'i, Maui, Hawai'i, O'ahu).

Modern Name: Japanese Quail
Scientific Name: Coturnix japonica
Folknames and Names: -
* introduced into Hawai'ian Islands,(Kaua'i, Moloka'i, Maui, Hawai'i,)

Modern Name: Kalij Pheasant
Scientific Name: Lophura leucomelana
Folknames and Names: -
* introduced into Hawai'ian Islands, (Hawai'i)

Modern Name: Red Junglefowl
Scientific Name: Gallus gallus
Folknames and Names: Chicken, Domestic Fowl, Gallina, Gallo,
Moa, Rooster.
*introduced into Hawai'i by early Polynesians (Kaua'i, O'ahu).

Modern Name: Ring-necked Pheasant

Scientific Name: Phasianus colchicus
Folknames and Names: Cackle-bird, Chinese Pheasant, Common Pheasant, English Pheasant, Faisan, Kolo-hala, Mongolian Pheasant, Pheasant, Ring-neck.
*introduced into Hawai'ian Islands: (Hawai'i, Kaua'i, Lana'i).

Modern Name: Peacock
Scientific Name: Pavo cristatus
Folknames and Names: Common Peafowl, Peafowl, Peahen.
*introduced into Hawai'ian Islands (Maui, O'ahu and Hawai'i).

Grouse (Subfamily Tetraoninae)

Modern Name: Spruce Grouse
Scientific Name: Canachites canadensis
Folknames and Names: Alaska Spruce Partridge, Black Grouse, Black Partridge, Canada Grouse, Cedar Partridge, Chicken, Crazy Grouse, Fool Cock, Fool Hen, Fool Partridge, Franklin's Grouse, Franklin's Spruce Grouse, Hen and Dick, Hudsonian Spruce, Mountain Grouse, Partridge, Perdrix, Perdrix d'Epinette, Perdrix de Savane, Perdrix Sapineuse, Peurdag, Pine Grouse, Pine Partridge, Soft-wood Partridge, Spotted Grouse, Spruce Chicken, Spruce Grouse, Spruce Hen, Spruce Partridge, Sprucer, Swamp Grouse, Swamp Partridge, Tyee Grouse, Wood Grouse, Wood Partridge, Yukon Chicken.

Modern Name: Blue Grouse
Scientific Name: Dendragapus obscurus
Folknames and Names: Black Partridge, Blue Grouse, Dusky Grouse, Fool Hen, Gray Grouse, Hooter, Partridge, Pine Grouse, Pine Hen, Sooty Grouse, Timber Grouse.

Modern Name: Willow Ptarmigan
Scientific Name: Lagopus lagopus
Folknames and Names: Alaska Ptarmigan, Alexander's Ptarmigan, Allen's Ptarmigan, Arctic Grouse, Browse Partridge, Common Ptarmigan, Eskimo Chicken, Foo-hen, Grouse, Moor Cock, Partridge, Perdix Blanche, Ptarmigan, Snow Grouse, Snow Hen, Snow Partridge, White Bird, White Grouse, Willow Bird, Willow Grouse, Willow Partridge.

Modern Name: Rock Ptarmigan
Scientific Name: Lagopus mutus
Folknames and Names: Arctic Grouse, Barren-ground Bird, Barren Partridge, Croaker, Mountain Partridge, Nelson Ptarmigan, Partridge, Patridge, Pattermegan, Perdrix Blanche, Ptharmakin, Polar Grouse, Reinhardt Ptarmigan, Rocker, Rock Grouse, Rock

Partridge, Small Grouse, Snow Grouse, Townsend Ptarmigan, Turner Ptarmigan, White Grouse.

Modern Name: White-tailed Ptarmigan
Scientific Name: Lafopus leucurus
Folknames and Names: Mountain Quail, Rock Ptarmigan, Rocky Mountain Snow Grouse, Rocky Mountain Snow Partridge, Snow Grouse, Snow Partridge, Snow Quail, White Quail, Whitetail.

Modern Name: Ruffed Grouse
Scientific Name: Bonasa umbellus
Folknames and Names: Birch Partridge, Bircher, Brown Grouse, Brown Partridge, Brush Partridge, Bush Partridge, Canada Ruffed Grouse, Canadian Partridge, Carpenter Bird, Cearc-thomain, Chicken, Common Partridge, Copper-rufferd Partridge, Drummer, Drumming Grouse, Drumming Pheasant, Fesond, French Hen, Gray Ruffed Grouse, Grey Partridge, Grouse, Hardwood Partridge, Moor Fowl, Mountain Pheasant, Oregon Ruffed Grouse, Partridge, Pheasant, Perdrix, Perdrix Bois Franc, Perdrix Franche, Perdrix Grise, Pine Hen, Pine Pheasant, Quail, Red Grouse, Red-ruffed Partridge, Ruffed Heathcock, Ruffled Grouse, Shoulder-knot Grouse, Spring Drummer, Spruce Partridge, Tippet, White-fleshed Partridge, White-flesher, White-meat Partridge, Willow Grouse, Willow Partridge, Wood Grouse, Wood Hen, Woodpile Quarker, Woods Pheasant.

Modern Name: Sage Grouse
Scientific Name: Centrocercus urophasianus
Folknames and Names: Cock of the Plains, Fool Hen, Sage Chicken, Sage Cock, Sage Grouse, Sage Hen, Spiny-tailed Pheasant.

Modern Name: Greater Prairie Chicken
Scientific Name: Tympanuchus cupido
Folknames and Names: Attwater's Prairie Chicken, Chicken, Common Prairie Chicken, Eastern Pinnated Grouse, Faisan, Grouse, Heath Hen, Louisiana Prairie Chicken, Pinnated Grouse, Pinnated Grouse, Prairie Chicken, Prairie Grouse, Prairie Hen, Square-tailed Grouse.

Modern Name: Lesser Prairie Chicken
Scientific Name: Tympanuchus pallidicinctus
Folknames and Names: Prairie Hen, Pinnated Grouse, Prairie Hen.

Modern Name: Sharp-tailed Grouse
Scientific Name: Tympanuchus phasianellus
Folknames and Names: Blackfoot, Brush Grouse, Chicken, Columbian Sharp-tailed Grouse, Faisan, Northern Sharp-tailed Grouse, Partridge, Pheasant, Pintail Grouse, Pintailed Grouse, Poule de Prairies, Prairie Chicken, Prairie Chicken of the Northwest,

Prairie Grouse, Prairie Hen, Prairie Pheasant, Prairie Sharp-tailed Grouse, Pin-tail, Sharp-tail, Sharp-tailed Grouse, Spike-tail, Sprig-tailed Grouse, White-belly, White Grouse, Willow Grouse.

Modern Name: Chestnut-bellied Sandgrouse
Scientific Name: Pterocles exustus
Folknames and Names: -
*Introduced to Hawai'ian Islands (Hawai'i)

Turkeys (Subfamily Meleagridinae)

Modern Name: Turkey
Scientific Name: Meleagris gallopavo
Folknames and Names: American Turkey, American Wild Turkey, Bronze Turkey, Cocoano, Cocono, Common Wild Turkey, Coq d'In-de, Dinde Saurage, Dindon, Eastern Turkey, Florida Wild Turkey, Gallina de la Tierra, Ganso, Gobbler, Guajalote, Guajolote, Guijalo, Merriam Turkey, Northern Turkey, Palahu, Peacock, Pelehu, Plain Turkey, Poule d'Inde, Rio Grande Turkey, Torque, Turkey Gobbler, Wild Turkey, Wilte Welshhinkel, Wood Turkey.
*introduced into Hawai'ian Islands: (Hawai'i, Lana'i, Maui, Moloi-ka'i, Niihau).

Quail (Subfamily Odontophorinae)

Modern Name: Montezuma Quail
Scientific Name: Cyrtonyx montezumae
Folknames and Names: Black Quail, Crazy Quail, Fool Quail, Fool Hen, Harlequin, Harlequin Quail, Massena Quail, Mearns' Har-liquin Quail, Mearns' Quail.

Modern Name: Northern Bobwhite
Scientific Name: Colinus virginianus
Folknames and Names: Bob, Bobwhite, Bobwhite Quail, Bodreesel, Caille, Colin, Common Bobwhite, Codorniz, Feldhinkel, Florida Bobwhite, Partridge, Perdrix, Quail, Quail-dle, Texan Bobwhite, Virginia Partridge.

Modern Name: Scaled Quail
Scientific Name: Callipepla squamata
Folknames and Names: Blue Quail, Blue Racer, Codorniz Cresti-blanca, Cotton-top, Cotton-top Quail, Mexican Quail, Scaled Par-tridge, Scaly, Top-knot Quail.

Modern Name: Gambel's Quail

Scientific Name: Callipepla gambelii
Folknames and Names: Arizona Quail, Codorniz Desertica, Desert Quail, Gambel's Valley Quail, Manu-Kapalulu, Olanthe Quail.
*introduced into Hawai'ian Islands (Lana'i, Kaho'olawe).

Modern Name: California Quail
Scientific Name: Lohortyx californicus
Folknames and Names: California Partridge, Catalina Quail, Crested Quail, Helmet Quail, Top-knot Quail, Valley Partridge, Valley Quail.
*introduced into Hawai'ian Islands (Lana'i, Hawai'i, Kaua'i)

Modern Name: Mountain Quail
Scientific Name: Oreortyx pictus
Folknames and Names: Mountain Partridge, Painted Quail, Plumed Partridge, Plumed Quail, San Pedro Quail.

Guineafowl (Subfamily Numidinae)

Modern Name: Helmeted Guineafowl
Scientific Name: Numida meleagris
Folknames and Names: Common Guineafowl, Guinea Bird, Guinea Hen, Guinea Torcaz.
*introduced into Hawai'ian Islands (Hawai'i).

Cranes, Rails and Allies (Order Gruiformes)
Rails, Gallinules and Coots (Family Rallidae)

Rails, Gallinules and Coots (Subfamily Rallinae)

Modern Name: Yellow Rail
Scientific Name: Coturnicops noveboracensis
Folknames and Names: Clicker, Little Yellow Rail, Water Sparrow, Yellow Crake.

Modern Name: Black Rail
Scientific Name: Laterallus jamaicensis
Folknames and Names: Black Crake, Gallito Negro, Little Black Rail.

Modern Name: Corn Crake
Scientific Name: Crex crex
Folknames and Names: Land Rail.

Modern Name: Clapper Rail
Scientific Name: Rallus longirostris
Folknames and Names: Common Clapper, Light-footed Rail, Loui-

siana Clapper Rail, Mangrove Hen, Marsh Clapper, Marsh Hen, Meadow Hen, Mud Hen, Pollo De Mangle, Prairie Hen, Rale, Rattling Rail, Salt-water Marsh Hen, Sedge Hen, Yuma Clapper Rail.

Modern Name: King Rail
Scientific Name: Rallus elegans
Folknames and Names: Big Virginia Rail, Freshwater Marsh Hen, Grand Rale de Prairie, Great Red-breasted Rail, King Rail, Marsh Hen, Meadow Hen, Mud Hen, Prairie Chicken, Red-breasted Rail, Stage Driver.

Modern Name: Virginia Rail
Scientific Name: Rallus limicola
Folknames and Names: Bull Rale, Freshwater Marsh Hen, Little Red-breasted Rail, Long-billed Rail, Small Mud Hen, Water Hen.

Modern Name: Sora
Scientific Name: Porzana carolina
Folknames and Names: Carolina Crake, Carolina Rail, Chickenbill, Chicken-billed Rail, Common Rail, Gallito, Little American Water Hen, Little Rice Bird, Meadow Chicken, Mud Hen, Ortolan, Plover, Railbird, Rale Musque, Ricefield Rail, Sora Crake, Sora Rail, Soree, Tinsmith, Water Partridge, Water Rail, Widgeon.

Modern Name: Purple Gallinule
Scientific Name: Porphyrula martinica
Folknames and Names: Blue Pate Coot, Blue Pete, Blue Peter, Bonnet-walker, Gallareta Azul, Gallareta Inglesa, La Poule Sultana, Marsh Guinea, Marsh Hen, Pond Guinea, Rale Heae, Sultana.

Modern Name: Common Moorhen
Scientific Name: Gallinula chloropus
Folknames and Names: Alae 'ula, American Gallinule, Antillean Gallinule, Blue Peter, Blue Rail, Bonnet-walker, Chicken-foot Coot, Common Gallinule, Florida Gallinule, Gallareta Comun, Moorhen, Mud Hen, Pond Guinea, Poule d Eau, Poule d'Eau de Marquis, Poule de Lac, Rail Hen, Rale Poule d'Eau, Red-billed Mud Hen, Red-seal Coot, Rice Bird, Rice Hen, Sedge Peter, Water Chicken, Water Fowl, Water Hen.
*introduced into Hawai'ian Islands (Kaua'i, Moloka'i, O'ahu).

Modern Name: American Coot
Scientific Name: Fulica americana
Folknames and Names: Alae Ke 'oke'o, American Coot, Baldface, Bald-face Coot, Black Fish-duck, Blue Hen, Blue Pete, Blue Peter, Common Coot, Coot, Crow-bill, Crow-duck, Fish Duck, Flusterer, Fool Hen, Freshwater Coot, Gallareta Americana, Gallinazo Americano, Helldiver, Hen-bill, Ivory-billed Coot, Louse Bird, Marsh

Hen, Meadow Hen, Moor-head, Mud Coot, Mud Duck, Mud
Hen, Pelick, Pond Crow, Pond Hen, Poule d' Eau, Poule
de Marais, Pull-doo, Republican, Rice Hen, Sea-crow,
Spatterer, Shdink Ent, Shuffler, Water Chicken, Water
Fowl, Water Hen, White-bellied Mud Hen, White Bill,
White-faced Duck, White-seal Coot, Wosserhund.
*introduced into Hawai'ian Islands (Kaua'i, O'ahu, Moloka'i,
Maui, Hawai'i).

Limpkins (Family Aramidae)

Modern Name: Limpkin
Scientific Name: Aramus guarauna
Folknames and Names: Carau, Carrao, Clucking Hen, Courlan,
Crippled Bird, Crying Bird, Indian Pullet, Screamer, Speckled
Curlew.

Cranes (Family Gruidae)

Cranes (Subfamily Gruinae)

Modern Name: Sandhill Crane
Scientific Name: Grus canadensis
Folknames and Names: Alaska Turkey, Baldhead, Blue Crane,
Brown Crane, Brown Turkey, Field Crane, Florida Crane, Garoo,
Gray Crane, Greater Sandhill Crane, Grue Bleue, Lesser Sandhill
Crane, Little Brown Crane, North-west Turkey, Red Crane, San-
dhill Whooper, Southern Sandhill Crane, Turkey, Upland Crane,
Whooper, Whooping Crane, Wild Turkey.

Modern Name: Whooping Crane
Scientific Name: Grus americana
Folknames and Names: Flying Sheep, Garoo, Great White Crane,
Grus Blanche, White Crane, White Turkey, Whooper, Wild Tur-
key.

Shorebirds, Gulls, Auks and Allies (Order Charadriiformes)
Plovers and Allies (Suborder Charadrii)
Plovers and Lapwings (Family Charadri-idae)

Lapwings (Subfamily Vanellinae)

Modern Name: Lapwing
Scientific Name: Vanellus vanellus

Folknames and Names: Avefria, Green Plover, Northern Lapwing, Pewit.

Plovers (Subfamily Charadriinae)

Modern Name: Mountain Plover
Scientific Name: Charadrius montanus
Folknames and Names: Curlew, Feldhinkel, Field Plover, Long-baniche Feldhinkel, Plover, Prairie Plover, Prairie Turkey, Quail, Snipe, Upland Plover.

Modern Name: Lesser Golden Plover
Scientific Name: Pluvialis dominica
Folknames and Names: American Golden Plover, Black-breast, Brass-back, Bullhead, Bull-head Plover, Common Plover, Corbido, Dark Plover, Dore, Field-bird, Field Plover, Frost-bird, Golden-back, Golden Plover, Grand Chevalier, Greenback, Greenhead, Green Plover, Grosse-yeux, Ground Plover, Hawk's Eye, Kolea, Lesser Golden Plover, Little Ox-eye, Lowland Plover, Muddy-belly, Muddy-breast, Pacific Golden Plover, Pale-belly, Pale-breast, Pasture-bird, Pigeon de Mer, Playero Dorado, Pluvier Dore, Prairie-bird, Prairie Pigeon, Spotted Plover, Squealer, Three-toed Plover, Three-toes, Toad-head, Trout-bird, Whistling Plover, Yellow Back.
*native to Hawai'ian Islands

Modern Name: Black-bellied Plover
Scientific Name: Pluvalis squatarola
Folknames and Names: Beetle-head, Black-breast, Black-breasted Plover, Bottle-head, Bull Bird, Bullhead, Bull-head Plover, Chuckle-head, Chuckly-head, Corbido, Corbijo, Feadag, Field Plover, Four-toed Plover, Gray Plover, Grey Field Plover, Grosse-tete, Gump, Hollow-head, Lapwing, May Cock, Muddy-breast, Mud Plover, Owl-head, Ox-eye, Pale-belly, Pigeon de Mer, Pigeon Plover, Pilot, Playero Cabezon, Pot-head, Quebec Curlew, Sand Plover, Silverback, Swiss Plover, Toad-head, Ventra Noir, Whistling Field Plover, Whistling Plover.

Modern Name: Common Ringed Plover
Scientific Name: Charadrius hiaticula
Folknames and Names: Ringed Plover, Ringed Dotterel.

Modern Name: Piping Plover
Scientific Name: Charadrius melodus
Folknames and Names: Beach Bird, Beach Plover, Belted Piping Plover, Clam-bird, Mourning Bird, Pale Ring-neck, Playero Melodico, Ring-neck, Sand Plover, Tete de Pipe, Western Piping Plo-

ver, White Ringneck.

Modern Name: Snowy Plover
Scientific Name: Charadrius alexandrinus
Folknames and Names: Kentish Plover, Playero Blanco, Snowy Ringed Plover,
Western Snowy Plover.

Modern Name: Semipalmated Plover
Scientific Name: Charadrius semipalmatus
Folknames and Names: Alouette Cou Blanc, Beach Bird, Black Ringneck, Bodhag, Cou Blanc, Luatharan, Playero Acollarado, Red-eye, Redleg, Ringer, Ring-neck, Ring-necked Plover, Ring Plover, Semipalmated Ring Plover, Twillig.

Modern Name: Wilson's Plover
Scientific Name: Charadrius wilsonia
Folknames and Names: Belding's Plover, Collier, Little Ploward, Nit, Playero Maritimo, Sand Bird, Thick-billed Plover.

Modern Name: Killdeer
Scientific Name: Charadrius vociferus
Folknames and Names: Braillard, Chattering Plover, Chorlito Til-dio, Cou Collier, Corbijou, Field Plover, Gilderee, Gilleree, Jack-snipe, Killdee, Killdeer Plover, Marsh-hawk, Meadow Plover, Mosquito Hawk, Noisy Plover, Pasturebird, Playero Sabanero, Ploward, Pouvier Dore, Ringneck, Ring-neck Plover, Sand-run-ner, Soldier Bird, Tell-tale Killdeer, Tilderee, Tip-up.

Modern Name: Eurasian Dotteral
Scientific Name: Charadrius morinellus
Folknames and Names: Dotteral.

Oystercatchers (Family Haematopodidae)

Modern Name: American Oystercatcher
Scientific Name: Haematopus palliatus
Folknames and Names: Bank Bird, Brown-backed Oystercatcher, Caracolero, Common Oystercatcher, Frazar's Oystercatcher, Mantled Oyster-catcher, Ostrero, Oyster-catcher, Sea Crow, Whelkcracker.

Modern Name: Black Oystercatcher
Scientific Name: Haematopus bachmani
Folknames and Names: Redbill, Sea Parrot.

Stilts and Avocets (Family Recurvirostridae)

Modern Name: Black-necked Stilt

Scientific Name: Himantopus mexicanus
Folknames and Names: Ally-moor, Avocet, Becasse de Marais, Becassine de Marais, Becassine de Mer, Cap'n Lewis, Civil, Common Stilt, Crackpot Soldier, Daddy Longlegs, Lawyer, Longshanks, Ne 'o, Redshank, Religieuse, Soldat, Stilt, Telltale, Viuda, Yelper.
*native to Hawai'ian Islands (O'ahu, Maui, Kaua'i)

Modern Name: American Avocet
Scientific Name: Recurvirostra americana
Folknames and Names: Avocet, Avoceta, Becassine de Mer, Blueshanks, Bluestocking, Golden Plover, Irish Snipe, Lawyer, North American Avocet, Yellow-necked Snipe, Yelper.

Sandpipers, Jacanas and Allies (Suborder Scolopaci)
Jacanas (Superfamily Jacanoidea)
Jacanas (Family Jacanidae)

.Modern Name: Jacana
Scientific Name: Jacana spinosa
Folknames and Names: American Jacana, Lillytrotter, Lotus Bird, Mexican Jacana, North American Jacana, Northern Jacana, Pond Coot, Queen Coot, River Chink, Spanish Coot.

Sandpipers, Phalaropes and Allies (Superfamily Scolopacoidea)
Sandpipers, Phalaropes and Allies (Family Scolopacidae)

Sandpipers and Allies (Subfamily Scolopacoinae)

Modern Name: Long-billed Curlew
Scientific Name: Numenius americanus
Folknames and Names: Big Curlew, Corpigeon, Curlew, Guilbueach, Hen Curlew, Old Hen Curlew, Sabre-bill, Sickle-bill, Sickle-billed Curlew, Smoker, Spanish Curlew, Turkey Curlew.

Modern Name: Whimbrel
Scientific Name: Numenius phaeopus
Folknames and Names: American Whimbel, Big Curlew, Blue-legs, Corbigeau, Crooked-bill Marlin, Foolish Curlew, Guilueach, Hudsonian Curlew, Jack, Jack Curlew, Mountain Curlew, Playero Pico Corvo, Short-billed Curlew, Sickle-bill, Striped-head, Whimbrel.

Modern Name: Eskimo Curlew

Scientific Name: Numenius borealis
Folknames and Names: Corbigeau, Curlew, Doe-bird, Dough-bird, Fute, Guilbueach, Little Curlew, Little Sickle-bill, Playero Artico, Prairie Pigeon.

Modern Name: Bristle-thighed Curlew
Scientific Name: Numenius tahitiensis
Folknames and Names: Kioea.
*native to Hawai'ian Islands (NW islands)

Modern Name: Marbled Godwit
Scientific Name: Limosa fedoa
Folknames and Names: Badger-bird, Barga Jaspeada, Brant-bird, Brown Marlin, Curlew, i.Doe-bird;, Dotterel, Dough-bird, Great Godwit, Great Marbled Godwit, Marlin, Red Curlew, Red Marlin, Spike-bill, Spike-billed Curlew, Straight-billed Curlew.

Modern Name: Hudsonian Godwit
Scientific Name: Limosa haemastica
Folknames and Names: American Black-tailed Godwit, Barga Aliblanca, Black-tail, Black-tailed Godwit, Brant-bird, Dotterel, Field Marlin, Goose-bird, Little Curlew, Red-breasted Godwit, Ring-tailed Marlin, Smaller Doe-bird, Smaller Dough-bird, Spot-rump, Staight-billed Curlew, White-rump.

Modern Name: Bar-tailed Godwit
Scientific Name: Limosa lapponica
Folknames and Names: Pacific Godwit.

Modern Name: Upland Sandpiper
Scientific Name: Bartramina longicauda
Folknames and Names: Bartramian Sandpiper, Bartram's Plover, Bartram's Sandpiper, Field Plover, Ganga, Grass Plover, Highland Plover, Hill Bird, Papebotte, Pasture-bird, Pasture Plover, Prairie Plover, Prairie Snipe, Quaily, Uplander, Upland Plover.

Modern Name: Buff-breasted Sandpiper
Scientific Name: Tryngites subrufcollis
Folknames and Names: Hill Grass-bird, Robin Snipe.

Modern Name: Solitary Sandpiper
Scientific Name: Tringa solitaria
Folknames and Names: Alouette, Alouette Grise, American Green Sandpiper, American Wood Sandpiper, Barnyard Plover, Beachy Bird, Becassine Grosse-tete, Black Snipe, Bullhead, Green Sandpiper, Peet-weet, Playero Solitario, Shneb, Solitary Tattler, Swee-sweet, Tie-up, Wood Sandpiper, Wood Tattler.

Modern Name: Spotted Sandpiper

Scientific Name: Actitis macularia
Folknames and Names: Alouette, Alouette Branie Queue, Beachy Bird, Bowing Bird, Bow Snipe, Branie Queue, Chevalier de Batture, Chorook, Crooked-winged Bird, Curracag, Grey Snipe, Gutter Snipe, Maubeche, Peep, Peet-weet, Peeweet, Pewit, Playero coleador, River Snipe, Sand Lark, Sand Peep, Sand Snipe, Saute-queue, Seesaw, Shneb, Snipe, Swee-swee, Teeter, Teeter Bird, Teeterer, Teeterer Snipe, Teeter Peep, Teeter Snipe, Teeter-tail, Teeter-tip, Tilt-up, Tip-up, Wagtail.

Modern Name: Wandering Tattler
Scientific Name: Heteroscelus incana
Folknames and Names: Alaskan Tattler, Rock Snipe, 'Ulili.
*native to Hawai'ian Islands

Modern Name: Willet
Scientific Name: Catoptrophorus semipalmatus
Folknames and Names: Bill-willie, Bill-willy, Chevalier, Clewie, Curlew, Duck Snipe, Eastern Willet, Goose Bird, Humility, Kill-cu, Laughing Jackass, Longlegs, Old Humility, Pied-wing Curlew, Pillo-wee, Pill-willet, Pill-will-willet, Pilly-willick, Playero Aliblanco, Pond Bird, Semipalmated Snipe, Snipe, Spanish Plover, Stone Curlew, Tattler, Tell-bill-willy, Tell-tale, Tinkasheer, Turn a Vire, Virette, Vire-vire, Twillick, Western Willet, White-wing, White-winged Curlew, Will, Will-willet.

Modern Name: Greater Yellowlegs
Scientific Name: Tringa melanoleuca
Folknames and Names: Ansary, Aunt Sarah, Big Cucu, Big Tell-tale, Big Yellow-leg, Big Yellow-legged Plover, Big Yellow-legs, Chevalier, Chevalier Aux Pattes Jaunes, Corbido, Cucu, Daddy-longlegs, Golden Plover, Grand Pluvier, Greater Tattler, Greater Tell-tale, Greater Yellow-shanks, Horse Yellowlegs, Humility, Klook-klook, Lansary, Long-legged Tattler, Longlegs, Nansary, Patte Jaune, Pied Jaune, Playero Guineilla Grande, Plover, Shneb, Snipe, Stone-bird, Stone Curlew, Stone-snipe, Tattler, Tell-tale, Tell-tale Godwit, Twillick, Winter, Winter Yellowlegs, Woodcock, Yellow-leg, Yellow-leg Plover,
Yellow-shank, Yellow-shank Sandpiper, Yellow-shins, Yelper.

Modern Name: Lesser Yellowlegs
Scientific Name: Tringa flavipes
Folknames and Names: Aunt Sary, Common Yellowlegs, Lesser Long-legged Tattler, Lesser Tell-tale, Lesser Yellowshanks, Little Stone-bird, Little Stone Snipe, Little Tell-tale, Little Yellow-leg, Little Yelper, Petit Pluvier, Playero Guineilla Pequena, Plover, Saunder, Shneb, Small Cucu, Small Snipe, Small Tattler, Small Yellowleg, Small Yelper, Snipe, Summer Yellowlegs, Tattler, Tell-tale, Twillick, Yellow-leg, Yellow-legs, Yellow-legged Plover,

Yellow-shanks Tattler.

Modern Name: Stilt Sandpiper
Scientific Name: Micropalama himantopus
Folknames and Names: Bastard Yellowlegs, Frost Snipe, Long-legged Sandpiper, Mongrel, Playero Patilargo.

Modern Name: Short-billed Dowitcher
Scientific Name: Limnodromus griseus
Folknames and Names: American Dowitcher, Becassine de Mer, Becassine Grise, Brown-back, Brownback Dowitcher, Brown Snipe, Chorlo Pico Largo, Driver, Dormeur, Eastern Dowitcher, Gray-back, Gray Snipe, Jacksnipe, Red-breasted Snipe, Robin Snipe, Spotrump, Sea Pigeon, Summer Grey-back.

Modern Name: Long-billed Dowitcher
Scientific Name: Limnodromus scolopaceus
Folknames and Names: Greater Gray-back, Greater Long-beak, Red-bellied Snipe, Red-breasted Snipe.

Modern Name: Surfbird
Scientific Name: Aphriza virgata
Folknames and Names: Plover-billed Turnstone, Rock Plover, Roc Snipe.

Modern Name: Ruddy Turnstone
Scientific Name: Arenaria interpres
Folknames and Names: Akekeke, Bead-bird, Bishop Plover, Brant-bird, Brown Bird, Calico-back, Calico Bird, Calico Jacket, Calico Plover, Caraquet Plover, Checkered Snipe, Chicken, Chicken-bird Turnstone, Chicken Plover, Chickling, Chuckatuck, Common Turnstone, Creddock, Fat-oxen, Horsefoot Snipe, Jinny, King-crab Bird, Pied Plover, Playero Turco, Red-legged Plover, Red-legs, Redshank, Rock-bird, Rock Plover, Stone-pecker, Streaked-back, Tourne-pierre, Whale Bird.
*native to Hawai'ian Islands (main islands)

Modern Name: Black Turnstone
Scientific Name: Arenaria melanocephala
Folknames and Names: Rock Plover, Rock Snipe.

Modern Name: Purple Sandpiper
Scientific Name: Calidris maritima
Folknames and Names: Big Beachy Bird, Rock-bird, Rock Plover, Rock Sandpiper, Rock Snipe, Rockweed Bird, Sand Peep, Winter Rock-bird, Winter Snipe.

Modern Name: Rock Sandpiper
Scientific Name: Calidris ptiloenemis

Folknames and Names: Aleutian Sandpiper, Pribilof Sandpiper.

Modern Name: Pectoral Sandpiper
Scientific Name: Calidris melanotos
Folknames and Names: Alouette, Alouette de Pres, Beachy Bird, Brown-back, Brownie, Chevalier, Cow Snipe, Fat-bird, Grass-bird, Grass Plover, Grass-snipe, Hay-bird, Kreeker, Krieker, Marsh Plover, Meadow Snipe, Playero Manchado, Short-neck, Squat Snipe, Squatter, Triddler.

Modern Name: Red Knot
Scientific Name: Calidris canutus
Folknames and Names: Alouettte, American Knot, Ash-colored Sandpiper, Beach Robin, Black-cap, Blue Plover, Buff-Breast, Buff-breasted Plover, Canute's Sandpiper, Coochee, Freckled Sandpiper, Gray-back, Grey-neck, Horsefoot Snipe, Knot, Maubeche, Maybird, Playero Gordo, Redbreast, Red-breasted Plover, Red-breasted Sandpiper, Red Sandpiper, Robin Breast, Robin Snipe, Silver-back, Silver Plover, Wahquoit, White-bellied Snipe, White Robin Snipe.

Modern Name: Ruff
Scientific Name: Philomachus pugnax
Folknames and Names: Combatiente.

Modern Name: Curlew Sandpiper
Scientific Name: Calidris ferruginea
Folknames and Names: Pigmy Curlew.

Modern Name: Dunlin
Scientific Name: Calidris alpina
Folknames and Names: American Dunlin, Black-bellied Sandpiper, Black-breast, Black-crop, Black-heart, Black-heart Plover, Brant-bird, Crooked-bill, Crooked-bill Snipe, Fall Snipe, Lead-back, Lead-bird, Little Black-breast, Ox-bird, Playero Espaldi-colorado, Red-back, Red-backed Dunlin, Red-backed Sandpiper, Simpleton, Snippet, Stib, Winter Snipe.

Modern Name: Sanderling
Scientific Name: Calidris alba
Folknames and Names: Alouette, Alouette de Mer, Beach Bird, Beach Plover, Beach Snipe, Beachy Bird, Bull Peep, Hunakai, Lake Plover, Mud Snipe, Playero Arenero, Ruddy Plover, Sand Snipe, Snippet, Surf Snipe, White Snipe, White Oxeye, White Snipe, Whitey, Whiting.
*native to Hawai'ian Islands

Modern Name: White-rumped Sandpiper
Scientific Name: Calidris fuscicollis

Folknames and Names: Alouette, Beachy Bird, Bonaparte's Sand-
piper, Bull Peep, Mud Snipe, Peep, Playero Rabadilla Blanca,
Sand Bird, Sand Snipe, Snippet, Schinz's Sandpiper.
Modern Name: Baird's Sandpiper
Scientific Name: Calidris bairdii
Folknames and Names: Grass-bird, Mud Snipe, Sand Snipe, Snip-
pet.

Modern Name: Least Sandpiper
Scientific Name: Calidris minutilla
Folknames and Names: Alouette, American Stint, Beachy Bird,
Little Sandpeep, Little Sandpiper, Maringouin, Mud-peep, Mud-
picker, Mud Snipe, Ox-eye, Peep, Petite Alouette, Playerito
Menudo, Sand-peep, Sand Snipe, Snippet, Stint, Wilson's Stint.

Modern Name: Semipalmated Sandpiper
Scientific Name: Calidris pusillus
Folknames and Names: Alouette, Alouette de Mer, Beach Bird,
Beachy Bird, Black-legged Peep, Little Peep, Mud Snipe, Peep,
Playero Gracioso, Sand Ox-eye, Sand-peep, Sand Snipe, Snippet,
Stint.

Modern Name: Western Sandpiper
Scientific Name: Calidris mauri
Folknames and Names: Mud Snipe, Peep, Playero Occidental,
Sand Snipe, Snippet.

Modern Name: American Woodcock
Scientific Name: Philohela minor
Folknames and Names: Becasse, Becasse de Nuit, Becasse des Bois,
Becassine, Big-eyes, Big-headed Snipe, Big Mud Snipe, Big Snipe,
Blind Snipe, Bog-bird, Bog-borer, Bogsucker, Cache-cache Rouge,
Cock, English Snipe, Grosa Brouna Shneb, Hookum Pake, Labora-
dor Twister, Mudhen, Mudsnipe, Night Partridge, Night Peck,
Pewee, Schneb, Siphon Snipe, Snipe, Snipe Owl, Timber-doodle,
Whistler, Whistling Red Snipe, Whistling Snipe, Woodcock, Wood
Hen, Wood Snipe.

Modern Name: Common Snipe
Scientific Name: Capella gallinago
Folknames and Names: Alewife Bird, Alouette, American Snipe,
Bescasina, Becassine, Bleater, Bog Snipe, Cache-cache, Cohoon
Bird, Common Snipe, Croman-loin, Dodger, Englishe Schneb, En-
glish Snipe, Field Snipe, Gutter Snipe, Jacksnipe, Little Snipe,
Long-bill Snipe, Marsh Snipe, Meadow Hen, Meadow Snipe, Naosg,
Plover, Puta-puta Bird, Shad Bird, Shad Spirit, Shneb, Snipe,
Snite, Squatting Snipe, Twillic, Wilson Snipe, Wilson's Snipe.

Phalarope (Subfamily Phalaropodinae)

Modern Name: Wilson's Phalarope
Scientific Name: Phalaropus tricolor
Folknames and Names: Falaropo De Wilson, Grunter, Summer Phalarope.

Modern Name: Red Phalarope
Scientific Name: Phalaropus fulicarius
Folknames and Names: Bank-bird, Bird, Brown Bank-bird, Flat-billed Phalarope, Gale Bird, Gray Bank-bird, Gray Phalarope, Ground Bird, Gulf Bird, Herring Bird, Jersey Goose, Mackeral Goose, Red Coot-footed Tringa, Red-footed Tringa, Sea Goose, Sea-snipe, Swimming Snipe, Whale-bird.

Modern Name: Northern Phalarope
Scientific Name: Phalaropus lobatus
Folknames and Names: Bank-bird, Bird, Gale-bird, Ground Bird, Grunter, Gulf Bird, Goose, Gulf Bird, Hyper-borean Phalarope, Mackeral, Mackeral Goose, Red-necked Phalarope, Sea Goose, Sea-snipe, Swimming Snipe, Web-footed Peep, Whale-bird, White Bank-bird.

Skuas, Gulls, Terns and Skimmers (Suborder Lari) Skuas, Gulls, Terns and Skimmers (Family Laridae)

Skuas and Jaegers (Subfamily Stercorariinae)

Modern Name: Parasitic Jaeger
Scientific Name: Stercorarius parasiticus
Folknames and Names: Arctic Hawk Gull, Arctic Skua, Aret, Black-toed Gull, Boatswain, Bo's'n, Bosun Bird, Dung Hunter, Gull-chaser, Jiddy Hawk, Man-o'-war, Marlingspike, Mason, Marlinspike, Richardson's Jaeger, Sea Hawk, Skait-bird, Skua, Teaser, Whiptail.

Modern Name: Pomarine Jaeger
Scientific Name: Stercorarius pomarinus
Folknames and Names: Aret, Black Marling Spike, Bo's'n, Bosun Bird, Gull-chaser, Gull Hunter, Jaeger Gull, Jiddy Hawk, Marlingspike, Marlinspike, Mason, Pagalo Pomarino, Pomarine Skua, Pomatorhine Skua, Sea Hen, Sea Robber, Skuar, Whip-tail.

Modern Name: Long-tailed Jaeger
Scientific Name: Stercorarius longicaudus
Folknames and Names: Arctic Jaeger, Aret, Bo's'n, Buffon's Jae-

ger, Gull-chaser, Gull-teaser, Long-tailed Skua, Man of war, Marlinspike, Marlinspike Bird, Mason, Sea Hen, Skua, Whip-tail.

Modern Name: Skua
Scientific Name: Catharacta skua
Folknames and Names: Bonxie, Gran' Goose, Great Skua, Keeask Gull, Pagalo Grande, Sea Hawk, Sea Hen, Skua Gull.

Gulls (Subfamily Larinae)

Modern Name: Ivory Gull
Scientific Name: Larus glaucoides
Folknames and Names: Duck Gull, Ice Bird, Ice Gull, Ice Partridge, Slob Gull, Snow Grouse, Snow-white Gull, White-winged Gull, Winter Gull.

Modern Name: Glaucous Gull
Scientific Name: Larus hyperboreus
Folknames and Names: Blue Gull, Burgomaster, Burgomaster Gull, Glauocous-winged Gull, Harbor Gull, Ice Gull, Large Ice Gull, Minister Gull, Owl Gull, White Minister, White-winged Gull, White Winter Gull.

Modern Name: Iceland Gull
Scientific Name: Larus glauocoides
Folknames and Names: White-winged Gull.

Modern Name: Glaucous-winged Gull
Scientific Name: Larus glaucescens
Folknames and Names: Sea Gull, Sea Mew.

Modern Name: Great Black-backed Gull
Scientific Name: Larus marinus
Folknames and Names: Black Back, Black-backed Gull, Black Minister, Cobb, Coffin-carrier, English Gull, Farmer Gull, Gaviota Major Espaldinegra, Goeland Anglais, Goeland Noir, Great Grey Gull, Old Saddler, Old Settler, Porte-cercueil, Saddleback, Saddleback Gull, Saddler, Saddler Gull, Screecher, Wagell.

Modern Name: Western Gull
Scientific Name: Larus occidentalis
Folknames and Names: -

Modern Name: Herring Gull
Scientific Name: Larus argentatus
Folknames and Names: Big White Gull, Blue Gull, Bluey, Common Gull, Common Seagull, Faollin, Farspag, Gaviota Argentus, Goe-

land, Goeland de Fleuve, Grey Gull, Harbor Gull, Herring Gull, Lake Gull, Lookabout, Mackerel Gull, Mauve, Mouette, Sea Gull, Sea Mew, Winter Gull.

Modern Name: California Gull
Scientific Name: Larus californicus
Folknames and Names: Blue Gull, Sea Gull.

Modern Name: Ring-billed Gull
Scientific Name: Larus delawarensis
Folknames and Names: Common Gull, Gaviota Piquianillada, Goeland, Lake Gull, Pond Gull, Sea Gull, Squeaky Gull, Squeezy Gull.

Modern Name: Mew Gull
Scientific Name: Larus canus
Folknames and Names: Common Gull, Sea Mew, Short-billed Gull.

Modern Name: Heermann's Gull
Scientific Name: Larus heermanni
Folknames and Names: White-headed Gull.

Modern Name: Black-legged Kittiwake
Scientific Name: Rissa tridactyla
Folknames and Names: Annett, Atlantic Kittiwake, Coddy Moddy, Common Kittiwake, Fall Gull, Frost-bird, Frost Gull, Haddock Gull, Jack Gull, Kittiwake, Kittiwake Gull, Lady, Lady Bird, Mackerel Gull, Mauve, Mouette, Meterick, Pick-me-up, Pinny Owl, Pinyole, Snow Gull, Tarrock, Tickle-lace, Tickler, Winter Gull.

Modern Name: Red-legged Kittiwake
Scientific Name: Rissa brevirostris
Folknames and Names: -

Modern Name: Ross' Gull
Scientific Name: Rhodostethia rosea
Folknames and Names: Cuneate-tailed Gull, Ross' Rosy Gull, Rosy Gull, Wedge-tailed Gull.

Modern Name: Laughing Gull
Scientific Name: Larus atricilla
Folknames and Names: Black-headed Gull, Booby, Gallego Comun, Galleguito, Gaviota Boba, Gaviota Cabecinegra, Gaviota Gallega, Goeland Charogne, Gullie, Gullie, Laughing Bird, Mangui, Mauve a Tete Noire, Sea Gull, Zo-zo de Mer.

Modern Name: Franklin's Gull
Scientific Name: Larus pipixcan
Folknames and Names: Black-headed Gull, Franklin's Rosy Gull,

Goeland, Grasshopper Gull, Prairie Gull, Prairie Pigeon, Rosette, Sea Gull.

Modern Name: Bonaparte's Gull
Scientific Name: Larus philadelphia
Folknames and Names: Bonaparte's Rosy Gull, Blackhead, Black-headed Gull, Goeland, Mackerel Gull, Mauve, Sea Pigeon.

Modern Name: Sabine's Gull
Scientific Name: Xema sabini
Folknames and Names: Hawk-tailed Gull, Fork-tailed Gull.

Modern Name: Black-headed Gull
Scientific Name: Larus ridibundus
Folknames and Names: Gaviota Cabecinegra.

Modern Name: Little Gull
Scientific Name: Larus minutus
Folknames and Names: -

Terns (Subfamily Sterninae)

Modern Name: Least Tern
Scientific Name: Sterna albifrons
Folknames and Names: Egg Bird, Gaviota Chica, Gaviota Pequena, Gaviotica, Golondrina de Mar, Kill-'em-Polly, Killing-peter, Little Tern, Little Striker, Minute Tern, Oiseau Fou, Peterman, Petite Mauve, Pigeon de la Mer, Sea Swallow, Silver Ternlet, Silvery Tern, Ternlet, Zo-zo su Mer.

Modern Name: Arctic Tern
Scientific Name: Sterna paradisaea
Folknames and Names: Blackhead, Common Tern, Crimson-billed Tern, Hirondelle de Mer, Greenland Swallow, Long-tailed Tern, Mackerel, Paradise Tern, Paytrick, Pictar, Pike's Tern, Portland Tern, Rittick, Sea Pigeon, Sea Swallow, Short-footed Tern, Stearn, Steering, Steering Gull.

Modern Name: Common Tern
Scientific Name: Sterna hirundo
Folknames and Names: Bass Gull, Esterlet, Egg Bird, Gannett, Gaviota, Gaviota Comun, Gullie, Gull Pigeon, High Diver, Hirondelle de Mer, Lake Erie Gull, Little Gull, Mackerel Gull, Palometa, Paytrick, Petite Mauve, Pickatiere, Pictar, Pietrie, Rape, Redshank, Sea Swallow, Stearin, Striker, Summer Gull, Wilson's Tern.

Modern Name: Roseate Tern

Scientific Name: Sterna dougallii
Folknames and Names: Carite, David, Davie, Gaviota, Graceful Tern, Gullie, Mackerel Gull, Mauve Blanche, McDougall's Tern, Oiseau Fou, Palometa, Petite Mauve, Pigeon de la Mer, Sea Gull.

Modern Name: Forster's Tern
Scientific Name: Sterna forsteri
Folknames and Names: Davie, Esterlette, Gaviota de Forster, Gullie, Havell's Tern, High Diver, Marsh Tern, Pigeon de Mer, Queue-a-ciseau, Sea Swallow.

Modern Name: Sandwich Tern
Scientific Name: Thalasseus sandvicensis
Folknames and Names: Boys' Tern, Cabot's Tern, Cabot Tern, Ducal Tern, Egg Bird, Gaviota de Pico Agudo, Gaviota Piquiaguda, Gullie, Kentish Tern, Sea Swallow.

Modern Name: Gull-billed Tern
Scientific Name: Gelochelidon nilotica
Folknames and Names: Anglican Tern, Egg Bird, Egyptian Tern, Gaviota de Pico Corto, Gaviota Piquigorda, Gullie, Marsh Tern, Nile Tern, Nuttall's Tern, Oiseau Fou, Pigeon de la Mer.

Modern Name: Elegant Tern
Scientific Name: Thalasseus elegans
Folknames and Names: -

Modern Name: Royal Tern
Scientific Name: Thalasseus maximus
Folknames and Names: Big Striker, Cayenne Tern, Egg Bird, Foquette, Gabby. Gannet, Gannet Striker, Gaviota Real, Goeland a Bec Rouge, Gullie, Mauve, Oiseau Fou, Pigeon de la Mar, Redbill, Sprat, Sprat Bird.

Modern Name: Caspian Tern
Scientific Name: Hydroprogne caspia
Folknames and Names: Caspian Sea Tern, Gannet Striker, Gaviota de Capia, Goeland a Bec Rouge, Goeland Espagnol, Grand Esterlette, Imperial Tern, Mackerel Gull, Redbill, Sea Swallow.

Modern Name: Black Tern
Scientific Name: Chlidonias niger
Folknames and Names: American Black Tern, Black Gannett, Black Gull, Black Sea Swallow, Gaviota Ceniza, Gaviota Negra, Hirondelle de Mer, Marsh Tern, Sea Pigeon, Semipalmated Tern, Short-tailed Tern, Slough Pigeon, Surinam Tern.

Modern Name: Sooty Tern
Scientific Name: Sterna fuscata

Folknames and Names: Booby, Booby Bird, Bubi, Egg Bird, Ewa 'ewa, Gaviota Monja, Gaviota Oscura, Hurricane Bird, Oiseau Fou, Pigeon de Mer, Touaou, Wide-awake.
*native to Hawai'ian Islands (O'ahu, NW islands)

Modern Name: Aleutian Tern
Scientific Name: Sterna aleutica
Folknames and Names: -

Modern Name: Bridled Tern
Scientific Name: Sterna anaesthetus
Folknames and Names: Booby, Booby Bird, Bubi, Dongue, Egg Bird, Gaviota, Gaviota Monja, Gaviota Oscura, Oiseau Fou, Touaou.

Modern Name: Noddy Tern
Scientific Name: Anous stolidus
Folknames and Names: Booby Blackbird, Brown Noddy, Cervera, Egg Bird, Lark.

Modern Name: Black Noddy Tern
Scientific Name: Anous tenuirostris
Folknames and Names: Black Noddy.

Modern Name: Gray-backed Tern
Scientific Name: Sterna lunata
Folknames and Names: Pakalakala.
*native to Hawai'ian Islands (O'ahu, NW islands)

Modern Name: Brown Noddy
Scientific Name: Anous stolidus
Folknames and Names: Black Bird, Booby, Bubi, Cervera, Charles, Egg Bird, Gaviota Boba, Lark, Minime, Moine, Noio ko-ha, Severo, Zo-zo du Mer.
*native to Hawai'ian Islands (O'ahu, NW islands)

Modern Name: Black Noddy
Scientific Name: Anous minutus
Folknames and Names: Noio.
*native to Hawai'ian Islands (main islands, NW islands)

Modern Name: Blue-gray Noddy
Scientific Name: Procelsterna cerulea
Folknames and Names: Gray Ternlet.
*native to Hawai'ian Islands (NW islands)

Modern Name: White Tern
Scientific Name: Gygis alba
Folknames and Names: Manu-o-ku, White Noddy, Fairy Tern.

*native to Hawai'ian Islands (O'ahu, NW islands)

Skimmers (Subfamily Rynchopinae)

Modern Name: Black Skimmer
Scientific Name: Rynchops niger
Folknames and Names: Bec-a-ciseaux, Bec-a-lancet-de-mer,
Black Skimmer Gull, Cut-water, Flood Gull, Knifebill, Pico de
Tijera, Razor-bill, Scissorbill, Sea-dog, Shearwater, Storm Gull.

Auks and Allies (Suborder Alcae)
Auks, Murres and Puffins (Family Alcidae)

Modern Name: Razorbill
Scientific Name: Alca torda
Folknames and Names: Auk, Baccaloo, Backalew Bird, Gode, Hawk-
billed Murre, Ice Bird, Little Diver, Murre, Noddy, Penguin,
Pingouin, Pinwing, Razor-billed Auk, Sea-crow, Tinker, Turre,
York Penguin.

Modern Name: Common Murre
Scientific Name: Uria aalge
Folknames and Names: Atlantic Murre, Backaloo Bird, California
Egg Bird, California Murre, California Guillemot, Crow-billed
Murre, Farallon Bird, Foolish Guillemot, Frowl, Gode, Gudd,
Guillem, Guillemot, Gwilym, Kiddaw, Lavy, Loom, Marmette, Mar-
rock, Murre, Noddy, Scribe, Scout, Scuttock, Sea Pigeon, Skiddaw,
Southern Turr, Strany, Thin-billed Murre, Tinker, Tinkershire,
Turr, Willock.

Modern Name: Thick-billed Murre
Scientific Name: Uria lomvia
Folknames and Names: Baccelieu Bird, Brunnich's Murre, Brun-
nich's Guillemot, Crowbill, Egg Bird, Frank's Guillemot, Murre,
Noddy, Northern Turr, Pallas' Murre, Polar Guillemot, Thick-
billed Guillemot, Turr.

Modern Name: Dovekie
Scientific Name: Alle alle
Folknames and Names: Alle, Bonhomme, Bull, Bull Bird, Green-
land Dove, Ice Bird, John Bull, Knotty, Little Auk, Little Bull,
Little Noddy, Little Turre, Nunchie, Petit Bonhomme, Petit Bon-
homme de Misere, Petit Gode, Pigeon Diver, Pine Knot, Rotch, Sea
Dove.

Modern Name: Black Guillemot
Scientific Name: Cepphus grylle
Folknames and Names: Calman Muir, Dovekie, Dovekey, Geylle,

Greenland Dove, Mandt's Guillemot, Murre, Pigeon, Pigeon de Mer, Scapular Guillemot, Sea Pigeon, Sea Widgeon, Shore Duck, Spotted Greenland Dove, Turr, Tysty, Tystie, White Guillemot, White-winged Guillemot, Widgeon, Wild Pigeon.

Modern Name: Pigeon Guillemot
Scientific Name: Cepphus columba
Folknames and Names: Sea Pigeon, White Winged Diver.

Modern Name: Common Puffin
Scientific Name: Fratercula artica
Folknames and Names: Atlantic Puffin, Baccalieu Bird, Balgan Beiceach, Bottle-nose, Coulterner, Fachach, Greenland Parrot, Hatchet-bill, Hatchet-face, Laborador Auk, Laborador Parrot, Large-billed Puffin, Parakeet, Parrot, Parrot-bill Murr, Perro-quet, Perroquet de Mer, Pope, Puffin, Puffin Auk, Sea Parrot, Tammy Norie, Tammy Nory, Tinker.

Modern Name: Horned Puffin
Scientific Name: Fratercula corniculata
Folknames and Names: Old Man of the Sea, Sea Parrot, Toporkie.

Modern Name: Tufted Puffin
Scientific Name: Lunda cirrhata
Folknames and Names: Ikey, Jew Duck, Old Man of the Sea, Parrot-bill, Sea Parrot.

Modern Name: Rhinoceros Auklet
Scientific Name: Cerorhinca monocerata
Folknames and Names: Horn-bill Auk, Unicorn Auk.

Modern Name: Crested Auklet
Scientific Name: Aethia cristatella
Folknames and Names: Crested Stariki, Dusky Auklet, Kanooska, Sea Quail, Snub-nosed Auk, Snub-nosed Auklet.

Modern Name: Whiskered Auklet
Scientific Name: Aethia pygmaea
Folknames and Names: Red-nosed Auk, Sea Quail, Whiskered Auk.

Modern Name: Cassin's Auklet
Scientific Name: Ptychoramphus aleuticus
Folknames and Names: Aleutian Auk, Sea Quail, Wrinkle-nosed Auk.

Modern Name: Least Auklet
Scientific Name: Aethia pusilla
Folknames and Names: Choochkie, Knob-billed Auklet, Knob-

nosed Auklet, Minute Auklet.

Modern Name: Marbled Murrelet
Scientific Name: Brachyramphus marmoratus
Folknames and Names: Dabchick, Fog Bird, Long-billed Murrelet,
Sea Chick.

Modern Name: Kittlitz's Murrelet
Scientific Name: Brachyramphus brevirostris
Folknames and Names: Short-billed Murrelet.

Modern Name: Xantus' Murrelet
Scientific Name: Endomychura hypoleuca
Folknames and Names: -

Modern Name: Ancient Murrelet
Scientific Name: Synthliboramphus antiquus
Folknames and Names: Black-throated Guillemot, Black-throated
Murrelet, Gray-headed Murrelet, Old Man.

Modern Name: Parakeet Auklet
Scientific Name: Cyclorrhynchus psittacula
Folknames and Names: Baillie Brushkie, Paroquet Auklet, Pug-
nosed Auklet.

Sandgrouse, Pigeons and Doves (Order Columbi-formes)
Sandgrouse: (Suborder Pterocletes)
Sandgrouse (Family Pteroclididae)

Modern Name: Chestnut-sided Sandgrouse
Scientific Name: Pterocles exustus
Folknames and Names: -
*introduced into Hawai'ian Islands (Hawai'i)

Pigeons and Doves: (Suborder Columbae)
Pigeons and Doves: (Family Columbidae)

Modern Name: Rock Dove
Scientific Name: Columba livia
Folknames and Names: Blue Rock, Blue Rock Pigeon, Carrier Pi-
geon, Common Pigeon, Coo, Domestic Pigeon, Dove, Feral Pigeon,
Homing Pigeon, Paloma Casera, Pigeon, Rock Pigeon, Squab Pi-
geon, Street Pigeon, Wild Pigeon.
*introduced into the Hawai'ian Islands (Hawai'i, Kaua'i, Lana'i,
Maui, Moloka'i, O'ahu).

Modern Name: Band-tailed Pigeon

Scientific Name: Columba fasciata
Folknames and Names: Bandtail, Passenger Pigeon, White-collared Pigeon, Wild Pigeon, Wood Pigeon.

Modern Name: White-winged Dove
Scientific Name: Zenaida asiatica
Folknames and Names: Cactus Pigeon, Lapwing, Paloma Aliblanca, Singing Dove, Sonora Dove, Sonoran Dove, Tortola Aliblanca, White-wing, White-wing Dove.

Modern Name: Mourning Dove
Scientific Name: Zenaidura macroura
Folknames and Names: Carolina Dove, Colombe Sauvage, Dord'l Doub, Dove, Fifi, Long-tail Pea Dove, Moaning Dove, Paloma, Paloma Huilota, Pigeon Sauvage, Rabiche, Tortola, Tortola Rabilarga, Tourte, Tourterelle, Tourterelle Queue-fine, Turtle Dove, Wild Dove, Wild Pigeon, Wood Dove, Wood Pigeon.
*introduced into the Hawai'ian Islands (Hawai'i).

Modern Name: White-crowned Pigeon
Scientific Name: Columba leucocephala
Folknames and Names: Bald-pate, Blue Pigeon, White-head, Paloma Cabeciblanca, Paloma Casco Blanco, Toreaza Cabeciblanca, Ramier Tete-blanca.
Modern Name: Red-billed Pigeon
Scientific Name: Columba flavirostris
Folknames and Names: -

Modern Name: Spotted Dove
Scientific Name: Streptopelia chinensis
Folknames and Names: Chinese Dove, Chinese Spotted Dove, Lace necked Dove, Tortola Moteada.
*introduced into the Hawai'ian Islands (Hawai'i, Kaua'i, Lana'i, Maui, Moloka'i, O'ahu)

Modern Name: Zebra Dove
Scientific Name: Geopelia striata
Folknames and Names: Barred Dove.
*introduced into the Hawai'ian Islands (Hawai'i, Kaua'i, Lana'i, Maui, Moloka'i, O'ahu)

Modern Name: Ringed Turtle Dove
Scientific Name: Streptopelia risoria
Folknames and Names: Barbary Dove, Barble Dove, Domestic Ring Dove, Paloma Collarina, Tortola Collarina.

Modern Name: Ground Dove
Scientific Name: Columbina passerina
Folknames and Names: Duppy Bird, Little Dove, Moaning Dove,

Mourning Dove, Rolita, Tobacco Bird, Walking Dove.

Modern Name: Inca Dove
Scientific Name: Scardafella inca
Folknames and Names: Long-tailed Dove, Scaled Dove, Scaly Dove.,
Tortola Colilarga.

Modern Name: White-fronted Dove
Scientific Name: Leptotila verreauxi
Folknames and Names: Wood Pigeon.

Parrots and Allies (Order Psittaciformes)
Lories, Parakeets, Macaws and Parrots
(Family Psittacidae)

Modern Name: Budgerigar
Scientific Name: Melopsittacus undulatus
Folknames and Names: Budgerygah, Budgie, Grass Parakeet, Parakeet, Periquito De Australia, Shell Parakeet.

Modern Name: Rose-ringed Parakeet
Scientific Name: Psittacula krameri
Folknames and Names: Ring-necked Parakeet.
*Introduced into Hawai'i (Kaua'i, O'ahu, Hawai'i and Maui).

Modern Name: Monk Parakeet
Scientific Name: Myiopsitta monachus
Folknames and Names: Gray-breasted Parakeet, Gray-breasted
Parrot, Gray-headed Parakeet, Green Monk Parakeet, Monk, Periquito Monje, Quaker Conure, Quaker Parakeet.

Modern Name: Thick-billed Parrot
Scientific Name: Rhynchopsitta pachyrhyncha
Folknames and Names: -

Modern Name: Canary-winged Parakeet
Scientific Name: Brotogeris versicolurus
Folknames and Names: -

Modern Name: Red-crowned Parrot
Scientific Name: Amazona viridigenalis
Folknames and Names: Ootorra Coronirroja, Green-checked Amazon.
*Introduced into Hawai'i (O'ahu).

Modern Name: Lilac-crowned Parrot
Scientific Name: Amazona finschi
Folknames and Names: -

Modern Name: Yellow-headed Parrot
Scientific Name: Amazona oratrix
Folknames and Names: -

Cuckoos and Allies (Order Cuculiformes)
Cuckoos (Family Cuculidae)

New World Cuckoos (Subfamily Coccyzinae)

Modern Name: Mangrove Cuckoo
Scientific Name: Coccyzus minor
Folknames and Names: Arrierito, Arriero Chico, Bahama Mangrove Cuckoo, Black-eared Cuckoo, Boba, Carga Agua, Cat Bird, Coffin Bird, Coucon Manioe, Cowbird, Dumb Bird, Four o'Clock Bird, Gangan, Gogo, Guacaira, Mani-coco, May Bird, Maynard's Cuckoo, Pajaro Bobo, Pajaro Bobo Menor, Petit Tacot, Primavera, Rain Bird, Rain Crow, Rain Dove.

Modern Name: Yellow-billed Cuckoo
Scientific Name: Coccyzus americanus
Folknames and Names: Arrierito, Arriero Chico, Boba, California Cuckoo, Carga Agua, Chow-chow, Coffin Bird, Coucon Manioe, Coucou, Cow Bird, Cuckoo, Four o'Clock Bird, Gangan, Grand Queue, Guacaira, Gukuk, Kow-kow, Longue Queue, Mani-coco, May Bird, Pajaro Bobo, Pajaro Bobo Piquiamarillo, Petit Tacot, Primavera, Rain Bird, Rain Crow, Rain Dove, Raya Fogel, Storm Crow, Western Cuckoo, Wild Pigeon.

Modern Name: Black-billed Cuckoo
Scientific Name: Coccyzus erythrophthalmus
Folknames and Names: Cou-cou, Cow Bird, Grand Queue, Gukuk, Kow-kow, Longue Queue, Poule D'eau, Rain Bird, Rain Crow, Rain Dove, Raya Fogel.

Modern Name: Smooth-billed Ani
Scientific Name: Crotophaga ani
Folknames and Names: Ani, Bilbitin, Black Daw, Black Parakeet, Black Parrot, Black Witch, Bouts-Tabac, Chapman Bird, Corbeau, Cuban Parrot, Death-bird, Judio, Juif, Garrapatero, Long-tailed Crow, Merle Corbeau, Old Arnold, Old Slut, Parrot Blackbird, Savanna Blackbird, Tick Bird, Voodoo Bird.

Modern Name: Groove-billed Ani
Scientific Name: Crotophaga sulcirostris
Folknames and Names: Tick Bird, Black Witch, Jew Bird.

Modern Name: Roadrunner

Scientific Name: Geococcyx californianus
Folknames and Names: Chaparral Cock, Churca, Correo del Camino, Correcaminos Norteno, Cock of the Desert, Greater Roadrunner, Ground Cuckoo, Lizard Bird, Paisano, Snake Killer, Correcamino.

Owls (Order Strigiformes)
Barn-Owls (Family Tytonidae)

Modern Name: Common Barn Owl
Scientific Name: Tyto alba
Folknames and Names: American Barn Owl, Barn Owl, Chat-huant, Church Owl, Death Bird, Death Owl, Eil, Frezaic, Golden Owl, Grass Owl, Hibou Paille, Jumbie Bird, Lechuza, Monkey-faced Owl, Monkey-face Owl, Monkey-faced Owl, Monkey Owl, Night Owl, Owl, Patoo, Rat Owl, Screech Owl, Scritch Owl, Sheier Eil, Steeple Owl, Stone Owl, Straw Owl, White Owl, Tawny Owl.
*Introduced to the Hawai'ian Islands (Hawai'i, Kaua'i, Lana'i, Maui, Moloka'i, O'ahu)

Typical Owls (Family Strigidae)

Modern Name: Eastern Screech Owl
Scientific Name: Otus asio
Folknames and Names: Aiken's Screech Owl, Arizona Screech Owl, Barn Owl, Bendire's Screech Owl, California Coast Screech Owl, California Screech Owl, Cat Owl, Chat Haut, Chouette, Common Screech Owl, Death Owl, Eil, Florida Screech Owl, Glana Eil, Gray Owl, Hoot Owl, Little Cat Owl, Little Dukelet, Little Gray Owl, Little Horned Owl, Little Owl, McCally's Screech Owl, McFarlane's Screech Owl, Mexican Screech Owl, Mottled Owl, Nocht Eil, Red Owl, Rocky Mountain Screech Owl, Screech Owl, Scritch Owl, Shivering Owl, Shta Keitzel, Squinch Owl, Texas Screech Owl, Western Screech Owl, Whickering Owl, Whinneying Owl.

Modern Name: Western Screech Owl
Scientific Name: Otus kennicotti
Folknames and Names: Kennicott's Screech Owl.

Modern Name: Great Horned Owl
Scientific Name: Bubo virginanus
Folknames and Names: Arctic Horned Owl, Big Hoot Owl, Big Owl, Buho Cornado Americano, Cailleach-oidhche, Cat Owl, Cave-duc, Chaoin, Chat-huant, Chicken Owl, Common Owl, Duc, Dusty Horned Owl, Dwarf Horned Owl, Eagle Owl, Eared Owl, Eil, Grand Duck, Grand Hibou, Grosa Eil, Guibou, Harn Aowl, Hibou, Hibou Corne, Hoot Owl, Horn Coot, Horned Owl, Horn Owl, Labrador Horned Owl, King Owl, Meat Owl, Nocht Eil, Pacific Horned Owl,

Pallid Horned Owl, Saint Michael Horned Owl, Screech Owl, Tiger of the Air, Virginia Horned Owl, Virginia Owl, Western Horned Owl, White Owl.

Modern Name: Long-eared Owl
Scientific Name: Asio otus
Folknames and Names: American Long-eared Owl, Cat Owl, Cedar Owl, Coulee Owl, Eil, Horned Owl, Lesser Horned Owl, Little Horned Owl, Nocht Eil, Prairie Owl, Pussy Owl, Screech Owl, Wilson's Owl.

Modern Name: Short-eared Owl
Scientific Name: Asio flammeus
Folknames and Names: Bog Owl, Buho, Carabo, Cat Aowl, Cat Owl, Chat-haunt, Eil, Evening Owl, Flat-faced Owl, Hawk Owl, Leuhuza de Sabana, Marsh Owl, Mouse-hawk, Mucaro De Sabana, Mucaro Real, Nocht Eil, Prairie Owl, Pueo, Swamp Owl.
*Native to the Hawai'ian Islands (Hawai'i, Kaua'i, Lana'i, Maui, Moloka'i, O'ahu)

Modern Name: Snowy Owl
Scientific Name: Nyctea scandiaca
Folknames and Names: Arctic Owl, Ermine Owl, Great White Owl, Harfang, Hibou Blanc, Northern Owl, Snow Owl, Wapachthu, White Owl.

Modern Name: Barred Owl
Scientific Name: Strix varia
Folknames and Names: Black-eyed Owl, Bottom Owl, Chouette du Canada, Combachag, Crazy Owl, Eight Hooter, Eil, Grey Owl, Hibou a Grosse Tete, Hoot Owl, Laughing Owl, Mouse Owl, Nocht Eil, Old-folks Owl, Rain Owl, Round-headed Owl, Screech Owl, Southern Barred Owl, Swamp Owl, Wool Owl.

Modern Name: Spotted Owl
Scientific Name: Strix occidentalis
Folknames and Names: Brown-eyed Owl, Northern Spotted Owl, Western Barred Owl, Xantus's Owl, Hoot Owl, Wood Owl.

Modern Name: Great Gray Owl
Scientific Name: Strix nebulosa
Folknames and Names: Gray Owl, Speckled Owl, Spectral Owl, Spruce Owl.

Modern Name: Northern Hawk Owl
Scientific Name: Surnia ulula
Folknames and Names: American Hawk Owl, Canadian Owl, Chouette, Day Owl, Hawk Owl, Hibou, Hudsonian Owl, Toot-aowl, Tooting Owl.

Modern Name: Burrowing Owl
Scientific Name: Athene cunicularia
Folknames and Names: Badger-hole Owl, Billy Owl, Cuckoo Bird, Coucou, Coucouterre, Cucu, Florida Burrowing Owl, Ground Owl, Howdy Owl, Long-legged Owl, Prairie Dog Owl, Prairie Owl.

Modern Name: Boreal Owl
Scientific Name: Aegolius funereus
Folknames and Names: American Sparrow Owl, Arctic Saw-whet Owl, Barn Owl, Little Owl, Partridge-haw, Richardson's Owl, Sparrow Owl, Tengmalm's Owl.

Modern Name: Northern Saw-whet Owl
Scientific Name: Aegolius acadicus
Folknames and Names: Acadian Owl, Barn Owl, Blind Owl, Cop Owl, Kirtland's Owl, Limard, Little Owl, Pygmy Owl, Saw-filer, Saw-whet, Saw-whet Owl, Sawyer, Small Owl, Sparrow Owl, Tooting Owl, Whet-saw, White-fronted Owl.

Modern Name: Whiskered Owl
Scientific Name: Otus trichopsis
Folknames and Names: Spotted Screech Owl.

Modern Name: Flammulated Owl
Scientific Name: Otus flammeolus
Folknames and Names: Flammulated Screech Owl.

Modern Name: Northern Pygmy-owl
Scientific Name: Glaucidium gnoma
Folknames and Names: Pygmy-owl, Gnome Owl.

Modern Name: Elf Owl
Scientific Name: Micrathene whitneyi
Folknames and Names: Whitney's Owl.

Modern Name: Ferruginous Owl
Scientific Name: Glaucidium brasilianum
Folknames and Names: Ferruginous Pygmy Owl.

Goatsuckers, Oilbirds and Allies (Order Caprimulgilformes)
Goatsuckers (Family Caprimulgidae)

Nighthawks (Subfamily Chordeilinae)

Modern Name: Common Night Hawk

150

Scientific Name: Chordeiles minor
Folknames and Names: Booming Nighthawk, Booming Swallow, Bull-bat, Burnt-land Bird, Capacho, Chouette, Crapaud Volant, Engoulevent, Epervier de Nuit, Furze, Furzet, Gaspayo, Gie-me-me-bit, Goatsucker, Goatsucker of Carolina, Hawk, Killydadick, Long-winged Goatsucker, Mangeur Maringouins, Mange-maringouin, Mosquito Bird, Mosquito Catcher, Mosquito Hawk, Moth Hawk, Nighthawk, Night-jar, Peut-on-voir, Piramidig, Pisk, Pork'n'Beans, Querequeque, Querequeque Migratorio, Querequete, Seabhag Oidche, Swooper, Wib'rwil, Wib'rewil, Will-o'-the-Wisp.

Modern Name: Lesser Night Hawk
Scientific Name: Chordeiles acutipennis
Folknames and Names: Texan Nighthawk, Texas Nighthawk, Trilling Nighthawk.

Nightjars (Subfamily Caprimulginae)

Modern Name: Pauraque
Scientific Name: Nyctidromus albicollis
Folknames and Names: Merrill's Pauraque.

Modern Name: Chuck-will's Widow
Scientific Name: Caprimulgus carolinensis
Folknames and Names: Chick-a-willa, Chip-fell-out-of-a-oak, Chuck, Dutch Whip-poor Will, Guabairo Mayor, Manguer Maringouins, Mosquito Hawk, Nightjar, Spanish Whip-poor-will, The Great Bat.

Modern Name: Whip-poor-will
Scientific Name: Caprimulgus vociferus
Folknames and Names: Bois-pourri, Eastern Whip-poor-will, Engoulevent, Guabairo, Guabairo Chico, Mangeur Maringouins, Mimic, Mosquito Hawk, Nightjar, Stephen's Wib'rwil, Whip-her-well.

Modern Name: Poor-will
Scientific Name: Phalaenoptilus nuttallii
Folknames and Names: Common Poor-will, Dusky Poor-will, Northern Poor-will, Nuttall's Poor-will.

Swifts and Hummingbirds (Order Apodiformes)
Swifts (Family Apodidae)

Cypseloidine Swifts (Subfamily Sypseloidinae)

Modern Name: Black Swift
Scientific Name: Cypseloides niger
Folknames and Names: Black Cloud Swift, Black Swallow, Chique-
sol, Cloud Bird, Gros Martinet Noir, Hirondelle de Montagne,
Northern Black Swift, Oiseau de la Pluie, Rainbird, Swallow,
Vencejo, Vencejo Negro.

Modern Name: Chimney Swift
Scientific Name: Chaetura pelagica
Folknames and Names: American Swift, Bocanier, Chimney Bat,
Chimney-bird, Chimney Swallow, Chimney Sweep, Chimney-
sweep Swallow, Glohlan-gaoith, Hirondelle des Cheminee, Marti-
net, Martinet des Cheminees, Ramoneur, Ramono, Roos Shwolm,
Shornshte Shwolb, Swallow.

Modern Name: Vaux's Swift
Scientific Name: Chaetura vauxi
Folknames and Names: Chimney Swallow.

Modern Name: White-throated Swift
Scientific Name: Aeronautes saxatalis
Folknames and Names: -

Hummingbirds (Family Trochilidae)

Modern Name: Ruby-throated Hummingbird
Scientific Name: Archilochus colubris
Folknames and Names: Common Hummingbird, Colibri, Draund-
eun, Fly, Honey Bird, Honey-sucker, Hummer, Hummingbird, Le
Colibri, Mange-maringouins, Oiseau Mouche, Ruby-throat,
Shnaffag'le, Shnarrfagle, Suceur de Fleur.

Modern Name: Broad-tailed Hummingbird
Scientific Name: Selasphorus platycercus
Folknames and Names: Broad-tailed Hummer.

Modern Name: Calliope Hummingbird
Scientific Name: Stellula calliope
Folknames and Names: -

Modern Name: Anna's Hummingbird
Scientific Name: Calypte anna
Folknames and Names: Anna's Hummer.

Modern Name: Black-chinned Hummingbird
Scientific Name: Archilochus alexandri

Folknames and Names: Black-chin, Black-chinned Hummer, Colibri Gorjinegro.

Modern Name: Costa's Hummingbird
Scientific Name: Calypte costae
Folknames and Names: -

Modern Name: Rufous Hummingbird
Scientific Name: Selasphorus rufus
Folknames and Names: -

Modern Name: Allen's Hummingbird
Scientific Name: Selasphorus sasin
Folknames and Names: -

Modern Name: Lucifer Hummingbird
Scientific Name: Calothrax lucifer
Folknames and Names: -

Modern Name: Rivoli's Hummingbird
Scientific Name: Eugenes fulgens
Folknames and Names: Magnificent Hummingbird, Refulgent Hummingbird.

Modern Name: Blue-throated Hummingbird
Scientific Name: Lamporanis clemenciae
Folknames and Names: Blue-throated Casique, Blue-throated Hummer.

Modern Name: Violet-throated Hummingbird
Scientific Name: Amazilia verticalis
Folknames and Names: Salvin's Hummingbird, Violet-crowned Hummingbird.

Modern Name: Buff-bellied Hummingbird
Scientific Name: Amazilia yucatanensis
Folknames and Names: Fawn-breasted Hummingbird, Yucatan Hummingbird.

Modern Name: Broad-billed Hummingbird
Scientific Name: Cynanthus latirostris
Folknames and Names: -

Modern Name: White-eared Hummingbird
Scientific Name: Hylocharis leucotis
Folknames and Names: -

Trogons (Order Trogoniformes)
Trogons (Family Trogonidae)

Modern Name: Elegant Trogon
Scientific Name: Trogon elegans
Folknames and Names: Coppery-tailed Trogon.

Kingfishers, Rollers, Hornbills and Allies(Order Corachiiformes)
Kingfishers (Family Alcedinidae)

Modern Name: Belted Kingfisher
Scientific Name: Ceryle alcyon
Folknames and Names: Blue Diver, Cruidein, Fishroyer, Fly-up-the-creek, Halcyon, Kingfisher, Kingfisherman, Lazy-bird Halcyon, Martin Pecheur, Martin Pescador, Martin Pescador Norteno, Martin Plongeur, Martin Zambullidor, Murlach, Pajaro del Rey, Peche-martin, Pecheur, Pie, Pitirre de Agua, Pitirre de Mangle, Pitirre de Rio, Plongeur, Ringneck, Sanglode, The Halcyon.

Modern Name: Green Kingfisher
Scientific Name: Chloroceryle americana
Folknames and Names: Texas Kingfisher, Texan Green Kingfisher.

Woodpeckers and Allies (Family Picidae)

Modern Name: Flicker
Scientific Name: Colaptes auratus
Folknames and Names: Antbird, Ant Woodchuck, Big Sapsucker, Big Woodpecker, Black-heart Woodpecker, Boreal Flicker, Buidheag Bhuachair, Carpintero, Carpintero Coll Rejo, Carpintero Escapulario, Carpintero Ribero, Cave-duc, Clape, Claype, Common Flicker, Cotton-backed Yellowhammer, Cotton-rump, Cotton-tail, Crescent-bird, Eastern Flicker, English Woodpecker, Fiddler, Flicker, Flicker Woodpecker, Flitter, French Woodpecker, Gaffer Woodpecker, Gaffle Woodpecker, Gale Shbecht, Gallie, Gel Specht, Gelb Specht, Golden Sapsucker, Golden-shafted Flicker, Golden-shafted Woodpecker, Golden-wing, Golden-winged Flicker, Golden-winged Woodpecker, Gold-wing Woodpecker, Golden-wing Woodpecker, Gold-winged Woodpecker, Golden Woodpecker, Golden-winged Woodcock, Gold Woodpecker, Grasshopper Woodpecker, Gree Shbecht, Hairy-wicket, Harry-wicket, Hammerhead, He-hi-holder, Heigh-ho, Hexa Shbecht, Hick-wall, Highhole, High-holer, High-hold, High-holder, High-ho Woodpecker, Higholder, Hittock, Hittocks, Hittuck, Hivel, Hybrid Flicker, Jaune, Joune, Le pic aux ailes dores, Little Woodchuck, Meadow Partridge, Missouri Red-moustashed Woodpecker, Mo-ning-qua-

na, Northern Flicker, O-hi-o, Ome-tuc, On-thee-quan-nor-ow, O-
zaw-wan-day Paw-Paw-say, Partridge Woodpecker, Paw-Paw-say,
Paw-Paw-say-og, Peckwood, Peckerwood, Peerit, Pee-ut, Pe-up,
Pic-a-bois, Pique-bois Dore, Picque-bois-jaune, Pic Dore, Pie-
bis, Pie-bris, Pigeon, Pigeon Woodpecker, Pink-throat, Picque-
bois-jaune, Piut, Pi-ute, Pivart, Poule de Bois, Rain Bird, Rain
Fowl, Rampike, Red-shafted Flicker, Sapsuck, Sapsucker, Shad-
spirit, Sharp-billed Flicker, Silver Dollar Bird, Spotted Woodpecker, Sucker, Specht, Speckt, Speight, Spright, Southern Flicker, Southern Woodpecker, Talpa-na-ni, Taping-bird, Treepecker, Wa-cup, Wah-cup, Walk-up, Wake-up, Wa-wup, Weather
Bird, Weather-hen, Wheeler, Whittaker, Wild Hen, Will Crisson,
Winter Robin, Woodchuck, Woodcock, Wood-lark, Woodpeck,
Woodpecker, Woodpicker, Woodpecker Lark, Wood Pigeon, Woodquoi, Wood-wall, Xebec, Yacker, Yecker, Yucker, Yaffle, Yallow
Wheeler, Yallow Whicker, Yarrup, Yarup, Yar-rup, Yawker Bird,
Yaw-up, Yellow Flicker, Yellowhammer, Yellow-hammer High-
hole, Yellerhammer, Yallerhammer, Yellow-'ammer, Yellow Jay,
Yellow-shafted Flicker, Yellow-shafted Woodpecker, Yellow-
winged Woodpecker, Yellow Wing, Yellow-winged Sapsucker, Yel-
low-winged Woodcock, Yellow Woodpecker, Zebec.

Modern Name: Red-shafted Flicker
Scientific Name: Colaptes auratus cafer
Folknames and Names: California Flicker, Common Flicker,
Flicker, High-holder, High-hole, High-holer, Hybrid Flicker,
Mexican Flicker, Monterey Red-shafted Flicker, Northwestern
Flicker, Orange-shafted Woodpecker, Red-hammer, Red-
moustashed Woodpecker, Red-quilled Flicker, Red-shafted
Woodpecker, Wake-up, Wick-up, Yellow-shafted Flicker, Yucker.

Modern Name: Gilded Flicker
Scientific Name: Colaptes chrysoides mearnsi
Folknames and Names: Common Flicker, Mearns' Gilded Flicker,
Wakeup, Wick-up, Yucker.

Modern Name: Pileated Woodpecker
Scientific Name: Dryocopus pileatus
Folknames and Names: Big Black Woodpecker, Black Logcock,
Black Woodpecker, Carpenter Bird, Cock of the North, Cock of the
Woods, Cock-o'-the-woods, Coq, Coq de Bruyere, Coq des Bois,
Crow-with-the-hard-face, Devil's Woodpecker, Field Officer, Gi-
ant Woodpecker, Good-god, Good God Woodpecker, Grand Pique-
bois, Great Black Woodpecker, Gros Pie, Huls Hock, Indian Hen,
Large Red-headed Woodpecker, Laughing Woodpecker, Logcock,
Log-cock Woodchuck, Log-god, Lord God Woodpecker, Northern
Pileated Woodpecker, Pic, Pie a Tete Escarlate, Pic a Tete Rouge,
Pic Bois, Pie, Pique Bois, Poule de Bois, Rain Crow, Redhead, Red-
headed Woodpecker, Wood Cock, Woodchuck, Wood Hen, Wood

Kate.

Modern Name: Ivory-billed Woodpecker
Scientific Name: Campephilus principalis
Folknames and Names: Caip, Carpintero Real, Grand Pique-bois,
Indian Hen, Ivory-bill, Kate, Kent, King of the Woodpeckers, King
Woodchuck, Logcock, Log-god, Poule de Bois, Southern Giant
Woodpecker, White-billed Woodpecker, Woodchuck, Woodcock.
NOTE: The Ivory-billed Woodpecker is probably extinct in the
continential United States; a few of these birds may still live in
some mountain forests of Cuba.

Modern Name: Red-bellied Woodpecker
Scientific Name: Melanerpes carolinus
Folknames and Names: Chad, Cham-chack, Guinea Sapsucker,
Jam-jack, La Petite Pique-bois Barre, Orange Sapsucker, Ram-
shack, Sham-shack, Woodpecker, Zebra, Zebra-back, Zebra Bird,
Zebra Woodpecker.

Modern Name: Golden-fronted Woodpecker
Scientific Name: Melanerpes aurifrons
Folknames and Names: Golden-front.

Modern Name: Gila Woodpecker
Scientific Name: Melanerpes uropygialis
Folknames and Names: Banded Woodpecker, Brewster's Wood-
pecker, Cardon Woodpecker, Carpintero Pechileonado Desetico,
Saguaro Woodpecker.

Modern Name: Ladder-backed Woodpecker
Scientific Name: Picoides scalaris
Folknames and Names: Cactus Woodpecker, Carpinterillo Mexicano, Mexican Woodpecker, San Lucas Woodpecker, Speckle-
cheek, Texas Downy, Texas Woodpecker.

Modern Name: Red-cockaded Woodpecker
Scientific Name: Picoides borealis
Folknames and Names: Pique-bois, Sapsucker.

Modern Name: Nuttall's Woodpecker
Scientific Name: Picoides nuttalli
Folknames and Names: -

Modern Name: Red-headed Woodpecker
Scientific Name: Melanerpes erythrocephalus
Folknames and Names: Flag Bird, Half-a-shirt, Jelly Coat, Patri-
otic Bird, Pic-a-bois, Pique-bois a Tete Rouge, Red-head, Rodkup,
Rodkuppicher Shbecht, Shbecht, Shirt-tail, Shirttail Bird, Tri-
color, Tricolore, Tri-colored Woodpecker, White-shirt, Whitew-

ing, Woodcock, Woodpicker.

Modern Name: Acorn Woodpecker
Scientific Name: Melanerpes formicivorus
Folknames and Names: Ant-eating Woodpecker, California Wood-
pecker, Carpintero Arlequin, Mearn's Woodpecker.

Modern Name: Lewis' Woodpecker
Scientific Name: Melanerpes lewis
Folknames and Names: Black Woodpecker, Crow Woodpecker.

Modern Name: White-headed Woodpecker
Scientific Name: Piocides albolarvatus
Folknames and Names: Little White-headed Sapsucker, Northern
White-headed Woodpecker, Southern White-headed Woodpecker,
White-headed Sapsucker.

Modern Name: Yellow-bellied Sapsucker
Scientific Name: Sphyrapicus varius
Folknames and Names: Bawm Lawffer, Carpintero de Paso,
Carpintero Pechiamarillo, Charpentier, Pecker-wood, Pic-bois
a Tete Rouge, Pic Macule, Pie, Pique-bois, Red-breasted Sapsuck-
er, Red-headed Woodpecker, Red-head Woodpecker, Red-Naped
Sapsucker, Red-throated Sapsucker, Sapsucker, Spanish Wood-
pecker, Squealer, The Sapsucker, Woodpecker, Yellow-bellied
Woodpecker, Yellow-belly, Yellow-hammer.

Modern Name: Williamson's Sapsucker
Scientific Name: Sphyrapicus thyroideus
Folknames and Names: Black-crowned Sapsucker, Brown-headed
Woodpecker, Natalie's Sapsucker, Williamson's Woodpecker.

Modern Name: Arizona Woodpecker
Scientific Name: Picoides arizonae
Folknames and Names: Brown-backed Woodpecker.

Modern Name: Hairy Woodpecker
Scientific Name: Picodes villosus
Folknames and Names: Big Guinea Woodpecker, Big Sapsucker, Big
Woodpecker, Cabanis's Woodpecker, Chihuahua Woodpecker,
Grey Woodpecker, Guinea Woodpecker, Harry, Harris's Wood-
pecker, Iron-bill, Modec Woodpecker, Newfoundland Woodpeck-
er, Northern Hairy Woodpecker, Pic, Pique-bois, Queen Charlotte
Woodpecker, Red-headed Woodpecker, Rocky Mountain Hairy
Woodpecker, Sapsucker, Sook, Southern Hairy Woodpecker,
Spanish Woodpecker, Spotted Woodpecker, White-breasted
Woodpecker, White Woodpecker.

Modern Name: Downy Woodpecker

Scientific Name: Picoides pubescens
Folknames and Names: Batchelder's Woodpecker, Black and White Woodpecker, Gairdner's Woodpecker, Glaner Woodpecker, Little Guinea Woodpecker, Little Sapsucker, Little Woodpecker, Nelson's Downy Woodpecker, Northern Downy Woodpecker, Pic, Pique-bois, Red-headed Woodpecker, Sapsucker, Southern Downy Woodpecker, Spotted Woodpecker, Tommy Woodpecker, Black and White Driller, Willow Woodpecker.

Modern Name: Black-backed Three-toed Woodpecker
Scientific Name: Picoides arcticus
Folknames and Names: American Three-toed Woodpecker, Arctic Three-toed Woodpecker, Black-backed Woodpecker, Little Black Woodpecker, Pique-bois Noir.

Modern Name: Northern Three-toed Woodpecker
Scientific Name: Picoides tridactylus
Folknames and Names: Alaska Three-toed Woodpecker, Alpine Three-toed Woodpecker, American Three-toed Woodpecker, Common Three-toed Woodpecker, Ladder-back Woodpecker, Pique-bois, White-backed Three-toed Woodpecker.

Passerine Birds (Order Passeriformes)
Tyrant Flycatchers (Family Tyrannidae)

Tyrannine Flycatchers (Subfamily Tyranninae)

Modern Name: Rose-throated Becard
Scientific Name: Platypsairis aglaiae
Folknames and Names: Xantus' Becard.

Modern Name: Scissor-tailed Flycatcher
Scientific Name: Muscivora forficata
Folknames and Names: Swallow-tailed Flycatcher, Texan Bird of Paradise.

Modern Name: Kiskadee Flycatcher
Scientific Name: Pitangus sulphuratus
Folknames and Names: Bull-headed Flycatcher, Derby Flycatcher, Greater Kiskadee, Kiskadee.

Modern Name: Vermilion Flycatcher
Scientific Name: Pyrocephalus rebinus
Folknames and Names: Mosquero Cardenalito.

158

Modern Name: Sulphur-bellied Flycatcher
Scientific Name: Myiodynastes luteiventris
Folknames and Names: Arizona Sulphur-bellied Flycatcher.

Modern Name: Eastern Kingbird
Scientific Name: Tyrannus tyrannus
Folknames and Names: Barteur de Corbeaux, Bee Bird, Bee-eater, Bee Martin, Black Grasset, Butcher Bird, Eemafresser, Eema Woi, Field Martin, Flycatcher, Fouetteur de Corbeau, Fouetteur de Corville, Gros Grasset, Killer Bird, Kingbird, Mangeur D'abeilles, Tertri, Tritri, Tyrant Flycatcher.

Modern Name: Western Kingbird
Scientific Name: Tyrannus verticalis
Folknames and Names: Arkansas Kingbird, Bee Bird, Bee Martin, Flycatcher, Tirano Palido.

Modern Name: Cassin's Kingbird
Scientific Name: Tyrannus vociferans
Folknames and Names: -

Modern Name: Tropical Kingbird
Scientific Name: Tyrannus melancholicus
Folknames and Names: Couch's Kingbird, Lichtenstein's Kingbird, Olive-backed Kingbird, Pipiri Jaune, West Mexican Kingbird, Yellow Pipiri.

Modern Name: Gray Kingbird
Scientific Name: Tyrannus dominicensis
Folknames and Names: Bee Bird, Chinchary, Chinchery, Chinchiry, Fighter, Grey Petchary, Hard-head, Pestigre, Petchary, Pick-Peter, Pipiri, Pipirite, Pipiry Flycatcher, Pitirre, Pitirre Abejero, Rain Bird, Titirre.

Modern Name: Thick-billed Kingbird
Scientific Name: Tyrannus crassirostris
Folknames and Names: -

Modern Name: Great Crested Flycatcher
Scientific Name: Myiarchus crinitus
Folknames and Names: Crested Flycatcher, Crested Phoebe, Frate, Greatcrest, Great Crested Yellow-bellied Flycatcher, May-bird, Snakeskin Bird, Wheep, Yellow-bellied Flycatcher.

Modern Name: Wied's Crested Flycatcher
Scientific Name: Myiarchus tyrannulus
Folknames and Names: Arizona Crested Flycatcher, Brown-crested Flycatcher, Mexican Crested Flycatcher, Mexican Flycatcher,

Wied's Flycatcher.

Modern Name: Ash-throated Flycatcher
Scientific Name: Myiarchus cinerascens
Folknames and Names: -

Modern Name: Olivaceous Flycatcher
Scientific Name: Myiarchus tuberculifer
Folknames and Names: Dusky-capped Flycatcher.

Modern Name: Eastern Phoebe
Scientific Name: Sayornis phoebe
Folknames and Names: Barn Pewee, Bean Bird, Biwi, Bridge Pewee, Bridge Phoebe, Dusky Flycatcher, Fauvette, Pevrette, Pewee, Pewit Flycatcher, Phoebe, Phoebe Bird, Tick Bird, Wagtail, Water Pewee.

Modern Name: Black Phoebe
Scientific Name: Sayornis nigricans
Folknames and Names: Black-headed Flycatcher, Mosquero Negro, Western Black Pewee, Western Black Phoebe.

Modern Name: Say's Phoebe
Scientific Name: Sayornis saya
Folknames and Names: Flycatcher, Say's Pewee.

Modern Name: Yellow-bellied Flycatcher
Scientific Name: Empidonax flaviventris
Folknames and Names: -

Modern Name: Acadian Flycatcher
Scientific Name: Empidonax virescens
Folknames and Names: Green-crested Flycatcher, Green Flycatcher, Small Green-crested Flycatcher, Small Pewee.

Modern Name: Willow Flycatcher
Scientific Name: Empidonax trailii
Folknames and Names: Traill's Flycatcher.

Modern Name: Least Flycatcher
Scientific Name: Empidonax minimus
Folknames and Names: Chebec, Little Chebec, Pewee, Sewick.

Modern Name: Hammond's Flycatcher
Scientific Name: Empiconax hammondii
Folknames and Names: -

Modern Name: Dusky Flycatcher
Scientific Name: Empidonax oberholseri

Folknames and Names: Wright's Flycatcher.

Modern Name: Gray Flycatcher
Scientific Name: Empidonax wrightii
Folknames and Names: Wright's Flycatcher.

Modern Name: Western Flycatcher
Scientific Name: Empidonax difficilis
Folknames and Names: Santa Barbara Flycatcher.

Modern Name: Buff-breasted Flycatcher
Scientific Name: Empidonax fulvifrons
Folknames and Names: Fulvous Flycatcher, Ruddy Flycatcher.

Modern Name: Beardless Flycatcher
Scientific Name: Camptostoma imberbe
Folknames and Names: Beardless Tyrannulet, Northern Beardless Flycatcher.

Modern Name: Coues' Flycatcher
Scientific Name: Contopus pertinax
Folknames and Names: Coues' Pewee, Greater Pewee, Jose Maria.

Modern Name: Eastern Wood Pewee
Scientific Name: Contopus virens
Folknames and Names: Biwi, Eastern Pewee, Pewee, Pewee Fly-catcher, Pewit, Pewit Flycatcher, Small Pewee, Tick Bird.

Modern Name: Western Wood Pewee
Scientific Name: Contopus sordidulus
Folknames and Names: Large-billed Wood Pewee, Western Pewee.

Modern Name: Olive-sided Flycatcher
Scientific Name: Nuttallornis borealis
Folknames and Names: Nuttall's Pewee, Whip-poor-will.

Oscines (Suborder Passeres)
Larks (Family Alaudidae)

Modern Name: Skylark
Scientific Name: Alauda arvensis
Folknames and Names: European Skylark, Lark, Eurasian Sky-lark.
*Introduced to Hawai'ian Islands (Hawai'i, Kaua'i, Lana'i, Maui, Moloka'i, O'ahu)

Modern Name: Horned Lark
Scientific Name: Eremphila alpestris

Folknames and Names: Alouette Corne, California Horned Lark, Desert Horned Lark, Dusty Horned Lark, Grey Bird, Ground Bird, Hoyt Horned Lark, Island Horned Lark, Life Bird, Low Bird, Luatharan, Montezuma Horned Lark, Mud Lark, Northern Horned Lark, Ortolan, Prairie Bird, Prairie Horned Lark, Pallid Horned Lark, Quaker, Road Chippie, Road Lark, Road Trotter, Ruddy Horned Lark, Scorched Horned Lark, Shore Lark, Skylark, Spring Bird, Streaked Horned Lark, Texan Horned Lark, Wheat Bird, Winter Horned Lark.

Swallows (Family Hirundinidae)

Typical Swallows (Subfamily Hirundininae)

Modern Name: Purple Martin
Scientific Name: Progne subis
Folknames and Names: Barn Swallow, Black Martin, Blue Bird, Golondrina Azul, Golondrina de Iglesias, Golondrina Grande, Golondrina Purpura, Gourd Martin, Great Blue Swallow, Hirondelle, Hirondelle Bleue, Hirondelle Pourpree, House Martin, Large Black Martin, Martin, Martinet, Purple Swallow, Swallow, Western Martin.

Modern Name: Barn Swallow
Scientific Name: Hirundo rustica
Folknames and Names: American Barn Swallow, Barn-loft Swallow, Common Swallow, Eave Swallow, European Swallow, Forktailed Swallow, Gobhlan-gaoith, Golondrina De Horquilla, Golondrina Tijerata, Hirondelle Rousse, Inside Barn Swallow, Mud Swallow, Swallow.

Modern Name: Cliff Swallow
Scientific Name: Petrochelidon pyrrhonta
Folknames and Names: Barn Swallow, Colon, Crescent Swallow, Eave Swallow, Eaves Swallow, Golondrina De Penasco, Golondrina Risquera, House Swallow, Jug Swallow, Martin, Moon-fronted Swallow, Mud Swallow, Northern Cliff Swallow, Republican Swallow.

Modern Name: Cave Swallow
Scientific Name: Petrochelidon fulva
Folknames and Names: Buff-throated Swallow, Colahuila Cliff Swallow, Cuban Cliff Swallow, Golondrina de Cuevas, Hirondelle, Rain Bird, Swallow.

Modern Name: Violet-green Swallow
Scientific Name: Tachycineta thalassina
Folknames and Names: Martin, Northern Violet-green Swallow.

Modern Name: Tree Swallow
Scientific Name: Iridoprocne bicolor
Folknames and Names: Blue-backed Swallow, Blue Martin, Eave Swallow, Flycatcher, French Swallow, Golondrina Vientriblanca, Martin, Singing Swallow, Stump Swallow, Tree Swallow, Water Swallow, White-bellied Martin, White-bellied Swallow, White-breasted Swallow, Wood Swallow.

Modern Name: Bank Swallow
Scientific Name: Riparia riparia
Folknames and Names: Ainleag, Bank Martin, Golondrina Parda, Hirondelle de Rivage, Sand Martin, Sand Swallow, Stairneal.

Modern Name: Rough-winged Swallow
Scientific Name: Stelgidopteryx ruficollis
Folknames and Names: Bridge Swallow, Gully Martin, Rough-wing.

Jays, Magpies and Crows (Family Corvidae)

Modern Name: Blue Jay
Scientific Name: Cyanocitta cristata
Folknames and Names: Blue Coat, Common Jay, Corn Thief, Florida Blue Jay, Gudhaar, Heckert, Herrafogel, Jay, Jay-bird, Nest Robber, Northern Jay, Southern Jay.

Modern Name: Steller's Jay
Scientific Name: Cyanocitta stelleri
Folknames and Names: Aztec Jay, Black-headed Jay, Blue Bird, Blue-crested Jay, Blue-fronted Jay, Blue Jay, Chara Copetona, Coast Jay, Conifer Jay, Eun Gorm, Geai, Geai Bleu, Grinell's Jay, Jay, Jay-bird, Long-crested Jay, Mountain Jay, Pigheid, Queen Charlotte Jay, Rain Bird, Screech Bird, Screuch Ancoille, Sierra Nevada Jay, Silken Jay, Silk Jay.

Modern Name: Scrub Jay
Scientific Name: Aphelocoma coerulescens
Folknames and Names: Belding Jay, Belding's Jay, Blue-eared Jay, Blue Jay, Blue-grey Jay, California Jay, California Scrub Jay, Chara Pechirrayada, Florida Jay, Grinnell's California Jay, Island Jay, Long-tailed Jay, Nicasio Jay, Santa Cruz Island Jay, Santa Cruz Jay, Smooth-headed Jay, Swarth's California Jay, Texan Jay, Texas Jay, Woodhouse Jay, Woodhouse's Jay, Xantus Jay, Xantus' Jay.

Modern Name: Gray-breasted Jay
Scientific Name: Aphelocoma ultramarina
Folknames and Names: Arizona Jay, Chara Pechigris, Couch Jay, Couch's Jay, Mexican Jay, Ultramarine Jay.

Modern Name: Pinyon Jay
Scientific Name: Gymnorhinus cyanocephalus
Folknames and Names: Blue Crow, Cassin's Jay, Maximilian's Crow, Maximilian's Jay, Pine Jay, Piñon Jay, Piñon Crow, Piñonero.

Modern Name: Gray Jay
Scientific Name: Perisoreus canadenis
Folknames and Names: Alaska Jay, Butcher Bird, Butcher's Boy, Camp Bird, Camp Robber, Canada Jay, Carrion Bird, Cat Bird, Cat Jay, Coastal Gray Jay, Deer Hunter, Dumb Jay, Eun Gorm, Geai, Geai Bleu, Gorby, Grease Bird, Grey Jay, Gut-eater, Hudson Bay Bird, Jay-bird, Jay-jack, Lumberjack, Magpie, Meat Bird, Meat Hawk, Meat Jay, Mohawk, Molly Bird, Moon Bird, Moose Bird, Oregon Gray Jay, Oregon Jay, Pie, Pigheid, Potato Bird, Rocky Mountain Jay, Screuch Ancoille, Snow Bird, Tallow Bird, Thief, Venison Jay, Whiskey Jack, Whiskey John.

Modern Name: Green Jay
Scientific Name: Cyanocorax yncas
Folknames and Names: Rio Grande Jay.

Modern Name: Black-billed Magpie
Scientific Name: Pica pica
Folknames and Names: A'dn, Aiarat, American Magpie, Apishka-gogi, Atat, Atce'tc, Heart-bird, Kwi´ti wut, Magpie, Ma'quits, Ootaw-kee-ackee, Otcotc, Pie, Pyet, Que´-tou-gih gih, Rudder-bird, Shepecum-mewuck, Tah´-tut.

Modern Name: Yellow-billed Magpie
Scientific Name: Pica nuttalli
Folknames and Names: California Magpie.

Modern Name: Clark's Nutcracker
Scientific Name: Nucifraga columbiana
Folknames and Names: Camp Robber, Clark's Crow, Grey Crow, Pine Crow, Meat Bird, Meat Hawk, Whiskey Jack, Woodpecker Crow.

Modern Name: Common Raven
Scientific Name: Corvus corax
Folknames and Names: American Raven, Black Bird, Caw, Coirbidh, Corbeau, Corbeau de Mer, Crow, Cuervo Grande Ronco, Fang, Giant Crow, Holarctic Raven, Mexican Raven, Northern Raven, Raven, Rook, Sheeps Crow, Western Raven.

Modern Name: Chihuahuan Raven
Scientific Name: Corvus cryptoleucus

Folknames and Names: American White-necked Raven, Crow, Cuervo Llanero, White-necked Raven.

Modern Name: American Crow
Scientific Name: Corvus brachyrhynchos
Folknames and Names: California Crow, Carrion Crow, Caw, Common Crow, Corbeau, Creamhach, Crow, Crow Bird, Eastern Crow, Fitheach, Florida Crow, Grob, Jim Crow, Kraa, Krop, Northwestern Crow, Otter Crow, Raven, Rocais, Rook, Southern Crow, Western Crow, Corn-Thief.

Modern Name: Northwestern Crow
Scientific Name: Corvus caurinus
Folknames and Names: -

Modern Name: Fish Crow
Scientific Name: Corvus ossifragus
Folknames and Names: -

Modern Name: Hawai'ian Crow
Scientific Name: Corvus hawaiiensis, Corvus tropicus
Folknames and Names: Alala.
*native in Hawai'ian Islands (Hawa'i)

Titmice (Family Paridae)

Modern Name: Black-capped Chickadee
Scientific Name: Parus atricapillus
Folknames and Names: Black-capped Tit, Black-capped Titmouse, Black-cap Tit, Blackhead Chickadee, Chickadee, Common Chickadee, Eastern Chickadee, Florida Chickadee, Long-tailed Chickadee, Mesange, Oregon Chickadee, Phoebe, Pig-a-pee, P'tit Pinpin, Qui-es-tu, Sow-the-wheat, Sweet Weather Bird, Tchicadee, Tchick-a-didi, Thick-a-di-di, Tiny Mite, Tit, Titmouse, Tom-tee, Tom-tit, Western Black-capped Chickadee, Yukon Chickadee.

Modern Name: Carolina Chickadee
Scientific Name: Parus carolinensis
Folknames and Names: Florida Chickadee, Plumbeous Chickadee, Texan Chickadee.

Modern Name: Mountain Chickadee
Scientific Name: Parus gambeli
Folknames and Names: Bailey's Chickadee, Grinnell's Chickadee, Inyo Chickadee, Inyo Mountain Chickadee, Mrs. Bailey's Mountain Chickadee, Short-tailed Chickadee.

Modern Name: Mexican Chickadee
Scientific Name: Parus sclateri

Folknames and Names: Sclater's Chickadee.

Modern Name: Boreal Chickadee
Scientific Name: Parus hudsonicus
Folknames and Names: Acadian Chickadee, Blackcap, Brown-cap, Brown-capped Chickadee, Brownie, Hudsonsian Chickadee, Tomtit.

Modern Name: Chestnut-backed Chickadee
Scientific Name: Parus rufescens
Folknames and Names: Barlow's Chickadee, California Chickadee, Chestnut-sided Chickadee, Marin Chickadee, Nicasio Chickadee, Santa Cruz Chickadee.

Modern Name: Gray-headed Chickadee
Scientific Name: Parus cinctus
Folknames and Names: Alaska Chickadee, Siberian Chickadee.

Modern Name: Tufted Titmouse
Scientific Name: Parus bicolor
Folknames and Names: Crested Titmouse, Crested Tomtit, Pete Bird, Peter Bird, Peto Bird, Tufted Chickadee, Tufted Tit.

Modern Name: Black-crested Titmouse
Scientific Name: Parus bicolor atricristatus
Folknames and Names: Sennett's Titmouse

Modern Name: Plain Titmouse
Scientific Name: Parus inornatus
Folknames and Names: Gray Titmouse, Oregon Titmouse, San Diego Titmouse.

Modern Name: Bridled Titmouse
Scientific Name: Parus wollweberi
Folknames and Names: Wollweber's Titmouse.

Penduline Tits and Verdins (Family Remizidae)

Modern Name: Verdin
Scientific Name: Auriparus flaviceps
Folknames and Names: Bushtit, Eastern Verdin, Goldtit, Yellow-headed Bust-tit.

Long-tailed Tits and Bushtits (Family Aegithalidae)

Modern Name: Common Bushtit

Scientific Name: Psaltriparus minimus
Folknames and Names: Bushtit, Black-eared Bushtit, Black-tailed Bushtit, California Bushtit, Coast Bushtit, Lead-colored Bushtit, Lloyd's Bushtit, Plumbeous Bushtit.

Nuthatches (Family Sittidae)

Modern Name: White-breasted Nuthatch
Scientific Name: Sitta carolinensis
Folknames and Names: Big Quank, Carolina Nuthatch, Common Nuthatch, Devil Downhead, Florida Nuthatch, Glaner Bloer Wood-picker, Inyo Nuthatch, Inyo Slender-billed Nuthatch, Rocky Mountain Nuthatch, Sapsucker, Sita Pechiblanca, Slender-billed Nuthatch, Tip-up, Tom-tit, Topsy-turvy-bird, Tree-mouse, White-bellied Nuthatch, Yank.

Modern Name: Red-breasted Nuthatch
Scientific Name: Sitta canadensis
Folknames and Names: Canada Nuthatch, Canadian Nuthatch, Cardy Bird, Devil-down-head, Little Quank, Red-bellied Nuthatch, Sapsucker, Tip-up, Tomtit, Topsy-turvy-bird, Upside-down Bird.

Modern Name: Brown-headed Nuthatch
Scientific Name: Sitta pusilla
Folknames and Names: Gray-headed Nuthatch.

Modern Name: Pygmy Nuthatch
Scientific Name: Sitta pygmaea
Folknames and Names: Black-eared Nuthatch, California Nuthatch, Nevada Nuthatch, Nevada Pigmy Nuthatch, Pine Nuthatch, White-naped Nuthatch.

Creepers (Family Certhiidae)

Typical Creepers (Subfamily Certhiinae)

Modern Name: Brown Creeper
Scientific Name: Certhia familiaris
Folknames and Names: American Creeper, American Brown Creeper, California Creeper, Common Creeper, Creeper, Little Brown Creeper, Mexican Creeper, Nevada Creeper, Rocky Mountain Creeper, Sierra Creeper, Tree Creeper, Woodpecker.

Bulbuls (Family Pychnonotidae)

Modern Name: Red-vented Bulbul
Scientific Name: Pycnonotus cafer

Folknames and Names: -
*Introduced to the Hawai'ian Islands (O'ahu)

Modern Name: Red-whiskered Bulbul
Scientific Name: Pycnonotus jocosus
Folknames and Names: -
*Introduced to the Hawai'ian Islands (O'ahu)

Wrens (Family Troglodytidae)

Modern Name: House Wren
Scientific Name: Troglodytes aedon
Folknames and Names: Apache Wren, Brown Wren, Common Wren, God Bird, Jenny Wren, Mangeur de Gadelles, Mouskanich, Pacific House Wren, Oiseau Bon Dieu, Parkman's Wren, Rock Bird, Roitelet, Roitelet de Maison, Rossignol, Short-tailed House Wren, Short-tailed Wren, Stump Wren, Wall Bird, Western Wren, Western House Wren, Wood Wren, Wren, Zaw Shlibber, Zounshlibber.

Modern Name: Brown-throated Wren
Scientific Name: Troglodytes bruneicollis
Folknames and Names: -

Modern Name: Winter Wren
Scientific Name: Troglodytes troglodytes
Folknames and Names: Alaska Wren, Aleutian Wren, Attu Wren, House Bird, Kiska Wren, Kodiak Winter Wren, Mouse Wren, Poulette de Bois, Semidi Wren, Short-tailed Wren, Spruce Wren, Stevenson's Wren, Tanaga Wren, Unalaska Wren, Western Winter Wren, Wood Wren.

Modern Name: Bewick's Wren
Scientific Name: Thryomanes bewickii
Folknames and Names: Baird's Wren, Catalina Island Wren, Desert Wren, Long-tailed House Wren, Long-tailed Wren, Nicasio Wren, San Clemente Wren, San Diego Wren, San Joaquin Wren, Santa Cruz Island Wren, Seattle Wren, Song Wren, Sooty Wren, Texas Wren, Vigor's Wren.

Modern Name: Carolina Wren
Scientific Name: Thryothorus ludovicianus
Folknames and Names: Florida Wren, Great Carolina Wren, Lomita Wren, Louisiana Wren, Mocking Wren, Teakettle Bird.

Modern Name: Cactus Wren
Scientific Name: Campylorhynchus brunneicapillus
Folknames and Names: Brown-headed Cactus Wren, Bryant's Cactus Wren, Coue's Cactus Wren, Matraca Desertica.

168

Modern Name: Rock Wren
Scientific Name: Salpinctes obsoletus
Folknames and Names: Common Rock Wren.

Modern Name: Canyon Wren
Scientific Name: Catherpes mexicanus
Folknames and Names: Auburn Wren, Cañon Wren, Dotted Wren, Nevada Wren, White-throated Wren.

Modern Name: Long-billed Marsh Wren
Scientific Name: Cistothorus palustris
Folknames and Names: Alberta Marsh Wren, California Marsh Wren, Cattail Wren, Louisiana Marsh Wren, Marian's Marsh Wren, Marsh Wren, Pacific Marsh Wren, Prairie Marsh Wren, Reed Wren, Saltwater Marsh Wren, Suisan Marsh Wren, Tule Wren, Wayne's Marsh Wren, Western Marsh Wren, Worthington's Marsh Wren.

Modern Name: Short-billed Marsh Wren
Scientific Name: Cistothorus platensis
Folknames and Names: Freshwater Marsh Wren, Grass Wren, Meadow Wren.

Dippers (Family Cinclidae)

Modern Name: Dipper
Scientific Name: Cinclus mexicanus
Folknames and Names: American Dipper, American Water Ouzel, Grey Singing Wren, Hell-diver, Slate Bobber, Water Ouzel, Water Witch.

Muscicapids (Family Muscicapidae)

Old World Warblers, Kinglets and Gnatcatchers (Subfamily Sylviinae)

Modern Name: Japanese Bush-warbler
Scientific Name: Cettia diphone
Folknames and Names: -
*introduced into Hawai'ian Islands (Lana'i, Moloka'i, Maui, O'ahu)

Modern Name: Blue-gray Gnatcatcher
Scientific Name: Polioptila coerulea
Folknames and Names: Cat Bird, Chay-chay, Chew Bird, Common Gnatcatcher, Cotton Bird, Little Blue-gray Wren, Little Bluish-gray Wren, Rabuita, Small Blue-gray Flycatcher, Spain-Spain, Sylvan Flycatcher, Western Gnatcatcher.

Modern Name: Black-tailed Gnatcatcher
Scientific Name: Polioptila melanura
Folknames and Names: California Gnatcatcher, Plumbeous Gnat-catcher.

Modern Name: Golden-crowned Kinglet
Scientific Name: Regulus satrapa
Folknames and Names: Fiery-crowned Wren, Flame-crest, Gold-crest, Golden-crested Kinglet, Golden-crowned Goldcrest, Gold-en-crowned Wren, Kingbird, Western Golden-crowned Kinglet.

Modern Name: Ruby-crowned Kinglet
Scientific Name: Regulus calendula
Folknames and Names: Foxy Chub, King Bird, Ruby-crown, Ruby-crowned Warbler, Ruby-crowned Wren.

Modern Name: Arctic Warbler
Scientific Name: Phylloscopus borealis
Folknames and Names: Arctic Willow Warbler, Evermann's War-bler, Kennicott's Willow Warbler.

Modern Name: Nihoa Millerbird
Scientific Name: Acrocephalus familiaris kingi
Folknames and Names: -
*native to Hawai'ian Islands (Nihoa)

Modern Name: Laysan Millerbird
Scientific Name: Telespiza cantans
Folknames and Names: -
*native to Hawai'ian Islands (Laysan)

Monarch Flycatchers (Subfamily Monarchinae)

Modern Name: Elepaio
Scientific Name: Chasiempis sandwichensis
Folknames and Names: -
*native to Hawai'ian Islands (Hawai'i, Kaua'i, O'ahu)

Solitaires, Thrushes and Allies (Subfamily Turdinae)

Modern Name: White-rumped Shama
Scientific Name: Copsychus malabaricus
Folknames and Names: Shama Thrush
*introduced to Hawai'ian Islands (Kaua'i, O'ahu)

Modern Name: Robin
Scientific Name: Merula migratoria

Folknames and Names: American Robin, Blackbird, Canada Robin, Carolian Robin, Common Robin, Fieldfare, Grive, Grive Rouge, Merle, Migratory Thrush, Mirlo Norteamericano, Northern Robin, Omshel, Redbird, Redbreast, Red-breasted Mockingbird, Red-breasted Thrush, Robin Redbreast, Roi, Rouge-gorge, San Lucas Robin, Smeorach, Southern Robin, Western Robin, Zoral Pechirrojo.

Modern Name: Varied Thrush
Scientific Name: Ixoreus naevius
Folknames and Names: Alaska Robin, Golden Robin, Hudson Bay Robin, Marsh Robin, Northern Varied Thrush, Oregon Robin, Pacific Varied Thrush, Pale Varied Thrush, Swamp Robin, Wood Robin.

Modern Name: Townsend's Solitaire
Scientific Name: Myadestes townsendi
Folknames and Names: Fly-catching Thrush, Townsend's Fly-catching Thrush.

Modern Name: Bluethroat
Scientific Name: Luscinina svercica
Folknames and Names: -

Modern Name: Wheatear
Scientific Name: Oenathe oenanthe
Folknames and Names: European Wheatear, Greenland Wheatear, Northern Wheatear.

Modern Name: Eastern Bluebird
Scientific Name: Sialia sialis
Folknames and Names: American Bluebird, Azure Bluebird, Blofogel, Bluebird, Blue Redbreast, Blue Robin, Common Bluebird, Eun Gorm, Grive, Grive Bleu, Oiseau Blue, Red-breasted Blue Bird, Rouge-gorge, Rouge-gorge Bleu, Wilson's Bluebird.

Modern Name: Western Bluebird
Scientific Name: Sialia mexicana
Folknames and Names: Azulejo Gorjiazul, California Bluebird, Chestnut-backed Bluebird, Mexican Bluebird, San Pedro Bluebird.

Modern Name: Mountain Bluebird
Scientific Name: Sialia currucoides
Folknames and Names: Arctic Bluebird, Rocky Mountain Bluebird.

Modern Name: Wood Thrush
Scientific Name: Turdus mustelinus

Folknames and Names: Bellbird, Brown Linnet, Drush'l, Flute, Frush, Grive de Bois, Hautbois, Hulsfrush, Merle, Song Thrush, Swamp Angel, Swamp Robin, Wood Robin.

Modern Name: Hermit Thrush
Scientific Name: Turdus aonalashkoe pallasii
Folknames and Names: American Nightingale, Cathedral Bird, Evening Bird, Flute, Hautbois, Little Thrush, Merle, Night Bird, Nightingale, Rain Bird, Rossignol, Rufous-tailed Thrush, Solitary Thrush, Swamp Angel, Swamp Robin.

Modern Name: Swainson's Thrush
Scientific Name: Cathaarus ustulatus
Folknames and Names: Alma's Thrush, Ciarsach, Merle, Olive-backed Thrush, Russet-back, Russet-backed Thrush, Smeorach, Swamp Robin.

Modern Name: Gray-cheeked Thrush
Scientific Name: Catharus minimus
Folknames and Names: Alice's Thrush, Bicknell's Thrush, Merle.

Modern Name: Veery
Scientific Name: Catharus fuscescens
Folknames and Names: Cathedral Bird, Flute, Gound Thrush, Merle, Nightingale, Piou-piou, Swamp Robin, Tawny Thrush, Willow Thrush, Wilson's Thrush.

Modern Name: Hawai'ian Thrush
Scientific Name: Phaeornis obscurus
Folknames and Names: Oma'o
*native to Hawai'ian Islands (Hawai'i, Kaua'i, Moloka'i)

Modern Name: Small Kaua'i Thrush
Scientific Name: Phaeornis palmeri
Folknames and Names: Puaiohi
*native to Hawai'ian Islands (Kaua'i)

Babblers (Subfamily Timaliinae)

Modern Name: Wrentit
Scientific Name: Chamaea fasciata
Folknames and Names: Coast Wren-tit, Gambel's Wren-tit, Pallid Wren-tit.

Modern Name: Melodious Laughing-thrush
Scientific Name: Garrulax canorus
Folknames and Names: Chinese Thrush, Hwa-mei, Spectacled Laughing-thrush.

*introduced to Hawai'ian Islands (Hawai'i, Kaua'i, Maui, O'ahu)

Modern Name: Greater Necklaced Laughing-thrush
Scientific Name: Garrulax pectoralis
Folknames and Names: Black-gorgeted Laughing-thrush.
*introduced to Hawai'ian Islands (Kaua'i)

Modern Name: Red-billed Leiothrix
Scientific Name: Leiothrix lutea
Folknames and Names: Japanese Hill-robin, Pekin Nightingale, Pekin Robin.
*introduced to Hawai'ian Islands (Hawai'i, Kaua'i, Maui, Moloka'i, O'ahu)

Mockingbirds, Thrashers and Allies (Family Mimidae)

Modern Name: Mockingbird
Scientific Name: Mimus polyglottus
Folknames and Names: Centzontle Aliblanco, English Thrasher, Jamaica Nightingale, Northern Mockingbird, Mimic Thrush, Mock Bird, Mocker, Mocking Thrush, Nightingale, Rossignol, Ruisenor, Sinsonte, Sinsonte Norteno, The Singing Bird.
*introduced into the Hawai'ian Islands (Hawai'i, Kaua'i, Lana'i, Maui, Moloka'i, Maui, O'ahu)

Modern Name: Catbird
Scientific Name: Dumetalla carolinenis
Folknames and Names: Black-capped Thrush, Black Mockingbird, Black Thrush, Cat Flycatcher, Chat, Chicken Bird, Gray Catbird, Kotsafogel, Lazy Bird, Mary Bird, Merle Chat, Mockingbird, Oiseau-chat, Slate-colored Mockingbird, Taylor-made Bird, Zorzal Gato.

Modern Name: Brown Thrasher
Scientific Name: Toxostonia rufum
Folknames and Names: Brown Mocker, Brown Mocking Bird, Brown Thrush, Cane-bird, Death Bird, Drush'l, Drushdel, Fox-colored Thrush, French Mocking Bird, Grive Rousse, Ground Thrush, Mavis, Mockingbird, Planting Bird, Red Mavis, Red Thrush, Robin, Sandy Mocker, Sandy Mockingbird, Shpottfogel, Song Thrush, Thrasher.

Modern Name: Long-billed Thrasher
Scientific Name: Toxostonia longirostre
Folknames and Names: Sennett's Thrasher.

Modern Name: Sage Thrasher
Scientific Name: Oreoscoptes montanus

Folknames and Names: Mountain Mockingbird, Sage Mockingbird, Sage Thrush.

Modern Name: Bendire's Thrasher
Scientific Name: Toxostoma bendirei
Folknames and Names: -

Modern Name: Curve-billed Thrasher
Scientific Name: Toxostoma curvirostre
Folknames and Names: Cuitiacoche Comun, Palmer's Thrasher.

Modern Name: California Thrasher
Scientific Name: Toxostoma redivivum
Folknames and Names: Pasadena Thrasher, Sonoma Thrasher.

Modern Name: Le Conte's Thrasher
Scientific Name: Toxostoma lecontei
Folknames and Names: Desert Thrasher.

Modern Name: Crissal Thrasher
Scientific Name: Toxostoma dorsale
Folknames and Names: Red-vented Thrasher.

Wagtails and Pipits (Family Motacillidae)

Modern Name: White Wagtail
Scientific Name: Motacilla alba
Folknames and Names: Pied Wagtail.

Modern Name: Yellow Wagtail
Scientific Name: Motacilla flava
Folknames and Names: -

Modern Name: Red-throated Pipit
Scientific Name: Anthus cervinus
Folknames and Names: -

Modern Name: Sprague's Pipit
Scientific Name: Anthus spragueii
Folknames and Names: Missouri Skylark, Prairie Skylark, Sky-jingler, Skylark, Titlark.

Modern Name: Water Pipit
Scientific Name: Anthus spinoletta
Folknames and Names: Alouette Pipi, American Pipit, American Titlark, Brown Lark, Hudsonian Lark, Lark, Louisiana Lark, Pip-it, Red Lark, Rock Pipit, Titlark, Wagtail.

Waxwings (Family Bombycillidae)

Modern Name: Bohemian Waxwing
Scientific Name: Bombycilla garrulus
Folknames and Names: Black-throated Waxwing, Bohemian Chatterer, Cherry Bird, Greater Waxwing, Lapland Waxwing, Silktail, Northern Chatterer, Northern Waxwing, Recollet, Waxwing.

Modern Name: Cedar Waxwing
Scientific Name: Bombycilla cedrorum
Folknames and Names: Apple Bird, Basque, Blockhead, Blossom Bird, Canada Robin, Canadian Robin, Carolina Waxwing, Cedar Bird, Cherry-bird, Cherry Robin, Cherry Waxwing, Comb-wing Bird, Huppe, Lesser Waxwing, Mangeur de Cerises, Picotera, Recellet, Recollet, Spider Bird, Southern Waxwing.

Silky Flycatchers (Family Ptilogonatidae)

Modern Name: Phainopepla
Scientific Name: Phainopepla nitens
Folknames and Names: Black Flycatcher, Black-crested Flycatcher, Capulinero Negro, Shining Crested Flycatcher, Shining Flysnapper, Silky Flycatcher.

Shrikes (Family Laniidae)

Typical Shrikes (Subfamily Laniinae)

Modern Name: Northern Shrike
Scientific Name: Lanius excubitor
Folknames and Names: Butcher Bird, Devil's Bird, Devil's Whiskey-jack, Ecorcheur, Great Gray Shrike, Great Northern Shrike, Joy-killer, Mockingbird, Nine Killer, Northern Butcher Bird, Northwestern Shrike, Pie Boreale, Silky Jay, Whiskey Jack, White Jay, White Whiskijohn, Winter Butcher Bird, Winter Shrike.

Modern Name: Loggerhead Shrike
Scientific Name: Lanius ludovicianus
Folknames and Names: Anthony's Shrike, Butcher Bird, California Shrike, Cotton-picker, Ecorcheur, French Mockingbird, Gambel's Shrike, Island Shrike, Migrant Loggerhead, Migrant Shrike, Mouse-bird, Nelson's Shrike, Nine-killer, Southern Butcher Bird, Southern Loggerhead Shrike, Summer Butcher Bird, Verdugo Americano, White-rumped Shrike.

Starlings and Allies (Family Sturnidae)

Starlings (Subfamily Sturninae)

Modern Name: European Starling
Scientific Name: Sturnus vulgaris
Folknames and Names: Church Martin, Common Starling, English Starling, Estornino, Etourneau, Starling.
* introduced into the Hawai'ian Islands (O'ahu)

Modern Name: Common Myna
Scientific Name: Acridotheres tristis
Folknames and Names: Indian Myna, House Myna, Piha 'e-Kelo.
* introduced into the Hawai'ian Islands (Hawai'i, Kaua'i, Lana'i, Maui, Moloka'i, O'ahu)

Modern Name: Crested Myna
Scientific Name: Acridotheres cristatellus
Folknames and Names: Chinese Crested Myna, Chinese Starling, Japanese Starling.

Modern Name: Hill Myna
Scientific Name: Gracula religiosa
Folknames and Names: Grackle, Indian Hill Myna, Talking Myna.
*possible introduction to Hawai'ian Islands (O'ahu).

Honeyeaters (Family Meliphagidae)

Modern Name: Kaua'i O'o
Scientific Name: Moho braccatus
Folknames and Names: O'o'a'a
*native to Hawai'ian Islands (Kaua'i)

Modern Name: Bishop's O'o
Scientific Name: Moho bishopi
Folknames and Names: -
*native to Hawai'ian Islands (Maui).

White-eyes (Family Zoesteropidae)

Modern Name: Japanese White-eye
Scientific Name: Zosterops japonicus
Folknames and Names: -
*native to Hawai'ian Islands (Hawai'i, Lana'i, Kaua'i, Moloka'i, O'ahu, Maui).

Vireos (Family Vireonidae)

Modern Name: Black-capped Vireo

Scientific Name: Vireo atricapilla
Folknames and Names: Black-capped Greenlet.

Modern Name: Gray Vireo
Scientific Name: Vireo vicinior
Folknames and Names: -

Modern Name: Solitary Vireo
Scientific Name: Viveo solitarius
Folknames and Names: Blue-headed Vireo, Blue-headed Greenlet,
Cassin's Vireo, Mountain Vireo, Plumbeous Vireo, Western Blue-
headed Vireo.

Modern Name: White-eyed Vireo
Scientific Name: Vireo griseus
Folknames and Names: Basket-bird, Bermuda Vireo, Hanging
Bird, Julian Chivi Ojiblanco, Key West Vireo, Maynard's Vireo,
Politician, Rio Grande Vireo, Small White-eyed Vireo, White-
eyed Greenlet.

Modern Name: Bell's Vireo
Scientific Name: Vireo belli
Folknames and Names: Arizona Least Vireo, Arizona Vireo, Bell's
Greenlet, California Least Vireo, Least Vireo, Texas Vireo.

Modern Name: Hutton's Vireo
Scientific Name: Vireo huttoni
Folknames and Names: Anthony Vireo, Hutton Vireo, Stephens'
Vireo.

Modern Name: Yellow-throated Vireo
Scientific Name: Vireo flavifrons
Folknames and Names: Julian Chivi Gargantiamarillo, Yellow-
throated Greenlet.

Modern Name: Black-whiskered Vireo
Scientific Name: Vireo altiloquus
Folknames and Names: Bien-te-veo, Greenlet, John-chew-it, John
Phillips, John-to-whit, Julian Chivi Bigotinegro.

Modern Name: Yellow-green Vireo
Scientific Name: Vireo flavorviridis
Folknames and Names: -

Modern Name: Philadelphia Vireo
Scientific Name: Vireo philadelphicus
Folknames and Names: Brotherly-love Vireo, Philadelphia Green-
let.

Modern Name: Red-eyed Vireo
Scientific Name: Vireo olivaceus
Folknames and Names: Hangnest, Julian Chivi Ojirojo, Little Hang-nest, Preacher, Preacher Bird, Red-eye, Red-eyed Greenlet, Teacher, The Preacher.

Modern Name: Warbling Vireo
Scientific Name: Vireo gilvus
Folknames and Names: Eastern Warbling Vireo, Warbling Green-let, Western Warbling Vireo.

Emberizids (Family Emberizidae)

Wood-Warblers (Subfamily Parulinae)

Modern Name: Black-and-white Warbler
Scientific Name: Mniotilta varia
Folknames and Names: Anse-bird, Ant Bird, Ant-eater, Ants Bird, Ants Picker, Bijirita Trepadora, Black-and-white Creeper, Black-and-white Creeping Warbler, Blue-and-white Pied Creep-er, Blue-and-white Striped Creeper, Christmas Bird, Creeper, Creeping Warbler, Japanese Canary, Madras, Mi-Deuil, Reinita Trepadora, Striped Warbler, Tree Creeper, Varied Creeping Warbler, Whitepoll Warbler.

Modern Name: Prothonotary Warbler
Scientific Name: Protonotaria citrea
Folknames and Names: Golden Warbler, Golden Swamp Warbler, Reinita Anaranjada, Willow Warbler.

Modern Name: Swainson's Warbler
Scientific Name: Limnothlypis swainsonii
Folknames and Names: -

Modern Name: Worm-eating Warbler
Scientific Name: Helmitheros verminorus
Folknames and Names: Reinita Gusanera, Worm-eater, Worm-eat-ing Swamp Warbler.

Modern Name: Golden-winged Warbler
Scientific Name: Vermivora chrysoptera
Folknames and Names: Blue Golden-winged Warbler, Golden-winged Flycatcher, Golden-winged Swamp Warbler, Reinita Ali-dorada.

Modern Name: Blue-winged Warbler
Scientific Name: Vermivora pinus
Folknames and Names: Blue-winged Swamp Warbler, Blue-winged

Yellow Warbler.

Modern Name: Bachman's Warbler
Scientific Name: Vermivora bachmanii
Folknames and Names: -

Modern Name: Tennessee Warbler
Scientific Name: Vermivora peregrina
Folknames and Names: Swamp Warbler, Tennessee Swamp War-
bler.

Modern Name: Orange-crowned Warbler
Scientific Name: Vermivora celata
Folknames and Names: Dusky Orange-crowned Warbler, Dusky
Warbler, Eastern Orange-crowned Warbler, Lutescent Orange-
crowned Warbler, Lutescent Warbler, Orange-crown, Rocky
Mountain Orange-crowned Warbler.

Modern Name: Nashville Warbler
Scientific Name: Vermivora ruficapilla
Folknames and Names: Birch Warbler, Calaveras Warbler, Nash-
ville Swamp Warbler, Red-crowned Warbler.

Modern Name: Olive Warbler
Scientific Name: Peucedramus taeniatus
Folknames and Names: Northern Olive Warbler.

Modern Name: Virginia's Warbler
Scientific Name: Vermiviroa virginiae
Folknames and Names: -

Modern Name: Colima Warbler
Scientific Name: Vermivora crissalis
Folknames and Names: -

Modern Name: Lucy's Warbler
Scientific Name: Vermivora luciae
Folknames and Names: Desert Warbler.

Modern Name: Parula Warbler
Scientific Name: Parula americana
Folknames and Names: Blue Yellowback, Blue Yellow-backed
Warbler, Finch Creeper, Northern Parula, Reinita Pechidorada,
Southern Parula Warbler.

Modern Name: Olive-backed Warbler
Scientific Name: Parula pitiayumi
Folknames and Names: Olive-backed Warbler, Sennett's Warbler,
Sennett's Olive-backed Warbler.

Modern Name: Yellow Warbler
Scientific Name: Dendroica petechia
Folknames and Names: Bastard Canary, Blue-eyed Yellow War-
bler, Canario, Canario de Manglar, Canario de Mangle, Canary,
Canary Bird, Chippin' Chick, Didine, Fauvette Jaune, Golden
Warbler, Mangrove Canary, Mangrove Warbler, Oiseau Jaune,
Petit-jaune, Rossignol, Seaside Canary, Serin Sauvage, Spider
Bird, Sucrier Barbade, Sucrier Mangle, Summer Warbler, Sum-
mer Yellowbird, Thumb Bird, Toute Jaune, Wild Canary, Willow
Warbler, Yellow Titmouse, Yellowbird, Yellow Poll.

Modern Name: Magnolia Warbler
Scientific Name: Dendroica magnolia
Folknames and Names: Black-and-yellow Warbler, Blue-headed
Yellow-rumped Warbler, Spotted Warbler.

Modern Name: Cape May Warbler
Scientific Name: Dendroica tigrina
Folknames and Names: Reinita Tigre, Spotted Creeper.

Modern Name: Black-throated Blue Warbler
Scientific Name: Dendroica caerulescens
Folknames and Names: Black-throat, Blue Flycatcher, Reinita
Azul.

Modern Name: Yellow-rumped Warbler
Scientific Name: Dendroica coronata
Folknames and Names: Audubon's Warbler, Black-fronted War-
bler, Golden-crowned Flycatcher, Golden-crowned Warbler,
Myrtle-bird, Myrtle Warbler, Reinita Coronada, Spider Bird,
Yellow-crowned Warbler, Yellow-rump, Yellow-rumped Warbler,
Western Yellow-rumped Warbler.

Modern Name: Townsend's Warbler
Scientific Name: Dendroica townsendi
Folknames and Names:-

Modern Name: Black-throated Green Warbler
Scientific Name: Dendroica virens
Folknames and Names: Evergreen Warbler, Green Black-throat,
Green Black-throated Flycatcher, Reinita Verdosa.

Modern Name: Golden-cheeked Warbler
Scientific Name: Dendroica chrysoparia
Folknames and Names: -

Modern Name: Hermit Warbler
Scientific Name: Dendroica occidentalis

Folknames and Names: -

Modern Name: Black-throated Gray Warbler
Scientific Name: Dendroica nigrescens
Folknames and Names: -

Modern Name: Cerulean Warbler
Scientific Name: Dendroica cerulea
Folknames and Names: Azure Warbler, Blue Warbler.

Modern Name: Yellow-throated Warbler
Scientific Name: Dendroica dominica, Geothlypus trichas
Folknames and Names: Chip-chip, Common Yellowthroat, Dominican Yellowthroat, Domino Bird, Eastern Yellow-throated Warbler, Maryland Yellowthroat, Reinita Gargantiamarilla, Reinita Pica Tierra, Sycamore Yellow-throated Warbler, Sycamore Warbler, Yellow-throated Creeper, Yellow-throated Gray Warbler.

Modern Name: Grace's Warbler
Scientific Name: Dendroica graciae
Folknames and Names: Grace Warbler, Northern Grace's Warbler.

Modern Name: Blackburnian Warbler
Scientific Name: Dendroica fusca
Folknames and Names: Fire-brand, Hemlock Warbler, Orange-throated Warbler, Reinita De Fuego, Torch Bird.

Modern Name: Chestnut-sided Warbler
Scientific Name: Dendroica pennsylvanica
Folknames and Names: Bloody-sided Warbler, Golden-crowned Flycatcher, Quebec Warbler, Reinita Costadicastana, Yellow-Crowned Warbler.

Modern Name: Bay-breasted Warbler
Scientific Name: Dendroica castanea
Folknames and Names: Autumnal Warbler, Bay-breast, Little Chocolate-breast Titmouse, Reinita Castana.

Modern Name: Blackpoll Warbler
Scientific Name: Dendroica striata
Folknames and Names: Autumnal Warbler, Blackpoll, Black-polled Warbler, Reinita Rayada.

Modern Name: Pine Warbler
Scientific Name: Dendroica pinus
Folknames and Names: Chip-chip, Petit-Chiittte de Bois Pin, Pine Creeper, Pine-creeping Warbler, Siguita del Pinar.

Modern Name: Kirkland's Warbler
Scientific Name: Dendroica kirtlandii
Folknames and Names: Jack-pine Bird, Jack-pine Warbler.

Modern Name: Prairie Warbler
Scientific Name: Dendroica discolor
Folknames and Names: -

Modern Name: Palm Warbler
Scientific Name: Dendroica palmarum
Folknames and Names: Redpoll Warbler, Reinita Palmera, Tip-up Warbler, Wag-tail Warbler, Western Palm Warbler, Yellow Palm Warbler, Yellow Redpoll Warbler, Yellow Redpoll, Yellow Tip-up, Yellow Tip-up Warbler.

Modern Name: Ovenbird
Scientific Name: Seiurus aurocapillus
Folknames and Names: Betsy Kick-up, Golden-crowned Accentor, Golden-crowned Thrush, Golden-crowned Wagtail, Ground Bird, Nightingale, Night-walker, Pizpita Dorada, Teacher, Teacher-bird, The Teacher, Thrush, Wood Bird, Wood Wagtail.

Modern Name: Northern Waterthrush
Scientific Name: Seiurus noveboracensis
Folknames and Names: Aquatic Thrush, Aquatic Wood Thrush, Aquatic Wood Wagtail, Grinnell's Waterthrush, New York Warbler, New York Waterthrush, Northern Small-billed Water-thrush, Wagtail, Wagtail Warbler, Water-thrush, Water Wagtail.

Modern Name: Louisiana Waterthrush
Scientific Name: Seiurus motacilla
Folknames and Names: Large-billed Waterthrush, Pizpita De Rio, Southern Waterthrush, Wagtail, Wagtail Warbler, Water Wagtail.

Modern Name: Yellowthroat
Scientific Name: Geothlypis trcihas
Folknames and Names: Black-cheeked Yellow-throat, Black-masked Ground Warbler, Florida Yellowthroat, Ground Warbler, Maryland Yellowthroat, Northern Maryland Yellowthroat, Northern Yellowthroat, Olive-colored Yellow-throated Wren, Pacific Yellow-throat, Salt Marsh Yellow-throat, Southern Yellow-throat, , Salt Marsh Yellowthroat, Western Yellowthroat.

Modern Name: Yellow-breasted Chat
Scientific Name: Icteria virens
Folknames and Names: Polyglot Chat, Yellow Mocking Bird, Chat, Common Chat, Yellow Chat, Long-tailed Chat.

Modern Name: Kentucky Warbler

Scientific Name: Oporornis formosus
Folknames and Names: Kentucky Wagtail, Reinita De Kentucky.

Modern Name: MacGillivray's Warbler
Scientific Name: Oporornis tolmiei
Folknames and Names: Northern MacGillivray's Warbler, Tolmie Warbler.

Modern Name: Mourning Warbler
Scientific Name: Oporonis philadelphia
Folknames and Names: Black-throated Ground Warbler, Crape Warbler, Mourning Ground Warbler, Philadelphia Warbler, Reinita Enlutada.

Modern Name: Connecticut Warbler
Scientific Name: Oporonis aglis
Folknames and Names: Bog Black-throat, Swamp Warbler, Reinita De Connecticut, Tamarack Warbler.

Modern Name: Hooded Warbler
Scientific Name: Wilsonia citrina
Folknames and Names: Black-headed Warbler, Hooded Flycatching Warbler, Hooded Titmouse, Mitered Warbler, Reinita De Capucha.

Modern Name: Wilson's Warbler
Scientific Name: Wilsonia pusilla
Folknames and Names: Black-capped Fly-catching Warbler, Black-capped Warbler, Golden Pileolated Warbler, Green Black-capped Warbler, Northern Pileolated Warbler, Pileolated Warbler, Wilson's Black-cap, Wilson's Black-capped Flycatching Warbler, Wilson's Pileolated Warbler, Black-cap, Black-capped Warbler, Wilson's Blackcap, Wilson's Flycatcher, Wilson's Flycatching Warbler, Yellowhammer.

Modern Name: Canada Warbler
Scientific Name: Wilsonia canadensis
Folknames and Names: Canada Flycatcher, Canada Necklace, Canadian Flycatching Warbler, Canadian Warbler, Necklace Warbler, Necklaced Warbler, Reinita De Canada, Speckled Canada Warbler, Spotted Canadian Warbler.

Modern Name: Red-faced Warbler
Scientific Name: Cardellina rubrifrons
Folknames and Names: -

Modern Name: American Redstart
Scientific Name: Setophaga ruticilla
Folknames and Names: Alder Bird, Bean Bird, Bijirita, Butterfly

Bird, Christmas Bird, Candelita, Carougette, Carte, Common Red-start, Fire-tail, Gabriel du Feu, Goldfinch, Mariposera, Officier, Petit du Feu, Redstart Flycatcher, Redstart Warbler, Yellow-tailed Warbler.

Modern Name: Painted Redstart
Scientific Name: Myioborus pictus
Folknames and Names: -

Bananaquits (Subfamily Coerebinae)

Modern Name: Bananaquit
Scientific Name: Coereba flavola
Folknames and Names: Bahama Bananaquit, Bahama Honeycreep-er, Bahaman Honeycreeper, Banana Bird, Banana Quit, Banana Yoky, Beany Bird, Beeny Bird, Beeny Quit, Bessie Bird, Bessie Coban, Black and Yellow Creeper, Black See-see, Gusanero, Hon-ey-sucker, John Cropple, Marley Quit, Paw-paw Bird, Psyche, Reinita, Reinita Comun, See-see, Siguita, Sucrier, Sugar Bird, Teasy, Yellow-breast, Yellow See-see.

Tanagers (Subfamily Thraupinae)

Modern Name: Western Tanager
Scientific Name: Piranga ludoviciana
Folknames and Names: Louisiana Tanager.

Modern Name: Scarlet Tanager
Scientific Name: Piranga olivacea
Folknames and Names: Black-winged Redbird, Bludfink, Bludfo-gel, Canada Tanager, Cardinal, Cardinal Bird, Escarlatina, Fire-bird, King Bird, Oiseau Rouge, Pocket-bird, Red Bird, Scarlet Sparrow, Soldier Bird, Summer Redbird, War Bird.

Modern Name: Summer Tanager
Scientific Name: Piranga rubra
Folknames and Names: Redbird, Smooth-headed Redbird, Bee Bird, Calico Warbler, Cooper's Tanager, Crimson Tanager, Rose Tanager, Summer Redbird, Western Summer Tanager.

Modern Name: Hepatic Tanager
Scientific Name: Piranga flava
Folknames and Names: -

Modern Name: Blue-gray Tanager
Scientific Name: Tharaupis virens
Folknames and Names: -

Cardinals, Grosbeaks and Allies (Subfamily Cardinalinae)

Modern Name: Cardinal
Scientific Name: Cardinal cardinalis
Folknames and Names: Arizona Cardinal, Cardenal Rojo, Cardinal Bird, Cardinal Grosbeck, Cardinal Redbird, Common Cardinal, Crested Redbird, Florida Cardinal, Gray-tailed Cardinal, Kentucky Cardinal, Redbird, Red Bluejay, Red Cardinal, Red Grosbeak, Rota Fogel, Virginia Cardinal, Virginia Nightingale, Virginia Redbird.
*introduced into the Hawai'ian Islands (Hawai'i, Kaua'i, Lana'i, Maui, Moloka'i, Maui, O'ahu).

Modern Name: Red-crested Cardinal
Scientific Name: Paroaria coronata
Folknames and Names: Brazilian Cardinal
*introduced into the Hawai'ian Islands (Kaua'i, Lana'i, Maui, Moloka'i, O'ahu).

Modern Name: Yellow-billed Cardinal
Scientific Name: Paroaria capitata
Folknames and Names: -
*introduced into the Hawai'ian Islands (Hawai'i, Maui).

Modern Name: Pyrrhuyloxia
Scientific Name: Cardinal sinuata
Folknames and Names: Arizona Pyrrhuyloxia, Bullfinch, Bullfinch Cardinal, Gray Cardinal, Gray Grosbeak, Parrot-bill, Texan Cardinal, Texas Cardinal, Texas Pyrrhuyloxia.

Modern Name: Rose-breasted Grosbeak
Scientific Name: Pheucticus ludovicianus
Folknames and Names: Common Grosbeak, Degollado, Linnet, Piquigrueso Rosado, Potato-bug Bird, Rose-breast, Summer Grosbeak, Throat-cut.

Modern Name: Black-headed Grosbeak
Scientific Name: Pheucticus melanocephalus
Folknames and Names: Black-head, Common Grosbeak, Rocky Mountain Grosbeak, Western Grosbeak.

Modern Name: Evening Grosbeak
Scientific Name: Hesperiphona vespertina
Folknames and Names: American Hawfinch, Columbian Evening Grosbeak, Eastern Evening Grosbeak, Mexican Evening Grosbeak, Sugar Bird, Western Evening Grosbeak, Winter Canary.

Modern Name: Blue Grosbeak
Scientific Name: Guiraca caerulea
Folknames and Names: Azulejo, California Blue Grosbeak, Blue Pop, Big Indigo, Western Blue Grosbeak.

Modern Name: Indigo Bunting
Scientific Name: Passerina cyanea
Folknames and Names: Azulejo, Blofogel, Blue Bird, Blue Canary, Blue Finch, Gorrion Azul, Indigo Bird, Indigo Bluebird, Indigo Finch, Indigo Painted Bunting, Oiseau Bleu, Oiseau de Montreal.

Modern Name: Lazuli Bunting
Scientific Name: Passerina amoena
Folknames and Names: Lazuli Painted Finch.

Modern Name: Varied Bunting
Scientific Name: Passerina versicolor
Folknames and Names: Beautiful Bunting.

Modern Name: Painted Bunting
Scientific Name: Passerina ciris
Folknames and Names: Arco-iris, Mariposa, Mexican Canary, Nonpareil, Painted Finch, Paradise Finch, Pope, Red Pop, Texas Canary, Verderon.

Modern Name: Dickcissel
Scientific Name: Spiza americana
Folknames and Names: Black-throated Bunting, Judas-bird, Little Meadowlark, Sabanero Americano.

Emberizines (Subfamily Emberizinae)

Modern Name: Red-crested Cardinal
Scientific Name: Paroaria coronata
Folknames and Names: Brazilian Cardinal.
*introduced to the Hawai'ian Islands (O'ahu, Maui, Lana'i, Hawai'i)

Modern Name: Yellow-billed Cardinal
Scientific Name: Paroaria capitala
Folknames and Names: -
*introduced to the Hawai'ian Islands (Hawai'i)

Modern Name: Olive Sparrow
Scientific Name: Arremonopos rufivigatus
Folknames and Names: Green Finch, Texas Sparrow.

Modern Name: Green-tailed Towhee
Scientific Name: Pipilo chlorurus
Folknames and Names: Blanding's Finch, Chestnut-crowned To-
whee, Green-tailed Bunting.

Modern Name: Rufous-sided Towhee
Scientific Name: Pipilo erythrophthalmus
Folknames and Names: Arctic Towhee, Brush Robin, Bullfinch,
Bush-bird, Bush Robin, Catbird, Chewink, Eastern Towhee, Flor-
ida Towhee, Ground Robin, Joree, Joreetz, Low-ground-Stephen,
Marsh Robin, Mountain Towhee, Oregon Towhee, Red-eyed To-
whee, San Clemente Towhee, San Diego Towhee, Spotted Towhee,
Spurred Towhee, Swamp Robin, Towhee, Towhee Bird, Towhee
Bunting, To-whitt To-whee, Turkey Sparrow, White-eyed Towhee,
Wood Robin.

Modern Name: Brown Towhee
Scientific Name: Pipilo fuscus
Folknames and Names: Anthony Towhee, Brown Chippy, Califor-
nia Towhee, Canon Towhee, Canyon Bunting, Canyon Towhee,
Catbird, Crissal Bunting, Fuscous Towhee, Ground Robin, La Vie-
jita, Rascador Pardo, Sacramento Brown Towhee, Swamp Robin.

Modern Name: Abert's Towhee
Scientific Name: Pipilo aberti
Folknames and Names: Gray Towhee.

Modern Name: Saffron Finch
Scientific Name: Sicalis flaveola
Folknames and Names: Gorrion Zafran.
*introduced to Hawai'ian Islands (Hawai'i, O'ahu)

Modern Name: Savannah Sparrow
Scientific Name: Passerculus sandwichensis
Folknames and Names: Aleutian Savannah Sparrow, Belding's
Sparrow, Field Sparrow, Grass Sparrow, Grey Bird, Ground-bird,
Ground Sparrow, Large-billed Sparrow, Meadow Bird, Savannah
Bunting, Western Savannah Sparrow.

Modern Name: Ipswich Sparrow
Scientific Name: Passerculus sandwichensis princeps
Folknames and Names: Gray Bird, Ipswich Savannah Sparrow,
Maynard's Sparrow, Pallid Sparrow, Sable Island Sparrow.

Modern Name: Grasshopper Sparrow
Scientific Name: Ammodramus savannarum
Folknames and Names: Chamberguito, Chingolo Chicharra, Gor-
rion de Chicharra, Grass Dodger, Grass Pink, Oiseau Canne,

Quail Sparrow, Savanna Bird, Tichicro, Tumbarocio, Yellow-winged Sparrow.

Modern Name: Baird's Sparrow
Scientific Name: Ammodramus bairdii
Folknames and Names: -

Modern Name: Henslow's Sparrow
Scientific Name: Ammondramus henslowii
Folknames and Names: Henslow's Bunting.

Modern Name: LeConte's Sparrow
Scientific Name: Ammospiza leconteii
Folknames and Names: Le Conte's Bunting.

Modern Name: Sharp-tailed Sparrow
Scientific Name: Ammospiza caudacuta
Folknames and Names: Nelson's Sparrow, Nelson's Finch, Nelson's Sharp-tailed Sparrow, Acadian Sharp-tailed Sparrow.

Modern Name: Seaside Sparrow
Scientific Name: Ammospiza maritima
Folknames and Names: Meadow Chippy, Seaside Finch.

Modern Name: Dusky Seaside Sparrow
Scientific Name: Ammospiza maritima nigrescens
Folknames and Names: Black Shore Finch, Merritt Island Sparrow.

Modern Name: Cape Sable Sparrow
Scientific Name: Ammospiza maritima mirabilis
Folknames and Names: -

Modern Name: Lark Bunting
Scientific Name: Calamospiza melanocorys
Folknames and Names: Bobolink, Buffalo Bird, Prairie Bobolink, White-winged Blackbird, White-winged Prairie Bird, White-winged Bunting.

Modern Name: Vesper Sparrow
Scientific Name: Poocaetes gramineus
Folknames and Names: Bay-winged Bunting, Bay-winged Finch, Grass-finch, Grass-bird, Grass Sparrow, Gray-bird, Ground-bird, Oregon Vesper Sparrow, Pasture-bird, Western Vesper Sparrow.

Modern Name: Lark Sparrow
Scientific Name: Chondestes grammacus
Folknames and Names: Lark Finch, Little Meadowlark, Quail-head, Road-bird, Western Lark Sparrow.

Modern Name: Black-throated Sparrow
Scientific Name: Amphispiza bilineata
Folknames and Names: Black-throat, Desert Black-throated Sparrow, Desert Sparrow, Gorrion Gorjinegro Carirrayado.

Modern Name: Sage Sparrow
Scientific Name: Amphispiza belli
Folknames and Names: Bell's Sparrow, Gray Sage Sparrow, Northern Sage Sparrow.

Modern Name: Dark-eyed Junco
Scientific Name: Junco hyemalis
Folknames and Names: Bad-weather Bird, Black Chipping Bird, Black Snowbird, Blue Bird, Blue Snowbird, Blue Sparrow, Carolina Junco, Cassiar Junco, Chip Bird, Chipping Bird, Chippy, Common Snowbird, Eastern Junco, Goose Bird, Gray-headed Junco, Gray Snowbird, Grey Bird, Guadalupe Junco, Hen Bird, Ivory-billed Bluebird, Junco, Male Bird, Montana Junco, Mountain Junco, Nevada Junco, Nonne, Nonette, Point Lobos Junco, Pink-sided Junco, Red-backed Junco, Ridgway's Junco, Sierra Junco, Shufeldt's Junco, Slate-colored Junco, Slate-colored Snowbird, Snowbird, Snow Sparrow, Thurber's Junco, Tip, Titoc, Tomtit, White-bill, White-tail, White-winged Junco.

Modern Name: Yellow-eyed Junco
Scientific Name: Junco phaeonotus palliatus
Folknames and Names: Arizona Junco, Red-backed Junco, Mexican Junco, Baird's Junco, Townsend's Junco.

Modern Name: Rufous-winged Sparrow
Scientific Name: Aimophila carpalis
Folknames and Names: -

Modern Name: Cassin's Sparrow
Scientific Name: Aimophila cassinii
Folknames and Names: -

Modern Name: Botteri's Sparrow
Scientific Name: Aimophila botterii
Folknames and Names: -

Modern Name: Bachman's Sparrow
Scientific Name: Aimophila aestivalis
Folknames and Names: Pine-woods Sparrow, Southern Pine Finch.

Modern Name: Tree Sparrow
Scientific Name: Spizella arborea
Folknames and Names: Canada Sparrow, Winter Chippy, Tree

Bunting, Winter Chip-bird, Arctic Chipper, Snow Chippy, Winter Sparrow.

Modern Name: Chipping Sparrow
Scientific Name: Spzella passerina
Folknames and Names: Chip-bird, Chipper, Chippy, Chip Sparrow, Field Sparrow, Grey Bird, Hair-bird, Hair Sparrow, Hay Bird, Little Grey Bird, Little House Sparrow, Moineau, Red-headed Grass Bird, Serin du Pays, Social Sparrow, Tsitcha, Titit, Western Chipping Sparrow.

Modern Name: Clay-colored Sparrow
Scientific Name: Spizella pallida
Folknames and Names: -

Modern Name: Brewer's Sparrow
Scientific Name: Spizella breweri
Folknames and Names: Brewer Sparrow, Roadrunner.

Modern Name: Field Sparrow
Scientific Name: Spizella pusilla
Folknames and Names: Field Bunting, Wood Sparrow, Bush Sparrow, Field Chippy, Ground-bird, Ground Sparrow, Huckleberry-bird, Rush Sparrow.

Modern Name: Black-chinned Sparrow
Scientific Name: Spizella atrogularis
Folknames and Names: Arizona Black-chinned Sparrow, California Black-chinned Sparrow.

Modern Name: Harris' Sparrow
Scientific Name: Zonotrichia querula
Folknames and Names: Black-hood, Hooded Sparrow, Hooded-crowned Sparrow, Mourning Sparrow.

Modern Name: White-crowned Sparrow
Scientific Name: Zonotrichia leucophrys
Folknames and Names: Chip-bird, Gambel's Sparrow, Grey Bird, Hedge Sparrow, Jockey-cap, Muee, Nuttall's Sparrow, Rain Bird, Scratch Sparrow, Striped-head, White-cap, White-crown.

Modern Name: Golden-crowned Sparrow
Scientific Name: Zonotrichia atricapilla
Folknames and Names: Golden-crown, Rain Bird.

Modern Name: White-throated Sparrow
Scientific Name: Zonotrichia albicollis
Folknames and Names: Canada Bird, Canada Sparrow, Canada Whitethroat, Canadian Song Sparrow, Cherrybird, Chingolo Gar-

gantiblanco, Frederic, Hard-times Canada Bird, Kennedy Bird, Linotte, Nighingale, Night-singer, Old Sam Peabody, Old Tom Peabody, Paddy-whack, Peabiddy Bird, Peabody, Peabody Bird, Peverly Bird, Poor Kennedy Bird, Poor Sam Peabody, P' Tit Frederic, Rossignol, Siffleur, Striped-head, Sweet Pinkey, Sweet Sweet Canada Bird, Tom Peabody, White-throat, White-throated Crown Sparrow, Widow Woman.

Modern Name: Fox Sparrow
Scientific Name: Passerella iliaca
Folknames and Names: Bobby-rooter, Brown Bobber, Ferruginous Finch, Fox Bird, Fox-colored Sparrow, Fox-tail, Foxy Finch, Foxy Tom, Gratteur, Great Sparrow, Hedge Sparrow, Kodiak Fox Sparrow, Partridge Bird, Red Singer, Red Thrush, Rossignol, Rossignol Francais, Shumagin Fox Sparrow, Slate-colored Fox Sparrow, Stephen's Fox Sparrow, Sooty Fox Sparrow, Swamp Sparrow, Thick-billed Fox Sparrow, Tom Fox, Townsend's Fox Sparrow, Yakutat Fox Sparrow, Wilderness Sparrow.

Modern Name: Lincoln's Sparrow
Scientific Name: Melospiza lincolnii
Folknames and Names: Lincoln's Finch, Lincoln's Song Sparrow, Tom's Finch.

Modern Name: Swamp Sparrow
Scientific Name: Melospiza georgiana
Folknames and Names: Grey Bird, Marsh Sparrow, Red Grass-bird, Swamp Finch, Swamp Song Sparrow.

Modern Name: Song Sparrow
Scientific Name: Melospiza melodia
Folknames and Names: Alameda Song Sparrow, Aleutian Song Sparrow, Bischoff's Song Sparrow, Brown Song Sparrow, Bush Sparrow, Desert Song Sparrow, Dakota Song Sparrow, Everybody's Darling, Gealbhonn, Glaiseun, Grass Bird, Grey Bird, Ground-bird, Ground Sparrow, Hedge Sparrow, Heermann Song Sparrow, Heiermann's Song Sparrow, Kenai Song Sparrow, Kodiak Song Sparrow, March Sparrow, Mendocino Song Sparrow, Merrill Song Sparrow, Mountain Song Sparrow, Red Grass-bird, Rossignol, Rusty Song Sparrow, Sooty Song Sparrow, Samuel's Song Sparrow, San Diego Song Sparrow, San Clemente Song Sparrow, Santa Barbara Song Sparrow, Shbeds'l, Silver Tongue, Song Sparrow, Spring Bird, Swamp Finch, Yakutat Song Sparrow.

Modern Name: McCown's Longspur
Scientific Name: Calcarius mccownii
Folknames and Names: Black-breasted Longspur, Ground Lark, McCown's Bunting, Rufous-winged Lark Bunting.

Modern Name: Chestnut-collared Longspur
Scientific Name: Calcarius ornatus
Folknames and Names: Butterfly Bird.

Modern Name: Lapland Longspur
Scientific Name: Calcarius lapponicus
Folknames and Names: Alaska Lark Bunting, Alaska Longspur, Chiddick Bird, Common Lark Bunting, Common Longspur, Dirty-face, Labrador Bunting, Lapland Lark Bunting, Lapland Snowbird, Stubble Sparrow.

Modern Name: Smith's Longspur
Scientific Name: Calcarius pictus
Folknames and Names: Painted Longspur.

Modern Name: Snow Bunting
Scientific Name: Plectrophenax nivalis
Folknames and Names: Arctic Sparrow, Common Snow Bunting, Little White Bird, Oiseau Blanc, Oiseau de Misere, Oiseau de Neige, Ortolon, Snow Bird, Snowdrift, Snow Lark, Snowbird, Snow-flake, Waddlin, Whitebird, White Snowbird.

Modern Name: McKay's Bunting
Scientific Name: Plectrophenax hyperboreus
Folknames and Names: McKay's Snow-bunting, Snowflake.

Icterines (Subfamily Icterinae)

Modern Name: Bobolink
Scientific Name: Dolichonyx aryzivorus
Folknames and Names: American Bobolink, American Ortolan, Bob, Bob-lincoln, Butter-bird, Chambergo, Chatter Bird, Goglu, May-bird, Meadow-bird, Meadow-wink, October Bird, October Pink, Ortolan, Pink, Reed-bird, Reedfogel, Rice-bird, Robert, Roberti Towhee, Skunk Bird, Skunk Blackbird, Skunk-head Blackbird, Towhee, White-winged Blackbird.

Modern Name: Eastern Meadowlark
Scientific Name: Sturnella magna
Folknames and Names: Alouette, Alouette de Prairie, Arizona Meadowlark, Common Lark, Common Meadowlark, Crescent Stare, Grive, Field Lark, Florida Meadowlark, Larrich, Marsh Lark, Marsh Quail, Meadow Bird, Meadow Starling, Medlar, Medlark, Mudlark, Old Field Lark, Ortolan, Riabhag, Rio Grande Meadow-lark, Sabanero, Sedge Lark, Swamp Lark, Southern Meadowlark, Texas Meadowlark, Uiseag.

Modern Name: Western Meadowlark
Scientific Name: Sturnella neglecta
Folknames and Names: Common Meadowlark, Field Lark of the West, King Syble-a-bon, Lark of the West, Pradero Gorjeador, Prairie Lark.
*Introduced to Hawai'ian Islands (Kaua'i)

Modern Name: Yellow-headed Blackbird
Scientific Name: Xanthocephalus xanthocephalus
Folknames and Names: California Blackbird, Copperhead, Yellowhammer, Yellowhead.

Modern Name: Red-winged Blackbird
Scientific Name: Agelaius phoeniceus
Folknames and Names: Blackbird, Caporal, Chirriador, Etourneau, Field Officer, Field Officer Bird, Geai, Geai a Aile Rouge, Harper, Marsh Blackbird, Mayito de la Cienaga, Northwestern Red-wing, Officer Bird, Red-shouldered Blackbird, Red-shouldered Starling, Redwing, Red-winged Grackle, Red-winged Oriole, Red-winged Starling, Rice Bird, Rodfleeg'lter Shdawr, San Diego Red-wing, Soldier Bird, Soldier Blackbird, Swamp Blackbird, Thick-bill Red-wing, Toti de la Cienaga, Tordo Sargento.

Modern Name: Tri-colored Blackbird
Scientific Name: Agelaius tricolor
Folknames and Names: Tricolored Oriole, Tricolored Redwing.

Modern Name: Rusty Blackbird
Scientific Name: Euphaus carolina
Folknames and Names: Blackbird, Black Robin, Cattle Blackbird, Cowbird, Crow, Crow Blackbird, Etourneau, Little Blackbird, Marsh Blackbird, Rusty Crow, Rusty Grackle, Rusty Oriole, Swamp Blackbird, Thrush Blackbird.

Modern Name: Brewer's Blackbird
Scientific Name: Euphagus cyanocephalus
Folknames and Names: Brewer Blackbird, Glossy Blackbird, Satin Bird, Starling, Tordo Ojiclaro.

Modern Name: Boat-tailed Grackle
Scientific Name: Quiscalus major
Folknames and Names: Crow Blackbird, Daw, Great-tailed Grackle, Jackdaw, Mexican Blackbird, Saltwater Blackbird, Zanate Mexicano.

Modern Name: Common Grackle
Scientific Name: Quiscalus quiscula
Folknames and Names: Big Blackbird, Blackbird, Black Robin, Bronzed Grackle, China-eyed Blackbird, Crow Blackbird, Crow

Grackle, Etourneau, Eun Dubh, Fan-tailed Blackbird, Florida
Grackle, Geai, Keel-tailed Grackle, Maize Thief, Merle Noir, New
England Jackdaw, Oiseau Bleu, Purple Grackle, Purple Jackdaw,
Rudder Tail, Rudder-tail Blackbird, Shdawr, Shwortsa Fogel,
Small Crow Bird, Starling, Swamp Robin.

Modern Name: Great-tailed Grackle
Scientific Name: Quiscalus mexicanus
Folknames and Names: Crow Blackbird, Daw, Jackdaw, Zanate
Mexicano.

Modern Name: Brown-headed Cowbird
Scientific Name: Molothrus ater
Folknames and Names: Blackbird, Black Robin, Black Sparrow,
Brown-headed Blackbird, Brown-headed Oriole, Buffalo Bird,
Cuckold, Buffalo Bird, Cowbird, Cow Blackbird, Cow Bunting,
Cow-pen Bird, Dwarf Cowbird, Etourneau, Geai, Grey Cowbird,
Herd Bird, Kee Shdawr, Lazybird, Little Blackbird, Nevada Cow-
bird, Tordo Cabecicafe, Vacher.

Modern Name: Bronzed Cowbird
Scientific Name: Molothrus aeneus
Folknames and Names: Glossy Cowbird, Red-eye, Red-eyed Cow-
bird.

Modern Name: Orchard Oriole
Scientific Name: Isterus spurius
Folknames and Names: Basket-bird, Bastard Baltimore, Brown
Oriole, Orchard Hangnest, Orchard Starling, Swinger.

Modern Name: Spotted-breasted Oriole
Scientific Name: Icterus pestoralis
Folknames and Names: -

Modern Name: Aububon's Oriole
Scientific Name: Icterus graducauda
Folknames and Names: Aububon Oriole, Black-headed Oriole.

Modern Name: Scott's Oriole
Scientific Name: Icterus parisorum
Folknames and Names: Bolsero Parisino, Scott Oriole.

Modern Name: Hooded Oriole
Scientific Name: Icterus cucullatus
Folknames and Names: Arizona Hooded Oriole, Nelson's Oriole,
Palm-leaf Oriole, Sennett's Oriole.

Modern Name: Baltimore Oriole
Scientific Name: Isterus galbula

Folknames and Names: Baltimore-bird, Bolsero Colipinto, Calandria Del Norte, English Robin, Firebird, Fire-hang-bird, Golden Bird, Golden Oriole, Golden Robin, Guldt Omshel, Hammockbird, Hang-bird, Hang-nest, Loriot, Northern Oriole, Orange Bird, Pea-bird.

Modern Name: Bullock's Oriole
Scientific Name: Icterus galbula bullockii
Folknames and Names: Bolsero Colipinto, Bullock Oriole, Northern Oriole.

Modern Name: Lichtenstein's Oriole
Scientific Name: Icterus gularis
Folknames and Names: Alta Mira Oriole, Black-throated Oriole.

Modern Name: Spotted-breasted Oriole
Scientific Name: Icterus pectoralis
Folknames and Names: -

Fringilline and Cardueline Finches and Allies (Family Fringillidae)

Cardueline Finches (Subfamily Carduelinae)

Modern Name: Purple Finch
Scientific Name: Carpodacus purpureus
Folknames and Names: California Linnet, California Purple Finch, Eastern Purple Finch, Gray Linnet, Purple Linnet, Purple Grosbeak, Red Linnet.

Modern Name: Cassin's Finch
Scientific Name: Carpodacus cassinii
Folknames and Names: Cassin's Purple Finch

Modern Name: House Finch
Scientific Name: Carpodacus mexicanus
Folknames and Names: Burion, California Linnet, Carpodaco Domestico, Crimson-fronted Finch, Guadalupe House Finch, Hollywood Linnet, Linnet, McGregor's House Finch, Mexican House Finch, Mexican Rose Finch, Papayabird, Redhead, Red-headed Linnet.
*introduced into the Hawai'ian Islands (Kaua'i, Lana'i, Maui, Moloka'i, Maui, O'ahu).

Modern Name: Pine Grosbeak
Scientific Name: Pinicola enucleator
Folknames and Names: Alaska Pine Grosbeak, American Pine Grosbeak, California Pine Grosbeak, Canadian Grosbeak, Canadi-

an Pine Grosbeak, Kodiak Pine Grosbeak, Pine Bullfinch, Queen Charlotte Pine Grosbeak, Rocky Mountain Pine Grosbeak, Mope.

Modern Name: Gray-crowned Rosy Finch
Scientific Name: Leucosticte tephrocotis
Folknames and Names: Aleutian Rosy Finch, Brown Snow-bird, Gray-crowned Leucosticte, Hepburn's Rosy Finch, Pink Snow-bird, Probilof Rosy Finch, Sierra Nevada Rosy Finch.

Modern Name: Black Rosy Finch
Scientific Name: Leucosticte atrata
Folknames and Names: -

Modern Name: Brown-capped Rosy Finch
Scientific Name: Leucosticte australis
Folknames and Names: -

Modern Name: Hoary Redpoll
Scientific Name: Carduelis hornamanni
Folknames and Names: Arctic Redpoll, Coues' Redpoll, Greenland Redpoll, Hornomann's Redpoll.

Modern Name: Common Redpoll
Scientific Name: Carduelis flammea
Folknames and Names: Greater Redpoll, Holboell's Redpoll, Holbrook's Redpoll, Lesser Redpoll, Lintie, Little Meadowlark, Little Redpoll, Mealy Redpoll, Red-poll, Red-polled Linnet, Redpoll Linnet.

Modern Name: Pine Siskin
Scientific Name: Cardueis pinus
Folknames and Names: American Siskin, Gray Linnet, Northern Canary Bird, Pine Finch, Pine Linnet.

Modern Name: American Goldfinch
Scientific Name: Carduelis tristis
Folknames and Names: Beet Bird, Catnip, California Goldfinch, Common Goldfinch, Catnip Bird, Eastern Goldfinch, Gale Fogel, Goldfinch, Guldfink, Lettuce-bird, Pale Goldfinch, Salad-bird, Thistle Bird, Western Goldfinch, Wild Canary, Willow Goldfinch, Yellow Bird, Zolawd Fogel, Zolawd Shbeds'l.

Modern Name: Lesser Goldfinch
Scientific Name: Carduelis psaltria
Folknames and Names: Arkansas Goldfinch, Arkansas Greenback, Dark-eyed Goldfinch, Green-backed Goldfinch, Mexican Goldfinch, Shiner, Tarweed Canary.

Modern Name: Lawrence's Goldfinch

Scientific Name: Carduelis lawrencei
Folknames and Names: -

Modern Name: European Goldfinch
Scientific Name: Carduelis carduelis
Folknames and Names: Draw-water, Goldfinch, Thistle-bird, Thistle Finch.

Modern Name: American Crossbill
Scientific Name: Loxia curvirostra
Folknames and Names: Red Crossbill, Crossbill, Common Crossbill.

Modern Name: White-winged Crossbill
Scientific Name: Loxia leucoptera
Folknames and Names: Bee-croise, Periquito.

Modern Name: White-collared Seedeater
Scientific Name: Sporophila torqueola
Folknames and Names: Morrelet Seedeater, Sharpe's Seedeater.

Modern Name: Common Canary
Scientific Name: Serinus canaria
Folknames and Names: Canary.
*Introduced to the Hawai'ian Islands (Midway).

Modern Name: Yellow-fronted Canary
Scientific Name: Serinus mozambicus
Folknames and Names: Green Singing-finch.
*Introduced to the Hawai'ian Islands (Hawai'i, O'ahu).

Hawai'ian Honeycreepers (Subfamily Drepanidinae)

Modern Name: Laysan Finch
Scientific Name: Telespyza cantans
Folknames and Names: -
*native to Hawai'ian Islands (Laysan).

Modern Name: Nihoa Finch
Scientific Name: Telspyza ultima
Folknames and Names: -
*native to Hawai'ian Islands (Nihoa).

Modern Name: O'u
Scientific Name: Psittirostra psittacea
Folknames and Names: -
*native to Hawai'ian Islands (Kaua'i, Hawai'i).

Modern Name: Palila
Scientific Name: Loxiodes bailleui
Folknames and Names: -
*native to Hawai'ian Islands (Hawai'i).

Modern Name: Maui Parrotbill
Scientific Name: Pseudonestor xanthophrys
Folknames and Names: Pseudonestor.
*native to Hawai'ian Islands (Maui).

Modern Name: Common Amakihi
Scientific Name: Hemignathus virens
Folknames and Names: Amakihi.
*native to Hawai'ian Islands (Kaua'i, O'ahu, Lana'i, Moloka'i,
Maui, Hawai'i).

Modern Name: Anianiau
Scientific Name: Hemignathus parvus
Folknames and Names: Lesser Amakahi.
*native to Hawai'ian Islands (Kaua'i).

Modern Name: Kaua'i Akialoa
Scientific Name: Hemignathus procerus
Folknames and Names: -
*native to Hawai'ian Islands (Kaua'i).

Modern Name: Nuku Pu'u
Scientific Name: Hemignathus lucidus
Folknames and Names: -
*native to Hawai'ian Islands (Kaua'i, Maui).

Modern Name: Akia Pola'au
Scientific Name: Hemignathus munroi
Folknames and Names: -
*Native to Hawai'ian Islands (Hawai'i).

Modern Name: Kaua'i Creeper
Scientific Name: Oreomystis bairdi
Folknames and Names: Akikiki.
*native to Hawai'ian Islands (Kaua'i).

Modern Name: Hawai'i Creeper
Scientific Name: Oreomystis mana
Folknames and Names: -
*native to Hawai'ian Islands (Hawai'i).

Modern Name: Maui Creeper
Scientific Name: Paroreomytza montana

Folknames and Names: Alauahio, Maui Alauwahio.
*native to Hawai'ian Islands (Maui).

Modern Name: Moloka'i Creeper
Scientific Name: Paroreomyza flammea
Folknames and Names: Kakawahie.
*native to Hawai'ian Islands (Moloka'i).

Modern Name: O'ahu Creeper
Scientific Name: Paroremyza maculata
Folknames and Names: Alauahio.
*native to Hawai'ian Islands (O'ahu).

Modern Name: Akepa
Scientific Name: Loxops coccineus
Folknames and Names: Common Akepa, Kaua'i Akepa.
*native to Hawai'ian Islands (Hawai'i, Kaua'i, Maui).

Modern Name: I'iwi
Scientific Name: Vestiaria coccinea
Folknames and Names: -
*native to Hawai'ian Islands (Hawai'i, Kaua'i, Moloka'i, Maui, O'ahu).

Modern Name: Crested Honeycreeper
Scientific Name: Palmeria dolei
Folknames and Names: Akohekohe.
*native to Hawai'ian Islands (Maui).

Modern Name: Apapane
Scientific Name: Himatione sanguinea
Folknames and Names: Layson Honeycreeper.
*native to Hawai'ian Islands (Hawai'i, Lana'i, Kaua'i, Moloka'i, Maui, O'ahu).

Modern Name: Po'ouli
Scientific Name: Melamprosops phacosoma
Folknames and Names: Black-faced Honeycreeper.
*native to Hawai'ian Islands (Maui).

Old World Sparrows (Family Passeridae)

Modern Name: English Sparrow
Scientific Name: Passer domesticus
Folknames and Names: Bull Sparrow, Domestic Sparrow, European House Sparrow, Gamin, Glaiseun, Gorrion, Gorrion Domestico, Gorrion Ingles, Grey Bird, Hedge Sparrow, Hoodlum, House Bird, House Sparrow, Manu Liilii, Moineau, Moineau Anglais, Moineau Pierrot, Pinson Anglais, Sparrow, Town Sparrow, Tramp.

*introduced to Hawai'ian Islands (O'ahu, Kaua'i, Hawai'i, Maui).

Modern Name: Eurasian Tree Sparrow
Scientific Name: Passer montanus
Folknames and Names: European Tree Sparrow, Tree Sparrow.

Estrildid Finches (Family Estrildidae)
Estrildine Finches (Subfamily Estrildinae)

Modern Name: Lavender Waxbill
Scientific Name: Estrilda caerulescens
Folknames and Names: Lavender Fire-finch, Red-tailed Lavender
Waxbill.
*introduced to Hawai'ian Islands (Hawai'i, O'ahu).

Modern Name: Common Waxbill
Scientific Name: Estrilda astrild
Folknames and Names: Waxbill.
*introduced to Hawai'ian Islands (O'ahu).

Modern Name: Orange-cheeked Waxbill
Scientific Name: Estrilda melpoda
Folknames and Names: Veterano Mejillianaranjado.
*introduced to Hawai'ian Islands (O'ahu).

Modern Name: Warbling Silverbell
Scientific Name: Lonchura malabarica
Folknames and Names: Gorrion Picoplata, Indian Silverbell, Silverbell, White-throated Munia.
*introduced to Hawai'ian Islands (Hawai'i, Lana'i, Maui, Molo-
ka'i).

Modern Name: Red Avadavat
Scientific Name: Amandava amandava
Folknames and Names: Red Munia, Strawberry Finch.
*introduced to Hawai'ian Islands (O'ahu).

Modern Name: Java Sparrow
Scientific Name: Padda oryzivora
Folknames and Names: Java Finch, Java Temple Bird, Pinchon
Arrocero, Ricebird.
*introduced to Hawai'ian Islands (O'ahu).

Modern Name: Chestnut Mannikin
Scientific Name: Lonchura malacca
Folknames and Names: Black-headed Munia, Black-headed Nun,
Chestnut Munia, Monja Tricolor, Tricolored Mannikin.
*introduced to Hawai'ian Islands (Kaua'i, O'ahu).

Modern Name: Nutmeg Mannikin
Scientific Name: Lonchura punctulata
Folknames and Names: Gorrion Canela, Ricebird, Scaly-breasted Mannikin, Spice Finch, Spotted Munia.
*introduced to Hawai'ian Islands (Hawai'i, Kaua'i, Lana'i, Maui, Moloka'i, O'ahu).

Bibliography

Note: some of the references listed below are incomplete. The information listed was all that was available in the original source and in the library card catalogs/CD-ROM listings. Instead of making "educated guesses" about missing information, the author thought it best to let the reference listings remain as found.

Adams, George, *Birdscaping Your Garden*, Emmaus, Pennsylvania: Rodale Press, 1994.

American Ornithologists' Union, *Checklist of North American Birds*, 6th Edition, 1983.

Bair, James, "The Emergence of the Modern Bird Guide in America," *Snowy Egret*, Volume 42, Number 2, Autumn 1979.

Beck, Herbert H., "The Pennsylvania German Names of Birds," *The Auk*, Vol. XLI, American Ornithologists' Union, 1925.

Berger, Andrew J., *Hawaiian Birdlife*, Honolulu: The University Press of Hawaii, 1981.

Berger, Andrew J., *Bird Life in Hawaii*, Norfolk Island, Australia: Island Heritage Press Ltd., 1983.

Blanchan, Neltje, *The New Nature Library, Volume VI: Bird Neighbors*, Garden City, New York, Doubleday, Page & Co., 1922.

Bond, James, *Birds of the West Indies*, Boston: Houghton Mifflin Co., 1971.

Burns, Frank L., "A Monograph of the Flicker," *The Wilson Bulletin*. No. 31, Oberlin, Ohio: Wilson Ornithological Chapter of the Agassiz Association, 1900.

Cassidy, Frederic G., Le Page, R. B., *Dictionary of Jamaican English*, London: Cambridge University Press, 1967.

Chapman, Frank M., *Handbook of Birds of Eastern North America*, New York, D. Appleton & Co, 1895.

Chapman, Frank M., Reed, Chester A., *Color Key to North American Birds*, New York: Doubleday, Page & Co., 1903.

Choate, Ernest A., Paynter, Raymond A., Jr., *Dictionary of American Bird Names*, Boston, The Harvard Common Press, 1985.

Cuddihy, Linda W., Stone, Charles P., *Alteration of Native Hawaiian Vegetation*, Honolulu: University of Hawaii Cooperative National Park Studies Unit, 1990.

Cunningham, Richard L., *50 Common Birds of the Southwest*, Tucson: Southwest Parks and Monuments Association, 1990.

Dawson, William Leon, *The Birds of California, Volumes 1 to 3*, San Diego: South Mouton Co., 1923.

Department of Conservation, State of Louisiana, *The Birds of Louisiana*, New Orleans: Department of Conservation, 1931.

Downer, Audrey, Sutton, Robert, *Birds of Jamaica*, Cambridge: Cambridge University Press, 1990.

Elman, Robert, *The Hunter's Field Guide to the Game Birds and Animals of North America*, New York: Alfred A. Knopf, 1974.

Forbush, Edward, *Useful Birds and their Protection*, Boston: Massachusetts State Board of Agriculture, 1913.

Goodwin, Derek, *Crows of the World*, 2nd Edition, Seattle: University of Washington Press, 1986.

Gruson, Edward S., *Words for Birds: A Lexicon of North American Birds with Biographical Notes*, New York, Quadrangle Books, 1972.

Hausman, Leon Augustus, *The Illustrated Encyclopedia of Amerian Birds*, New York: Halycon House, 1944.

Hawai'i Audubon Society, *Hawaii's Birds*, Honolulu: The Hawai'i Audubon Society, 1989.

Helmericks, Constance, *We Live in Alaska*, Garden City: Garden City Publishing Co., 1944.

Howell, Arthur H., *Florida Bird Life*, Florida Dept. of Game and Fresh Water Fish, 1932.

Jackson, Christine, *British Names of Birds*, London, England, H. F. & H. Wertherby Ltd., 1968.

Jackson, Jerome A., "From Hollywood to Broadway: How the western House Finch became established on the East Coast," *Birder's World*, February, 1992, Vol. 6 No. 1.

Kortright, Francis H., *The Ducks, Geese and Swans of North*

America, Washington, DC: The American Wildlife Institute, 1943.

Leahy, Christopher, *The Birdwatcher's Companion: An Encyclopedic Handbook of North American Birds*, New York, Hill & Wang, 1982.

Limburg, Peter R., *What's-in-the-Names of Birds*, New York, Coward, McCann & Geoghegan, Inc., 1975.

Linsdale, Jean M., The Natural History of Magpies, Berkeley, CA, Cooper Ornithological Club, *Pacific Coast Avifuna No. 25*, 1937.

Linthicum, Leslie, "Say What?" *The Albuquerque Journal*, July 11, 1993.

Longstreet, R. J., Editor, *Birds in Florida*, Tampa: Trend House, 1969.

Macdonald, J. D., *The Illustrated Dictionary of Australian Birds by Common Name*, Frenchs Forest, NSW, Australia, Reed Books Pty Ltd., 1987.

McAtee, Waldo L., "Folk-names of Canadian Birds," Ottawa, Canada: National Museum of Canada, Dept. of Northern Affairs and National Resources, *Bulletin No. 149, Biological Series No. 51*, 1959.

McAtee, Waldo L., "Folk Names of Florida Birds," Maitland, Florida, *The Florida Naturalist*, Vol. 28, pg. 35 - 37, 64, 83 - 87, 91,Vol. 29, pg 25 -28; 1955 -1956.

McAtee, Waldo L., "Folk Names of Georgia Birds," Atlanta, Georgia, *The Oriole*, Vol. XX, No. 1 - 14, 1955.

McAtee, Waldo L., "Folk-names of New England Birds," *Bulletin of the Massachusetts Audubon Society*, Vol. XXXIX, No. 7, Oct. 1955; Nov. 1955; Dec. 1955; Jan. 1956; Feb. 1956; March 1956; May 1956.

McAtee, Waldo L., "Some Local Names of Birds," *The Wilson Bulletin*, 1917.

Munro, George C., *Birds of Hawaii*, Rutland, Vermont: Charles E. Tuttle Co., 1960.

National Geographic Society, *Field Guide to the Birds of North America*, Washington, DC, 1977.

Nature Encyclopedia, 1924.

Pearson, T. Gilbert, Ed., *Birds of America,* New York, Garden City Publications, 1936.

Pembleton, Seliesa, *The Pileated Woodpecker,* Minneapolis: Dillon Press, Inc., 1989.

Peterson, Roger Tory, Peterson, Virginia Marie, *Audubon's Birds of America,* New York: Abbeville Press, 1991.

Raffaele, Herbert A., *A Guide to the Birds of Puerto Rico and the Virgin Islands,* Rio Piedras, Puerto Rico: Fondo Educativo Interamericano, 1982 (?), (Distributed by Addison-Wesley Publishing Company, Reading, Massachusetts).

Reed, Chester A., *Bird Guide - Land Birds East of the Rockies,* Garden City, New York: Doubleday & Co., 1947.

Robbins, Bruun and Zim, *Birds of North America: A Golden Guide to Field Identification,* 1966.

Scott, Susan, *Plants and Animals of Hawai'i,* Honolulu: Best Press, 1991.

Seton, Ernest Thompson, *The Book of Woodcraft and Indian Lore,* Garden City, New York: Doubleday, Page & Company, 1921.

Shuman, Geo. L. & Co., *The New Wonder World: Volume III: The Nature Book,* Chicago: Geo. L. Shuman & Co. 1945.

Smith, R. R. Frances, *British Birds from Nature,* Salem, New Hampshire: Salem House.

State of Hawaii, Dept. of Land and Natural Resources, Div. of Forestry and Wildlife, *Hawai'i Wildlife Plan,* Honolulu: State of Hawaii, 1984.

Stauffer, Marty, *Quail, Wild America,* PBS Television, 1993.

Sutton, George Miksch, *Birds of Pennsylvania,* Harrisburg, PA: J. Horace Mcfarland Company, Mount Pleasant Press, 1928.

Taverner, P. A., *Birds of Western Canada,* Ottawa: Museum Bulletin No. 41, Victoria Memorial Museum, Canada Dept. of Mines, 1926.

Teal, Edwin Way, *Wandering Through Winter,* New York: Dodd, Mead & Co., 1965.

Terres, John K., *Audubon Society Encyclopedia of North American Birds*, 1980.

Trotter, Spencer, "An Inquiry into the History of the Current English Names of North American Land Birds," *The Auk* Vol. XXVI, American Ornithologists' Union, 1909.

Yust, Walter, Editor in Chief, *Encyclopaedia Britannica*, Chicago: William Benton, Publ, 1959.

Whelan, Peter, "Those predacious red squirrels," *The Globe and Mail*, Toronto, January 14, 1995.

Writers' Program of the Work Projects Administration in the City of New York, *American Wild Life Illustrated*,Wm. H. Wise & Co., Inc., New York, 1940.

Writers' Program of the Work Projects Administration in the State of Nevada, *Nevada - A Guide to the Silver State*, Portland, Oregon: Binfords & Mort, 1940.

Etymology References

Ayto, John, *Dictionary of Word Origins*, New York: Little, Brown Co., 1990.

Barnhart, Robert K., Editor, *The Barnhart Dictionary of Etymology*, Bronxville, New York: H. W. Wilson Co., 1988.

Brown, Lesley, Editor, *The New Shorter Oxford English Dictionary on Historical Principles*, Oxford: Clarendon Press.

Cassidy, Frederic G., Le Page, R. B., *Dictionary of Jamaican English*, London: Cambridge University Press, 1967.

Champlin, John D., Jr., *The Young Folks' Cyclopædia of Common Things*, New York: Henry Holt & Co., 1879.

Dodge, John V., Editor, *Encyclopædia Britannica*, Chicago: William Benton, 1964.

Dwelly, Edward, *The Illustrated Gaelic - English Dictionary*, Glasgow: Gairm Publications, 1971.

Fisher, John Raymond, *Frisian-English Dictionary*, Boulder, Colorado: John Raymond Fisher, 1986.

Flexner, Stuart Berg, *The Random House Dictionary of the English Language*, Second Edition, Unabridged, New York: Random House, 1987.

Fowler, H. W., Fowler F. G., *The Concise Oxford Dictionary of Current English*, Oxford: Clarendon Press, 1964.

Gooders, John, *British Birds*, London: Collins 1987.

Hoffmeister, Donald F., *Zoo Animals, A Golden Guide*, New York: Golden Press, 1967.

Hvass, Hans, *Birds of the World in Color*, New York: E. P. Dutton & Company, Inc., 1963.

Klein, Dr. Ernest, *A Comprehensive Etymological Dictionary of the English Language*, New York: Elservier Publishing Co., 1971.

Lewis, Charlton T., & Short, Charles, *A Latin Dictionary*, Oxford: Clarendon Press, 1966.

Marchant, J. R. V., Charles, Joseph F., *Cassell's Latin Dictionary*, New York: Funk & Wagnalls Company, 1955.

McArthur, Tom, Editor, *The Oxford Companion to the English Language*, New York: Oxford University Press, 1992.

McDonald, A. M., Editor, *Chamber's Etymological English Dictionary*, New York: Philosophical Library, Inc., 1960.

McKechnie, Jean L., Editor, *Webster's New Universal Unabridged Dictionary*, Second Edition, New York: Simon & Schuster, 1983.

Neufeldt, Victoria, Editor, *Webster's New World Dictionary of American English - Third College Edition*, Cleveland: Simon & Schuster, Inc., 1988.

Neilson, William Allan, Editor, *Webster's New International Dictionary of the English Language* - Second Edition, Unabridged, Springfield, Mass.: G. & C Merriam Co., 1954.

Onions, C. T., *The Oxford Dictionary of English Etymology*, Oxford: Clarendon Press, 1966.

Onions, C. T., *The Oxford Universal Dictionary on Historical Principles*, Oxford, England: Clarendon Press, 1955.

Partridge, Eric, *Origins, a Short Etymological Dictionary of Modern English*, New York: MacMillan Company, 1958.

Peterson, Roger, Mountfort, Guy, and Hollom, P. A. D., *A Field Guide to the Birds of Britain and Europe*, London: Collins, 1966.

Skeat, Walter W., *A Concise Etymological Dictionary of the English Language*, Oxford: University Press, 1958.

Soukhanov, Anne H., Editor, Webster's II New Riverside University Dictionary, Boston: Hougton Mifflin Co., 1988.

Soukhanov, Anne H., Editor, *The American Heritage Dictionary of the English Language - Third Edition*, Boston: Hougton Mifflin Co., 1992.

Swann, H. Kirke, *A Dictionary of English and Folk-names of British Birds*, London: Witherby & Co., 1913.

Sweet, Henry, *The Student's Dictionary of Anglo-Saxon*, Oxford: University Press, 1976.

Stratmann, Francis Henry, *A Middle-English Dictionary*,

Oxford: Oxford University Press, 1978 (1891).

Thatcher, Virginia S., Editor, *The New Webster Encyclopedia Dictionary of The English Language*, Chicago: Consolidated Book Publishers, 1971.

Vriends, Matthew M., *The New Bird Handbook*, Hauppauge, New York: Barron's Educational Series, Inc., 1989.

Weekley, Ernest, *An Etymological Dictionary of Modern English*, New York: Dover Publications, Inc., 1967, 1921.

Index

A

C

F

Garzon Cenizo 100
Gaspard 113
Gaspayo 150
Gaulching 101
Gaulin 100, 101, 102
Gaunt 97
Gavia adamsii 92
Gavia arctica 92
Gavia stellata 92
Gavilan De Cienaga 116
Gavilan De Sierra 116
Gaviota 138, 139, 140
Gaviota Argentus 136
Gaviota Boba 137, 140
Gaviota Cabecinegra 137, 138
Gaviota Caraclera 97
Gaviota Ceniza 139
Gaviota Chica 138
Gaviota Comun 138
Gaviota de Capia 139
Gaviota de Forster 139
Gaviota de Pico Agudo 139
Gaviota de Pico Corto 139
Gaviota Gallega 137
Gaviota Major Espaldinegra 136
Gaviota Monja 140
Gaviota Negra 139
Gaviota Oscura 140
Gaviota Pequena 138
Gaviota Piquiaguda 139
Gaviota Piquianillada 137
Gaviota Piquigorda 139
Gaviota Real 139
Gaviotica 138
Geai 163, 192, 193
Geai a Aile Rouge 192
Geai Bleu 163
Gealbhonn 191
Gee 105
Gel Specht 154
Gelb Specht 154
Gelochelidon nilotica 139
Geococcyx californianus 147
Geothlypis trihas 182
Geothlypus trichas 180
Geylle 142
Giadh Fiadh 104
Giant Crow 164
Giant Woodpecker 155

Gibier Gris 105
Gibier Noir 111, 112
Gie-me-me-bit 150
Gila Woodpecker 155
Gilded Flicker 155
Gilderee 128
Gilleree 128
Gironde 100
Glaiseun 191, 199
Glana Eil 148
Glaner Bloer Woodpicker 166
Glaner Woodpecker 157
Glaucidium brasilianum 150
Glaucidium gnoma 150
Glaucous Gull 136
Glaucous-winged Gull 136
Glauocous-winged Gull 136
Glohlan-gaoith 151
Glossy Blackbird 193
Glossy Cowbird 193
Glossy Ibis 102
Gnome Owl 150
Goard 103
Goatsucker 150
Goatsucker of Carolina 150
Gobbler 123
Gobhlan-gaoith 162
God Bird 167
God-damn 113
Gode 141
Goeland 136, 137, 138
Goeland a Bec Rouge 139
Goeland Anglais 136
Goeland Charogne 137
Goeland de Fleuve 137
Goeland Espagnol 139
Goeland Noir 136
Goggle-nose 112
Goglu 192
Gogo 146
Gold Woodpecker 154
Gold-crest 169
Golden Bird 194
Golden Eagle 117
Golden Oriole 194
Golden Owl 147
Golden Pileolated Warbler 182
Golden Plover 127, 129, 131
Golden Robin 170, 194

242

Gusanero 183
Gut-eater 163
Gutter Snipe 131, 134
Gwilym 141
Gygis alba 140
Gymnogyps californianus 114
Gymnorhinus cyanocephalus 163
Gyrfalcon 118

H

Haddock Gull 137
Haematopus bachmani 128
Haematopus palliatus 128
Hag 94
Hagden 94
Hagdon 94
Hagdown 95
Haglet 94
Haglin 94
Hair Sparrow 189
Hair-bird 189
Hairy Woodpecker 157
Hairy-crown 114
Hairycrown 113
Hairyhead 113, 114
Hairy-wicket 154
Halcon Cernicalo 119
Halcyon 153
Half-a-shirt 156
Half-mooneye 112
Haliacetus leycocephalus 118
Halocyptena microsoma 97
Hamlet-bud Dem 100
Hamlin 100
Hammer-head 154
Hammerhead 103
Hammock-bird 194
Hammond's Flycatcher 160
Hang-bird 194
Hanging Bird 176
Hang-nest 194
Hangnest 177
Harbor Gull 136, 137
Harcourt's Petrel 96
Hard-head 113, 159
Hard-headed Broadbill 113
Hard-times Canada Bird 190
Hardwood Partridge 122

Harfang 148
Harlan 106
Harlan Hawk 116
Harlan's Buzzard 116
Harlan's Hawk 116
Harlan's Red-tailed Hawk 116
Harle 113, 114
Harlequin 123
Harlequin Brant 105
Harlequin Duck 110
Harlequin Quail 123
Harn Aowl 148
Harper 192
Harrier 116
Harris' Buzzard 117
Harris' Hawk 117
Harris' Sparrow 190
Harris's Woodpecker 157
Harry 157
Harry-wicket 154
Hatchet-bill 142
Hatchet-face 142
Hautbois 171
Havell's Tern 139
Hawaii Creeper 198
Hawaiian Crow 164
Hawaiian Duck 106
Hawaiian Petrel 96
Hawaiian Storm Petrel 96
Hawk 150
Hawk Owl 148, 149
Hawk's Eye 127
Hawk-billed Murre 141
Hawk-tailed Gull 138
Hay Bird 189
Hay-bird 133
Heart-bird 163
Heath Hen 122
Heavy-tailed Coot 113
Heckert 162
Hedge Sparrow 190, 191, 199
Heermann Song Sparrow 191
Heermann's Gull 137
He-hi-holder 154
Heiermann's Song Sparrow 191
Heigh-ho 154
Hell Diver 93
Hell's Chicken 111
Hell-Diver 93

I

J

Merle 170, 171
Merle Chat 173
Merle Corbeau 147
Merle Noir 193
Merlin 118, 119
Merriam Turkey 123
Merrill Song Sparrow 191
Merrill's Pauraque 150
Merritt Island Sparrow 187
Merry-wing 110
Mershon Goose 104
Merula migratoria 170
Mesange 165
Mesquin 107
Meterick 137
Mew Gull 137
Mexican Black Hawk 117
Mexican Blackbird 193
Mexican Bluebird 171
Mexican Buzzard 118
Mexican Canary 185
Mexican Chachalaca 119
Mexican Chickadee 165
Mexican Cormorant 99
Mexican Creeper 167
Mexican Crested Flycatcher 159
Mexican Duck 106, 108
Mexican Eagle 118
Mexican Evening Grosbeak 185
Mexican Flicker 154
Mexican Flycatcher 159
Mexican Goldfinch 196
Mexican Goose 104, 105
Mexican Goshawk 117
Mexican Grebe 93
Mexican House Finch 195
Mexican Jacana 129
Mexican Jay 163
Mexican Junco 188
Mexican Mallard 106
Mexican Quail 123
Mexican Raven 164
Mexican Rose Finch 195
Mexican Screech Owl 148
Mexican Squealer 108
Mexican Wood Duck 108
Mexican Woodpecker 156
Micrathene whitneyi 150
Micropalama himantopus 132

Mi-Deuil 177
Migrant Loggerhead 175
Migrant Shrike 175
Migratory Thrush 170
Milouin 109
Mimic 151
Mimic Thrush 172
Mimus polyglottus 172
Minfolk 106
Minik 107
Minime 140
Minister Gull 136
Minute Auklet 143
Minute Tern 138
Mire Drum 101
Mirlo Norteamericano 170
Mississippi Kite 115
Missouri Red-moustashed Woodpecker
    154
Missouri Skylark 174
Mniotilta varia 177
Moa 120
Moaning Bird 95
Moaning Dove 144, 145
Mock Bird 172
Mocker 172
Mocking Thrush 172
Mocking Wren 168
Mockingbird 172, 173, 175
Modec Woodpecker 157
Mohawk 163
Moho bishopi 176
Moho braccatus 175
Moiaque Blanche 110
Moignac 110
Moine 140
Moineau 189, 199
Moineau Anglais 199
Moineau Pierrot 199
Mojak 110
Moli 93
Mollimoke 94
Molly 94
Molly Bird 163
Molly Hawk 94
Mollymake 94
Molokai Creeper 198
Molothrus aeneus 193
Molothrus ater 193

N

256

Nonpareil 185
North American Avocet 129
North American Jacana 129
North American Ruddy Duck 113
North Atlantic Shearwater 94
Northern Bald Eagle 118
Northern Beardless Flycatcher 160
Northern Black Mallard 106
Northern Black Swift 151
Northern Bobwhite 123
Northern Butcher Bird 175
Northern Canary Bird 196
Northern Chatterer 174
Northern Cliff Swallow 162
Northern Downy Woodpecker 157
Northern Eider 110
Northern Flicker 154
Northern Fulmar 94
Northern Gannet 97
Northern Goose 104
Northern Goshawk 115
Northern Grace's Warbler 180
Northern Hairy Woodpecker 157
Northern Hawk Owl 149
Northern Horned Lark 161
Northern Jacana 129
Northern Jay 162
Northern Lapwing 126
Northern MacGillivray's Warbler 182
Northern Mallard 105
Northern Maryland Yellowthroat 182
Northern Mockingbird 172
Northern Olive Warbler 178
Northern Oriole 194
Northern Owl 148
Northern Parula 179
Northern Phalarope 135
Northern Pileated Woodpecker 155
Northern Pileolated Warbler 183
Northern Pintail 107
Northern Poor-will 151
Northern Pygmy-owl 150
Northern Raven 164
Northern Robin 170
Northern Sage Sparrow 188
Northern Saw-whet Owl 149
Northern Sharp-tailed Grouse 122
Northern Shoveler 107
Northern Shrike 175

Northern Small-billed Waterthrush 181
Northern Spotted Owl 149
Northern Three-toed Woodpecker 157
Northern Turkey 123
Northern Turr 141
Northern Varied Thrush 170
Northern Violet-green Swallow 162
Northern Waterthrush 181
Northern Waxwing 174
Northern Wheatear 170
Northern White-headed Woodpecker 156
Northern Yellowthroat 182
North-west Turkey 126
Northwestern Coast Heron 100
Northwestern Crow 164
Northwestern Flicker 154
Northwestern Red-wing 192
Northwestern Shrike 175
Nucifraga columbiana 164
Nukupuu 198
Numenius americanus 129
Numenius borealis 129
Numenius phaeopus 129
Numenius tahitiensis 130
Numida meleagris 124
Nunchie 141
Nuttall's Poor-will 151
Nuttall's Sparrow 190
Nuttall's Tern 139
Nuttall's Woodpecker 156
Nuttallornis borealis 161
Nyctanassa violacea 101
Nyctea scandiaca 148
Nycticorax nycticorax 101
Nyctidromus albicollis 150

O

O'u 197
Oahu Creeper 198
Oceanites oceanicus 96
Oceanodroma castro 96
Oceanodroma furcata 96
Oceanodroma homochroa 96
Oceanodroma leucorhoa 96
Oceanodroma melania 96
October Bird 192
October Pink 192

Roseate Tern 139
Rose-breast 185
Rose-breasted Grosbeak 185
Rose-ringed Parakeet 145
Rose-throated Becard 158
Rosette 138
Ross' Gull 137
Ross' Rosy Gull 137
Ross's Goose 105
Rossignol 167, 171, 172, 179, 190, 191
Rossignol Francais 190
Rostrhamus sociabilis 115
Rosy Gull 137
Rosy Spoonbill 102
Rota Fogel 184
Rotch 141
Rouge-gorge 170, 171
Rouge-gorge Bleu 171
Rough-billed Pelican 98
Rough-leg 116
Rough-legged Buzzard 116
Rough-legged Falcon 116
Rough-legged Hawk 116
Rough-wing 162
Rough-winged Swallow 162
Round-crested Duck 114
Round-headed Owl 149
Royal Eagle 118
Royal Tern 139
Rubber Duck 113
Ruby-crown 169
Ruby-crowned Kinglet 169
Ruby-crowned Warbler 169
Ruby-crowned Wren 169
Ruby-throat 152
Ruby-throated Hummingbird 152
Rudder Bird 113
Rudder Tail 193
Rudder-bird 163
Rudder-tail Blackbird 193
Ruddy Diver 113
Ruddy Duck 112
Ruddy Flycatcher 160
Ruddy Horned Lark 161
Ruddy Plover 133
Ruddy Turnstone 132
Ruff 133
Ruffed Grouse 122
Ruffed Heathcock 122

Rufous Hummingbird 152
Rufous-sided Towhee 186
Rufous-tailed Thrush 171
Rufous-winged Lark Bunting 191
Rufous-winged Sparrow 189
Ruisenor 172
Rush Sparrow 189
Russet-back 171
Russet-backed Thrush 171
Rusty Blackbird 193
Rusty Crow 193
Rusty Grackle 193
Rusty Oriole 193
Rusty Song Sparrow 191
Rusty-crowned Falcon 119
Rynchops niger 141

S

Sabanero 192
Sabanero Americano 186
Sabine's Gull 138
Sable Island Sparrow 187
Sabre-bill 129
Sac a Plomb 112
Sac-a-plomb 93
Sacramento Brown Towhee 186
Saddleback 136
Saddleback Gull 136
Saddler 136
Saddler Gull 136
Sage Chicken 122
Sage Cock 122
Sage Grouse 122
Sage Hen 122
Sage Mockingbird 173
Sage Sparrow 188
Sage Thrasher 173
Sage Thrush 173
Saguaro Woodpecker 156
Saint Michael Horned Owl 148
Salad-bird 196
Salpinctes obsoletus 168
Salt Marsh Yellow-throa 182
Salt Marsh Yellowthroat 182
Saltwater Blackbird 193
Saltwater Broadbill 109
Salt-water Duck 112
Salt-water Loon 92

X

Xanthocephalus xanthocephalus 192
Xantus Jay 163
Xantus' Becard 158
Xantus' Jay 163
Xantus' Murrelet 143
Xantus's Owl 149
Xebec 154
Xema sabini 138

Y

Yaboa Americana 102
Yaboa Comun 101
Yaboa Real 101
Yacker 154
Yaffle 154
Yakutat Fox Sparrow 190
Yakutat Song Sparrow 191
Yallerhammer 154
Yaller-tail 100
Yallow Wheeler 154
Yallow Whicker 154
Yanguaza Dominicana 108
Yank 166
Yankee Duck 108
Yar-rup 154
Yarrup 154
Yarup 154
Yawker Bird 154
Yaw-up 154
Yecker 154
Yellerhammer 154
Yellow Back 127
Yellow Bird 196
Yellow Chat 182
Yellow Crake 124
Yellow Flicker 154
Yellow Jay 154
Yellow Mocking Bird 182
Yellow Palm Warbler 181
Yellow Pipiri 158
Yellow Poll 179
Yellow Rail 124
Yellow Redpoll 181
Yellow Redpoll Warbler 181
Yellow See-see 183

Yellow Tip-up 181
Yellow Tip-up Warbler 181
Yellow Titmouse 179
Yellow Wagtail 174
Yellow Warbler 179
Yellow Wing 154
Yellow Woodpecker 154
Yellow-'ammer 154
Yellow-beak 106
Yellow-bellied Fiddler Duck 108
Yellow-bellied Flycatcher 159
Yellow-bellied Sapsucker 156
Yellow-bellied Woodpecker 156
Yellow-belly 156
Yellow-bill 111
Yellow-billed Cardinal 186
Yellow-billed Coot 111
Yellow-billed Cuckoo 146
Yellow-billed Loon 92
Yellow-billed Magpie 164
Yellow-billed Tropicbird 97
Yellowbird 179
Yellow-breast 183
Yellow-breasted Chat 182
Yellow-crowned Night Heron 101
Yellow-Crowned Warbler 181
Yellow-crowned Warbler 180
Yellow-eyed Junco 188
Yellow-footed Booby 98
Yellow-green Vireo 177
Yellow-hammer 156
Yellowhammer 154, 183, 192
Yellow-hammer High-hole 154
Yellowhead 192
Yellow-headed Blackbird 192
Yellow-headed Bust-tit 166
Yellow-headed Parrot 146
Yellow-leg 131
Yellow-leg Duck 106
Yellow-leg Plover 131
Yellow-legged Goose 105
Yellow-legged Mallard 106
Yellow-legged Plover 131
Yellow-legs 131
Yellowlegs 105, 106
Yellow-necked Snipe 129
Yellow-nose 111
Yellow-pad 106
Yellow-rump 180

Z

Author's biography

James K. Sayre was born in Paterson, New Jersey on July 21, 1942. He showed great interest in nature at an early age, although he was not always a keen observer. In Ridgewood, New Jersey, at age six, he somehow decided that the "cawing" of some distant Crows was actually the "honking" of Canadian Geese.

In 1950, his family moved to Mount Lebanon, a suburb of Pittsburgh, Pennsylvania. There, upon his urgent entreaties, a large enclosed birdfeeder was built and attached to the side of the house framing a large window. This design yielded excellent closeup views of local birds. Bird seed could be easily distributed by merely opening the window. In the winter Blue Jays, Chickadees, Sparrows, Juncos were regular daily visitors to the feeding station. His "serious" bird watching began in eighth grade, with the purchase of 7 X 35 bionoculars and a 35mm camera. Unfortunately though, the result "bird" photographs taken with that camera were still the "dot in the tree" as he had obtained earlier with the fixed-focus Brownie camera.

Undergraduate university education was in physics and engineering at Carnegie Tech and the University of Michigan, culminating in a Bachelor of Science degree in Metallurgical Engineering granted by the Ann Arbor school. The author moved to California to attend graduate studies in engineering at Stanford, but withdrew after a year to experience life outside of academia.

His first two-month trip to Australia with backpack and bicycle in 1985 was a real eye-opener. Crested Pigeons, Lorikeets, Parrots, Cockatoos, Rosellas, Bee Eaters, Wagtails and Kingfishers including the Laughing Kookaburra were among the birding highlights seen. The glories of the nightly gathering of magnificent flocks of the Galah Parrots in the tall eucalypt trees at Boundary Bend, on the Murray River, in the rural northern part of New South Wales, Australia was the high point of the trip.

Recently, he has settled into middle age as a self-described "dilettante extraordinaire." His favorite authors are George Bernard Shaw, S. J. Perelman and Hendrik Van Loon. He currently earns his living as a contract technical writer in the Silicon Valley, California. He is also working part time on several natural history book projects.

His current apartment has a view of the San Francisco Bay with a constantly changing daily show of Sandpipers, Godwits, Willets, Gulls, Herons and other shore birds moving about with the tides.

The author

How this Book came to be

This book was written by an amateur birdwatcher to fill a void in modern American bird literature: a book devoted exclusively to the listing of North American bird folknames and names and a detailed study of the etymology of those names.

In the summer of 1992, the author was rummaging around in a used book sale put on by the Public Library in Menlo Park, California and he found and purchased a copy of an old book, entitled, *Bird Neighbors*, written by Neltje Blanchan about eighty years ago. He found that Blanchan listed several old folknames for the many of the birds. The author's literature search in public and university libraries showed that there was no single book that listed all the old folknames for birds in America.

At this time the author was enrolled in an Special Projects class using Microsoft Word on the Apple Macintosh Computer at Canada College in Redwood City, California. This evergrowing personal list of bird names became the advanced project. His girlfriend decided to purchase an Apple Macintosh Computer, so that he could continue his listmaking at home. After gathering up lists of folknames from several books, he decided to combine them all and create a book devoted solely to American bird folknames and their origins. The product of these four years of research is what you are now holding in your hands. Enjoy.

To order a copy of the book, *North American Bird Folknames and Names,* ISBN 0-945039-05, please fill out this order form and return it to the publisher's address listed below. Your payment cheerfully refunded if you are not completely satisfied with your purchase.

Bottlebrush Press
Post Office Box 4554
Foster City, CA 94404
Tel. 415-345-9964   Date _____

Dear Bottlebrush Press,

Please find my personal check enclosed for the following order of your book, ISBN 0-945039-05, **North American Bird Folknames and Names:**

Number of books _____ x $24.95   = _____

Shipping and Handling: Please add $4.00 for first book and $3.00/additional book   = _____

Please tick: USPS Priority Mail ___
                    or UPS Delivery ___

California residents please add 8.25% Sales tax. ($2.06/book)   = _____

Total Enclosed = $ _____
(checks or money orders in U. S. dollars)

Name _____

Street Address _____

City _____ State _____

Zip Code _____

(OPTIONAL) Day phone (   ) _____